Winnicott's Letter to Bion

Winnicott's Letter to Bion presents reflections on a fascinating moment in the history of psychoanalytic thinking.

Donald Winnicott's letter, sent on October 5, 1967, and conveying thoughts about two of Wilfred Bion's papers, never received a response. In this book, international contributors elaborate on the contents of the letter, overlapping and divergent projects of the two psychoanalysts, and the meaning of Bion's silence. The chapters consider topics including the historical context of their work, their focuses on play and reverie, and the question of the sensuous.

Winnicott's Letter to Bion will be of great interest to psychoanalysts in practice and in training, and to historians of psychoanalysis.

Steven H. Cooper is a Training and Supervising Analyst at the Boston Psychoanalytic Society and Institute, and the Columbia Centre for Psychoanalytic Training and Research. A recipient of the JAPA Prize in 1989, he is also Chief Editor Emeritus of *Psychoanalytic Dialogues*. He is the author of numerous papers and seven books on psychoanalysis.

Christopher G. Lovett trained at the Boston Psychoanalytic Society and Institute, where he currently serves on the faculty. A former member of the editorial boards of *The International Journal of Psychoanalysis* and *The Journal of the American Psychoanalytic Association*, he maintains a private practice in Newton Centre, Massachusetts.

The International Psychoanalytical Association
International Psychoanalysis Library Series
Series Editor: Silvia Flechner

IPA Publications Committee
Natacha Delgado, Nergis Güleç, Thomas Marcacci, Carlos Moguillansky, Rafael Mondrzak, Angela M. Vuotto, Gabriela Legoretta (consultant)

Titles in this series

Truth, Reality and the Psychoanalyst: Latin American Contributions to Psychoanalysis
Silvia Flechner

The Geography of Meanings: Psychoanalytic Perspectives on Place, Space, Land, and Dislocation
Salman Akhtar

Linking, Alliances, and Shared Space: Groups and the Psychoanalyst
Rene Kaes

Children in Genocide: Extreme Traumatization and Affect Regulation
Suzanne Kaplan

Resonance of Suffering: Countertransference in Non-Neurotic Structures
Andre Green

The First Dictionary of Psychoanalysis: A Gift for Sigmund Freud's 80th Birthday
Richard Sterba

The Letters of Sigmund Freud to Jeanne Lampl-de Groot, 1921-1939: Psychoanalysis and Politics in the Interwar Years
Edited by Gertie Bögels

Winnicott's Letter to Bion: Playing, Dreaming, and Beyond
Edited by Steven H. Cooper and Christopher G. Lovett

"Clapping with one hand—how do we understand the apparent ignoring by Wilfred Bion of D W Winnicott's attempts to communicate and even collaborate with him? In this fascinating volume, contemporary psychoanalytic scholars consider this question through the prism of letters from DWW to WB during the years 1951–67. These were unanswered by Bion, even though it was increasingly apparent that, working in the same milieu, albeit divided British Psychoanalytical Society, there was much similarity, even overlap in their areas of interest. From a plethora of perspectives, these papers explore many possible answers in their historical, political and theoretical context, at the same time as illuminating the relationship between these two giants of and within the British Psychoanalysis in the 20th century."

—**Angela Joyce,** Training and Supervising Psychoanalyst, BPAS; Past Chair, The Winnicott Trust

"*Beyond Playing and Dreaming: Reflections on a Note from Winnicott to Bion* is a remarkable collection of papers on the relationship of the thinking of Winnicott and Bion. While Winnicott and Bion were contemporaries, they rarely referred to one another in their published work. In this volume, fifteen leading Winnicott and Bion scholars create their own versions of the dialogue between the two analytic thinkers. The individual papers creatively use as their starting point a letter Winnicott wrote to Bion. The contributions to this volume are unusual in their combination of astute commentary and accessibility. These papers are a pleasure to spend time with and leave the reader with a greater depth of understanding of the work of both Winnicott and Bion."

—**Thomas Ogden, author,** *Coming to Life in the Consulting Room: Toward a New Analytic Sensibility* and *Reclaiming Unlived Life: Experiences in Psychoanalysis*

"It is exciting to see a group of American and European analysts/scholars tackle the fascinating relationship between D.W. Winnicott and W.R. Bion. As a result of the still burning embers of the Controversial Discussions in post-war London, we have seen precious little of either of these psychoanalytic pioneers' comments on the other's work. This road now leads us to the current moment, where two developments are admirably combined in these pages—the deconstruction of how each analyst regarded the work of the other as seen through their correspondence, combined with inferences drawn from their published papers.

This approach fosters a deeper appreciation of the particular contribution of each. This is a scholarly collection of papers. Well done!"

Winnicott's Letter to Bion

Playing, Dreaming, and Beyond

**Edited by Steven H. Cooper
and Christopher G. Lovett**

Routledge
Taylor & Francis Group

LONDON AND NEW YORK

Designed cover image: Getty | scisettialfio

First published 2026
by Routledge
4 Park Square, Milton Park, Abingdon, Oxon OX14 4RN

and by Routledge
605 Third Avenue, New York, NY 10158

Routledge is an imprint of the Taylor & Francis Group, an informa business

British Library Cataloguing-in-Publication Data
A catalogue record for this book is available from the British Library

ISBN: 9781032819235 (hbk)
ISBN: 9781032819211 (pbk)
ISBN: 9781003502067 (ebk)

DOI: 10.4324/9781003502067

Typeset in Palatino
by KnowledgeWorks Global Ltd.

Contents

Series Editor's Foreword   ix
Foreword: Beyond Playing and Dreaming: Reflections on a
Note from Winnicott to Bion   xi
Acknowledgment   xii

1 Bion's Letter   1
   NICOLA ABEL-HIRSCH

2 Imagining Engagement   8
   LESLEY CALDWEL

3 Melanie Klein Absolutely Would Not Allow This:
   Winnicott's Shadowboxing in His Letter to Bion,
   October 5, 1967   17
   GIUSEPPE CIVITARESE

4 Winnicott's Paradox: Being with and without
   Memory and Desire   33
   STEVEN H. COOPER

5 Winnicott's Research: Between Parallel
   Convergences and Uniqueness   45
   PAOLO FABOZZI

6 Pluperfect Errands in the Controversial Discussions
   of Bion and Winnicott   64
   JACK FOEHL

7 On the Question of the Sensuous in Winnicott/Bion   72
   PETER GOLDBERG

8 **Winnicott to Bion: Reflections on Winnicott's Letter**   80
   R.D. HINSHELWOOD

9 **On Not Playing with Winnicott: A Not-So-Curious
   Case of Non-Communication**   88
   CHRISTOPHER G. LOVETT

10 **An Oracle (Perhaps a Miracle) at the British
   Psychoanalytical Society: Winnicott's Letter
   to Bion of October 5, 1967**   99
   MAURO MANICA

11 **Reading What Is Not in a Book: Dreaming
   and Playing with Words**   113
   ELENA MOLINARI

12 **'What Life Itself Is About'**   123
   MICHAEL PARSONS

13 **Winnicott and Bion: Communicating and
   Not Communicating**   152
   BRUCE REIS

14 **Holding and Containing: Winnicott, Bion,
   and Klein on Infancy and the Infantile**   168
   STEPHEN SELIGMAN

   Index   182

Series Editor's Foreword

The Publications Committee of the International Psychoanalytic Association is pleased to present another volume of the International Psychoanalysis Library series: *Winnicott's Letter to Bion: Playing, Dreaming, and Beyond*, edited by Steven Cooper and Christopher Lovett.

The library's focus is on the scientific developments of today throughout the IPA, with an emphasis within the discipline on clinical, technical, and theoretical advances and empirical, conceptual, and historical research projects.

The authors centered their papers on the five letters Donald Winnicott sent to Wilfred Bion over more than a decade. L. Caldwell deepens on the one-sided correspondence between two greats of British psychoanalysis, which Chris Mawson called "the failed fraternal." Winnicott's letter is written in his typically personal style, allowing us to speculate about their relationship and what seems to be a particular rivalry in which Bion displaced Winnicott in the Klein group. The issue has not subsided, and a continuing rivalry existed between followers of Winnicott and of Bion with the invention of mythologies about each other.

The friction between Winnicott and Bion is apparent. Such a politely nuanced set of reactions to Bion's paper nevertheless illustrates the multiple personal and interschool rivalries that are unfortunately prevalent within psychoanalysis, as Hinshelwood states.

B. Reis takes his point of view about both Winnicott and Bion, stating that they shared a fractured and indirect dialogue around psychoanalytic topics and that the former's (1963) paper "Communicating and Not Communicating Leading to a Study of Certain Opposites" represented Winnicott's "indirect communication" with Bion (and Klein) in the complicated context of the British Psychoanalytic Society at the time; and serves as a counterpoint to the letters exchanged between them.

Issues of communication and reception in infancy and psychoanalysis, silence, the influence of sources within insight and outside of psychoanalysis, ontic matters, and the influence and rivalry between these figures are discussed.

Seligman centers his paper on Winnicott's critique of Bion's notion of listening "without memory or desire," reflecting the differences between his and

Bion's basic orientation, with the latter's greater loyalty to Kleinian theory. Seligman states that clinical implications are considered throughout Bion's stress on projective identification, and the analyst-mother's containing function reflects his view that frustration and absence are central to development and therapeutic action. At the same time, Winnicott's more robust and positive developmental model emphasizes the complex transactions among internal objects, relationships, and lived environments, including the analytic setting.

G. Civitarese states that in his October 5, 1967, letter to Bion, Winnicott critiques Bion's radical proposal that the analyst should engage memory, desire, or understanding. While Bion views this approach as a path to uncover deeper, unfiltered truths, Winnicott challenges its implications, suggesting it risks sidelining the vital influence of the environment. S. Cooper centered on Winnicott's (1967) letter, written to Bion after his lecture on the negative capability, to reflect on what he regarded as the most intriguing historical moment in post-Freudian psychoanalytic theory and practice. Despite its rather cryptic brevity, Goldberg states that Winnicott's note to Bion hints at a significant difference between these otherwise highly compatible thinkers—their differing views of the place of sensory experience in psychical life.

This book shows how Wilfred Bion's and Donald Winnicott's concepts have profoundly influenced the development of psychoanalysis over the last half-century. Although they are frequently used interchangeably in the literature and are often seen as denoting essentially the same clinical practice, this new book clarifies the substantial differences between the two authors, the models of mind that underpin them, and how they are translated into clinical practice.

Dra. Silvia Flechner
Chair, Publications Committee IPA
Asociación Psicoanalítica del Uruguay

Foreword: Beyond Playing and Dreaming: Reflections on a Note from Winnicott to Bion

We hope that this volume stimulates readers to reflect on the letter from Winnicott to Bion in October 1967 and four other letters from that period. In October 1967, Winnicott had heard Bion's lecture on negative capability, but his note seems more directed to the lecture Bion had previously published on "without memory and desire."

Part of the stimulus for the book was the nature of how, despite their respective work related to actual maternal function and environmental influence, each differed in their language, idiom, and metaphors in their work.

There is no written record of Bion responding to Winnicott's letter, so this volume follows in some sense from an unknowable, but likely rivalrous and fractured conversation about their work. We know how much they were each negotiating a path toward becoming the boldly creative thinkers who they were while adapting to the political exigencies within their psychoanalytic culture. In some ways, this unanswered correspondence marks a level of avoidance and censorship that may have been operating all along. Some writers in this volume note the institutional conditions that may have inhibited or even prevented their engagement about key psychoanalytic issues, especially matters of being and becoming, which they were each elaborating.

So in some ways the authors in this volume have entered into a conversation that might have been and never was. We have wished to open their unconsummated conversation through the clinical imagination of our contributors, each steeped in their individual ways in the work of Winnicott and Bion. Each have offered us personal and creative readings of that undeveloped conversation. We hope we will stimulate you the reader to do the same in kind.

Acknowledgment

For Gwen from Steven
For Kim from Chris

1 Bion's Letter

Nicola Abel-Hirsch

Although Bion did not write in reply to Winnicott's letter, he did write a letter after the meeting. Bion's letter was to his wife. After reading both Winnicott and Bion's letters, I had to double-check they were discussing the same presentation. One wouldn't have known it from what they have written.

Here is Bion's letter:

'To Los Angeles October 3 [1967]
… I am churning over the paper and feeling jolly glad I shan't have to give more. Wednesday. The 'paper'[1] (of course I didn't read it) went off all right. At first I thought no one was coming – only one or two there five minutes before the start. But it filled up. They all stayed (except about three) till past the end and there was no hostile demonstration. …

I thought the 'paper' went well. Of course I spoke direct; too many 'ers' I think, but I haven't spoken for a long time and I did not, as you know, relish the circumstances. I think I spoke to the point and a number of people seemed to feel that this time a lot more people grasped the general idea. It might have turned out anyhow – including a boycott. There is no doubt that the Klein Group has been very upset but I think they needed it. But there must have been about 130 people which is as much as anyone has a right to expect. Furthermore there was no nonsense about my going (tears of grief etc.). Just a straight forward exposition by me of my ideas about how things should go and how I at least tried to make that happen. I think the fact that it was straight forward talk, 'to be continued in our next', all helped. And as I say, they stayed to the end.

'Negative Capability', published as chap. 13, 'Prelude to or Substitute for Achievement', in Attention and Interpretation (London: Tavistock Publications, 1970) [Volume VI]'.

(Bion Vol. II p. 166).

Bion's paper on 'Negative Capability' was his last presentation to a Scientific Meeting of the British Society before leaving for Los Angeles. From Winnicott's letter, it seems, however, that Winnicott was unaware of this. We can wonder at the differences between their respective experiences of the meeting.

What did Bion actually say in his presentation that evening?

DOI: 10.4324/9781003502067-1

On Bion's Presentation to the Scientific Meeting that Evening

As was usual for him, Bion presented his thinking at the Scientific Meeting directly, instead of reading a paper. We are fortunate however that a version of this presentation was later published as the last chapter – Chapter 13 – of Bion's final book on psychoanalysis, *Attention and Interpretation* (1970). While Bion's presentation to the meeting was originally called 'Negative Capability', Chapter 13 of Attention and Interpretation is titled 'Prelude to or Substitute for Achievement'. Bion drew both titles from the Keats' quote the paper/chapter begins with:

> I had not a dispute but a disquisition with Dilke on various sub-
> jects; several things dove-tailed in my mind, and at once it struck
> me what quality went to form a Man of Achievement, especially
> in Literature, and which Shakespeare possessed so enormously – I
> mean Negative Capability, that is, when a man is capable of being in
> uncertainties, mysteries, doubts, without any irritable reaching after
> fact and reason.
>
> (John Keats)

Bion then states:

> Any session should be judged by comparison with the Keats formu-
> lation so as to guard against one commonly unobserved fault lead-
> ing to analysis 'interminable'. The fault lies in the failure to observe
> and is intensified by the inability to appreciate the significance of
> observation.
>
> (Bion, Vol. VI, p. 327)

Bion then gives an instruction; one that is significantly less well-known and almost counter to his instruction to put memory and desire from one's mind in sessions. Instead, here Bion instructs us to attend to material characterized either by the Language of Substitution or by the Language of Achievement. It is of note that Bion's last book on psychoanalysis, which he was likely working on around this time, is titled *Attention and Interpretation* (1970).

Here is Bion:

> The analyst's attention must not wander from areas of material char-
> acterized either by the Language of Substitution or by the Language
> of Achievement; he must remain sensitive to both.
>
> (Bion Vol. VI, p. 328) (emphasis added)

So, what does Bion mean by the Language of Substitution and the Language of Achievement?

About the Language of Achievement Bion says in his paper:

> The idea that is nourished by love develops from matrix to function in Language of Achievement; from which it can be transformed into achievement'.
>
> (Bion Vol. VI, p. 329) (emphasis added)

Bion's reference to 'love' is noteworthy. In his earlier work on the three links of K (knowing), L (loving), and H (hating), Bion instructs the analyst to work only in the register of K. However, in the quote above, Bion speaks of love nourishing the movement of an idea from inner (matrix, 'O') to outer. In the presentation, he also discusses 'envy and gratitude' as belonging to the Language of Achievement – the debt owed to love is recognised (see Klein on 'gratitude').

Bion further states that the Language of Achievement is an action or a prelude to action. Below, Francis Tustin describes his experience as Bion's patient in the 1960s:

> He provoked me to think for myself – to have a mind of my own. He did this by asking challenging questions and by making unexpected remarks rather than by imposing a rigid interpretive scheme on what I said and did. In so doing, he made me think about what was happening to me in my own terms.
>
> (Tustin 1981, p. 175)

We might describe Bion as an active analyst; he also encouraged (Tustin says 'provoked') his patients to be active.

The Language of Achievement includes the recognition that one's theory is a point of view or what Bion came to call 'vertex'. That is, the idea that despite a theory being based on proper observation, it remains a partial understanding.

On the Discussion in the Paper of the Language of Substitution

Set over against and in contrast with the Language of Achievement, I consider the language that is a substitute for, and not a prelude to, action (Vol. VI, p. 327).

When the Language of Substitution dominates, sessions repeat themselves 'despite the multitudinous changes in disguise', and ideas seem to proliferate while in fact being all the same. Bion refers to cancerous growth and the Language of Substitution as related to 'envy and greed' instead of 'envy and gratitude' ('envy and greed' is an unusual pairing and I think one that Klein didn't make).

So what kind of way of talking or working is the Language of Substitution?

In the presentation, Bion says there is a failure to observe, and even to appreciate the significance of observation. Dreams, he comments, can act as a useful filler to obscure the fact that work isn't actually being done. 'Current events can be transformed to expression in sado-masochistic terms or near psychopathological jargon; there is no limit to the forms of transformation' (Vol. VI, p. 328).

During a visit to Los Angeles shortly before the presentation, Bion made a comment that throws some light on this predicament:

> it is the easiest thing in the world, what with the patients trying to deny the reality of what we are trying to draw attention to, and our own dislike of what we feel we ought to draw attention to, that you can very easily get into a state in which you gradually drift into a position in which you talk not English, but jargon ….
>
> (LASS, pp. 37–38)

In the presentation he comments that:

> the human animal has not ceased to be persecuted by his mind and the thoughts usually associated with it – whatever their origin may be. Therefore I do not expect any psychoanalysis properly done to escape the odium inseparable from the mind.
>
> (Vol. VI, p. 328)

In Bion's view, both the analyst and patient are persecuted by what they are doing in analysis (as well as having a love of thinking and epistemological drive). We might say that we move between the Language of Achievement and the Language of Substitution as we manage to be analysts, then fall back into merely being 'substitutes for analysts', before regaining our catalytic function as analysts. It is simple enough to write these words, but Bion's presentation gives a sense of his deep struggle to understand and formulate this idea.

Bion goes on to say that analysts are working with states of mind that society has specific institutions to deal with, such as organised spying, police forces and religious organisations (and he touches on the issue of who comes to have authority in these institutions). One implication of this comparison may be that we need our Psychoanalytical Society to help prevent us from falling into substitution, even into some kind of lying.

Bion's final words, certainly of the chapter, and possibly of the presentation:

> What is required is not the decrease of inhibition but a decrease of the impulse to inhibit; the impulse to inhibit is fundamentally envy of the growth-stimulating objects. What is to be sought is an activity that is both the restoration of god (the Mother) and the evolution of god

(the formless, infinite, ineffable, non-existent), which can be found only in the state in which there is no memory, desire, understanding.
(Bion Vol. VI, p. 330)

Why the emphatic use of the double reference to 'god'? I am helped in approaching what Bion might mean by 'infinite' by something the philosopher Wittgenstein said:

If we take eternity to mean not infinite temporal duration but timelessness, then eternal life belongs to those who live in the present.
(Wittgenstein 1922, 6.4311)

What was Bion saying to the 'Klein Group'?

In the letter to his wife Bion comments: 'There is no doubt that the Klein Group has been very upset but I think they needed it'. What was he saying to upset the Klein group? In the presentation, he differentiates repeatedly between repetitive behaviours and behaviours that foster growth. He also points out that all theory is a partial view. With these points, he may have been implicitly talking about the dangers for the 'Klein group' of using their theory repetitively and as if it was all-encompassing.

What about his reference to 'envy and greed', in contrast to the central Kleinian concept of 'envy and gratitude'? Although it's not articulated by Bion here, there may be a link between 'envy and greed' and his view of 'memories and desires'. He views 'memories and desires' as pleasure principle possessions of the mind. In greed, more 'possessions' are craved, in contrast to feeling gratitude, or envy, towards the object. Bion comments that the repetitive splitting in the 'Language of Substitution' can result in more theories that are essentially all the same. I think Bion may be saying to the 'Klein group', that, without realising it, they are attacking newly emerging ideas.

Bion's letter to his wife conveys a sense of his being on a mission. I think he was. I think he saw us as a rather undisciplined, overly-defensive lot! At Northfield hospital during World War II, when Bion encountered a lack of discipline and purpose, he decided what was needed was a leader and an enemy. He identified the 'enemy' to be 'neurosis'. I think he may have been doing something similar here: attempting to rally the undisciplined hordes of analysts against the 'enemies' of memory and desire and now, rallying them against substitution and cancerous growth. The 'enemies' are real; what I'm drawing attention to here is his use of them.

At Northfield, Bion's leadership was formal and legitimate. He was in charge. By contrast, in the Psychoanalytic Society, he would behave with colleagues and audiences as if he were their leader or group analyst, when the other analysts had not granted him the authority to do so. It is useful to note this when understanding the dynamics of the conflictual situation that developed within the British Society towards Bion's later work.

Returning to Winnicott's Letter

In his letter to Bion, Winnicott addresses two subjects. Firstly, he expresses his caution regarding the phrase 'memory and desire'. He writes about how, on returning from the meeting, his wife reminded him that 'the phrase memory and desire, which you have used before, is a quotation from T. S. Eliot'. Did Bion come to his phrase 'memory and desire' through T. S. Eliot? Reading Bion's later work one is often reminded of Eliot's poetry, but, to my knowledge, Bion never mentions him. Instead, when discussing 'desire', Bion references the writings of St John of the Cross.

Winnicott then writes

I cannot help finding myself using the word intention and not feeling desire to be correct. ...For me, memory and desire is all right in a poem because it refers to an experience that is 100% subjective. In the application to psycho-analytic work I find I cannot allow that this is 100% subjective.

Winnicott seems to interpret Bion's use of the term in opposition to how Bion intended. In Winnicott's view, Bion does not make room for the patient as separate from what the analyst has in mind. I understand Bion as attempting to discipline the analyst's pleasure principle functioning (memories and desires as 'pleasure principle based possessions in the mind') so that the analyst can be more available to the patient. However, in Winnicott's view, Bion may be paying too much attention to his own mind. Winnicott then moves onto his second point:

The rest of this letter has to do with something quite separate. I am very interested in the way you bring in the Bible story in your paper on catastrophic change and also quite frequently when you are talking. I, like you, was brought up in the Christian tradition (Wesleyan) and I have no desire to throw away all that I listened to over and over again and tried to digest and sort out.

Winnicott recommends an 'amazing book' that deals with a reconstruction of the Jesus story – but was no longer available to buy. What struck me most about this part of the letter was the 'I, like you, was brought up in the Christian tradition'.

What might Winnicott be communicating to Bion in his preference for 'intention' over 'desire' and his drawing attention to their childhoods? I wonder if he means that Bion is too much in his own mind, is too 'poetic' and needs to get his feet back onto the ground. Childhood, implies Winnicott, is where we come from, and we cannot put our memories of it aside. Winnicott wants to remind Bion of their childhoods. Perhaps he is implying that Bion is not so different to him.

If this is right, it may be that Winnicott did not want to get caught up in the dynamics surrounding Bion's leaving and Bion's relation to the 'Klein group'. Instead, he wanted to send him a personal message about needing to be more down to earth.

Note

1 In the last chapter of his 1965 book *Transformation: Change from Learning to Growth* Bion says:
> Change from K to O is a special case of Transformation; it is of particular concern to the analyst in his function of aiding maturation of the personalities of his patients.
>
> My term 'psychological turbulence' needs elucidation. By it I mean a state of mind the painful quality of which may be expressed in terms borrowed from St John of the Cross. I quote:

> > The Ascent of Mount Carmel, 1, 1 and 2.
> > The process described by St John of the Cross involves a giving up of possessions. While the quote refers to 'worldly things', Bion draws on it in exploring ideas about 'mental possessions', and how these are different from thoughts. Secondly, there is an emphasis on our fear of ignorance and how we can advance 'precociously' to avoid the experience of ignorance. It is noteworthy that Bion's discussion of the discipline of 'memory and desire' directly in relation to the work of a mystic – so at it's most mystical point, he does so within the framework of the Grid (the instrument that enables scrutiny of one's work).

> The first (night of the soul) has to do with the point from which the soul goes forth, for it has gradually to deprive itself of desire for all the worldly things which it possessed, by denying them to itself; the which denial and deprivation are, as it were, night to all the senses of man. The second reason has to do with the mean, or the road along which the soul must travel to this union – that is, faith, which is likewise as dark as night to the understanding. The third has to do with the point to which it travels – namely, God, Who, equally, is dark night to the soul in this life.
>
> I use these formulations to express, in exaggerated form, the pain which is involved in achieving the state of naïvety inseparable from binding or definition (col. 1).

References

Bion, W. R. (2014). *The Complete Works of W. R. Bion* (CWB), ed. C. Mawson & F. Bion. London: Karnac.

Bion, W. R. (1970). *Attention and Interpretation: A Scientific Approach to Insight in Psycho-Analysis and Groups*, ed. C. Mawson & F. Bion (Eds.). Volume VI. London: Karnac.

Bion, W. R. (1975). *Caesura*. Volume X.

Kavanaugh, K., & Rodriguez, O. (Trans.) (1964). *The Collected Works of St. John of the Cross*. New York: Doubleday.

Keats, J. (1817). *Letter to George and Thomas Keats*, 21st December 1817. In: The Letters of John Keats, Vol. 1, ed. H. E. Rollins. Boston, MA: Harvard University Press, 1958; also in: The Letters of John Keats (4th ed.), ed. M. B. Forman. London: Oxford University Press, 1952.

2 Imagining Engagement

Lesley Caldwel

My title draws attention to the editors' invitation to elaborate our own fantasies of the one-sided correspondence between two greats of British psychoanalysis whose non-relation the late Chris Mawson called 'the failed fraternal.' At a pre-conference event he and I did together at the London IPA congress in 2019 he referred to the sheer profundity of their common interests, but also to their 'degrees of separation.' He added 'they were like ships passing in the night, and psychoanalysis would have been enriched by a fraternal and mutually affecting (♀♂) relationship between the two clinicians and theoreticians, and by the triangulation that never happened between their ideas and the perspective of ontological philosophy of Sartre and Heidegger' (spoken presentation, 2019).

In the past decade or so there has been an increasingly widespread interest in the overlap of ideas, of shared but never discussed themes in the work of Donald Winnicott and Wilfred Bion. For me this current project has encouraged not only a set of fantasised exchanges and the personal associations they develop but speculation about my (and our) reasons, wishes, motivations, reactions to filling out this one-sided correspondence. What first seemed an inspiring challenge set up by the sheer volume of resounding echoes between these two major figures of British and international psychoanalysis then began to register a developing sense of disappointment, impatience, even unease about the institutions and personalities active in the field that produced this regrettable if consistent anomaly. They did not do it. It was not done. Can this now be repaired by bringing them together and taking further their commitment to the psychoanalysis to which both dedicated their lives.

In that 2019 discussion, Chris Mawson and I agreed about what they had in common: they were both personally and professionally indebted to Melanie Klein, they both shared an interest in considering the early mental experience of the infant in the relationship with the mother, they both approached its connections with the analytic relationship through an interest in the being of the patient in analysis, they both wrote of the becoming that analysis can encourage.

Perhaps importantly for the work they each went on to do in their later years we also agreed that they both elaborated ways of thinking and

DOI: 10.4324/9781003502067-2

working gained from the kinds of clinical experiences for which they feared their colleagues' incomprehension or disapproval and both had what Chris called 'painful personal experience of the difficulties of 'lateral communication' with colleagues and the 'establishment.'

Chris's own interest in anxiety had led him to use the Winnicott of 1952 to further his profound knowledge of Bion in his book, *Psychoanalysis and Anxiety – from Knowing to Being (2019)*.

An infant has the capacity to feel awful as a result of the failure of something that is quite in another field, that is to say, that of infant care… I feel that there is urgent need for us to hammer away at the discussion of the meaning of anxiety when the cause is failure in the technique of infant care, as for instance, failure to give the continuous live support that belongs to mothering. We know that this subject can take us right back to the time of birth, that is to say, to the time when the foetus is ready to be born – at about the thirty-sixth week of intrauterine life. The question that I want to ask is this: Can anything be said about this anxiety, or is it just a physical thing, and no more? (Winnicott, 1952).

Mawson's book is based loosely upon a question Bion asks in *Transformations* (1965), regarding 'how to evolve as a psychoanalyst from "knowing" or "knowing about" phenomena to *being and becoming* that which is real' – from transformations in K to change in O (Donna Savery, personal communication). For Mawson *existential anxiety* is the unifying experience of the human condition, irreducible and unable to be transformed through interpretation: Britton's foreword to his book summarises this:

> Change in O, the ontological self, requires a repetition of an interaction of a comparable kind between patient and analyst. That implies that we need to meet and find the O of the patient, and not some more diplomatic representative of the person, such as that described by Winnicott as a *false self*, or Steiner as a *pathological organisation*
> (Britton foreword, 2019).

Winnicott and Bion would probably part company on what is to be done analytically if that meeting were to happen but it is undoubtedly a theme that invites continuing thought and exchange.

There are five letters from Winnicott to Bion in *The Collected Works of Donald Winnicott* (2016) only the earliest of which, January 1951, written after Bion's paper on the Imaginary Twin, had not previously been published. All five offer confirmation of Winnicott's active engagement with Bion's work over two decades of shared scientific debate; they reveal his sustained attention, openness and interest in following up specific psychoanalytic issues and matters of group dynamics and behaviour inside the British society. In this there is further confirmation of Winnicott's whole approach. That first letter is frank about finding Bion's work difficult while recognising, 'There is something essentially individual about whatever you do and write and eventually your contribution to the Society will be a big one. It is for us to gradually find out how to understand what you say' (CW 3:6:2).

Like other living practices, psychoanalysis and the language of psychoanalysis are conditioned historically and socially, and in his last letter to Bion in 1967, he writes, 'As you said we each have to find the word that fits for oneself.' Here he echoed his much earlier letter to Klein sent after giving the paper, 'Anxiety associated with insecurity' in 1952, quoted above, although it is clear from that letter to Klein that the paper was not well-received. There Winnicott was already insisting that each of us has to find our own way of speaking and writing or our words become lifeless, they constrain and smother creativity, inhibiting rather than enabling new directions and ideas to develop in taking analysts further towards meeting its continuing challenges, the challenges of working as a psychoanalyst, of doing what we do. He further wrote that it was not only to develop his own ideas but also Klein's that he had to speak and write in his own language. However, one understands Bion's departure from London there seems little doubt that the freedom to develop the difficult and potentially different results emanating from his own work and his honesty in pursuing it were significant.

We are all familiar with the extent to which the overuse of some terms makes it hard to breathe any life into them, and in his second letter, written in October 1955, following Bion's paper 'Differentiation of the psychotic from the non-psychotic personalities,' Winnicott addressed this in relation to the wider issue of group behaviour in the British Society and how, after a first comment from Klein followed by three more from the Klein group, it was impossible for anyone to have challenged Bion's account. His letter went on to do this by introducing the importance of analytic communication through his understanding of the multiple communications condensed in the words and actions of Bion's patient. While appreciating Bion's clinical material and accepting his interpretations, he nonetheless proposed that Bion had seriously missed his patient and, in outlining why he offered a summary of his own theories of early infantile development which may well have been irritating, even as it underlined the discussion that could, should? have been had. Perhaps contemporary work and this book constitute attempts to have some of these discussions now.

Winnicott wrote in 1955,

> Bion's material cried out for an interpretation about communication......
> if a patient of mine lay on the couch moving to and fro in the way your
> patient did and then said, "I ought to have telephoned my mother," I
> would know he was talking about communication and his incapacity
> for making communication... I would have made an interpretation of
> the analyst as the mother who failed to make communication possible.

He regarded 'the present relation as a sample of the original failure from the environment which contributed to your difficulty in communication.'

The part of that 1955 interpretation which included, 'Of course you could telephone your mother but this represents a failure of the more subtle communication which is the only basis for communication that does not violate the fact of the essential isolation of each individual,' anticipates some of the more challenging claims of his paper, 'Communicating and not Communicating,' given first in San Francisco in 1962, revised for its presentation to the British Society in 1963 and published in 1965 (CW6:4:8).

For Mawson, in 2019, Winnicott's thoughts about the 'should have telephoned my mother' communications from the patient 'should have rung a bell for Bion's obvious concern for the environmental factor in psychosis,' a link that he continued to develop, always without reference to Winnicott. Until recently this is an area that has been seriously undervalued in what Winnicott brings to the study of the difficult, the hard to reach, the borderline, the psychotic patient.

In that same letter Winnicott had commented on what he described as 'the plugging of terms,' illustrating it by reference to the use of the term 'projective identification' several hundred times in the past six months, and noting that envy was destined to have a similar fate, as had internal objects until projective identification took their place! In a letter to Donald Meltzer a decade later (1966), he again commented on the constant repetition of both 'internal world' and 'projective identification.' Regardless of school or orientation this raises a continuing issue in psychoanalytic discussion: how can the freshness and illumination initially provided by particular psychoanalytic ways of thinking be retained for ongoing work if they become taken-for-granted cliches. Reference to holding and containing, container-contained, a parallel now difficult to escape, though scarcely mentioned before 2010, is only the latest example of an overuse that empties an important insight and its recognition of multiple meanings. I fear that the easy recourse to playing or creativity risks a similar deadening.

To Meltzer Winnicott also wrote, 'I am longing for the day when one of the Kleinian group will be able to say that the dependability of the internal mother has a history in the actual dependability at the beginning,' adding, significantly for our current focus, 'Bion is the only Kleinian who has used a sentence which amounts to the same thing as I have written' (in Rodman, 1987, p. 159; CW 7:3:24).

Group thinking and allegiance seems to have stood in the way of a public acknowledgement of the origin of ideas by Bion himself, and by the British society, a general area Winnicott had tackled with the philosopher John Wisdom, the discussant for Bion's work in October 1964 (CW7:1:11, 95–99). For him, Wisdom's failure to contextualise the extensive history of the three aspects of Bion's work which he regarded as distinctive and which had all formed part of his own and Marion Milner's work over the preceding twenty years was more significant than Bion's own failure because as a philosopher and a researcher, Wisdom had failed comprehensively in his task of adequately surveying the field.

Mawson referred to 'the rather touching letters sent by Winnicott to Bion, revealing a brotherly reaching out over more than a decade' (spoken presentation, 2019) and that there is no record of Bion's ever having replied, is indeed a disappointment that has left us with a frustratingly one-sided set of responses to the exchange of psychoanalytic knowledge. For me it is Bion's failures to acknowledge the climate in which his ideas originated that constitute the major trajectory of Winnicott's direct communications, the failure of a potentially shared interest and its shared pursuit that Winnicott's correspondence so strongly conveys. It is a significant if understandable blindness from Bion, one that the subsequent direction of his work leads me to think he himself later may have taken steps to remedy were Winnicott to still have been living.

I especially miss any response to Winnicott's questions in the letters from November 1960 and October 1967 about Bion's psychotic patients and whether they are people who would have had the capacity to dream and lost it, or people who never achieved what Winnicott so beautifully calls, 'the elbow room between the concrete and the abstract, or between psychic reality and external reality'(1960). When Winnicott wonders 'what it is in the analysis that may possibly enable a patient who cannot dream and who cannot either sleep or wake to achieve at last the dream'(1960) these are the profound questions about different patients and their engagement in analysis to which he was, Bion was and we are committed and to which it would be wonderful to have Bion's response as part of a continuing dialogue.

What does an analytic relationship mean and how may it enable a patient's dreaming, how can it facilitate the alternation of sleeping and being awake in such a way as to encourage a dream space that can be entered to enrich both living and dreaming. How and why do we analysts value that and what it signifies. And, rather than stay on familiar known territory can we meet patients on the territory they themselves currently occupy, so that being and becoming can occur. Moreover, when do we agree that work cannot be done, without condemning patient or analyst? These are and were shared concerns that invite shared debate now, debate that does not only regard separate local groups and traditions, then and now, but continuing debate, a willingness to engage with very real similarities and very important differences, differences inscribed in these engaged letters from Winnicott to Bion, two London analysts who shared an analytic and a cultural history. What an immense loss at the time and for the psychoanalysis of the future, for us, of that absent fraternal exchange that group, psychoanalytic and personal histories all must have acted to prevent.

In their person-directedness, Winnicott's letters confirm an aspect of letters in general, the intimacy, dedication, and effort they can embody. Winnicott was a prolific letter writer who fired off many a response to a paper he had heard at a scientific meeting to which he may have already contributed in person or which was written soon after to lie in wait for the presenter. I wonder what sort of emotional response, pleasure, interest, alarm, a letter from Winnicott arriving in the days after a scientific meeting may have occasioned in the paper's author! Did Bion just dismiss these fraternal offerings? Did he even read them? In these days of texts, email, WhatsApp, the instant response of social media, the care and the time involved in letter writing, and the intensity letters can convey about the material their writers communicate indicates a different world, one where communication and its difficulties, the determined pursuit and exchange of thoughts and collaboration are pushed to the fore. But is this not the world of psychoanalysis then and now?

In the last letter(1967) we have, Winnicott describes himself as at odds with Bion's focus on memory and desire because he does not think of analytic work as totally subjective and what he regards memory as containing. He is uneasy with Bion's linking of memory with desire, preferring his own word, 'intention.' I wonder what he would have made of the preoccupations of contemporary psychoanalysis and of the reduction of the complexity he recognises to the facile repetition of memory and desire that is now regular.

But it is the second part of that letter which incorporates a very different offer through the invoked personal link of their non-conformist Christian origins as indicated by Winnicott's wish to share his own reading of the reconstruction of the Jesus story, *The Nazarene Gospel Restored by* Robert Graves and Joshua Podro, a British poet and a Jewish scholar working together. What is a definitely idiosyncratic work disputing the accepted account of the gospels of the new testament for me echoes both with the brotherly reaching out Mawson refers to and even perhaps with both men's positioning in the world of established psychoanalysis.

The care and the time involved in letter writing and the intensity through which letter writers convey the material of their communications is worth pausing over in returning to this one-sided correspondence and its emotional intensity, its undisguised passion for the project of psychoanalysis. While the temptation is to concentrate on the content and to imagine potential debates about that content I am struck more and more by the impression of one analytic sensibility attempting to engage with another, demonstrating the participant's taken-for-granted belief in their shared project and its vital importance.

In approaching the papers of the sixties collected in *Playing and Reality* together with the papers on fear of breakdown, of communicating, and of concern I have been persistently reminded of Edward Said's development of Adorno on late style.

> Each of us can readily supply evidence of how it is that late works crown a lifetime of aesthetic endeavour, Rembrandt and Matisse, Bach and Wagner. But what of artistic lateness not as harmony and resolution, but as intransigence, difficulty and unresolved contradiction.
>
> (Said, 2006)

I have been seriously considering this as an assessment of *Playing and Reality*, the most popular psychoanalytic book ever, yet one whose popularity has always left me somewhat mystified, given the difficulty, the very inaccessibility of some of those papers, the contested clinical practices they report, the challenging ideas they contain. Perhaps those papers, in their difficulty, their challenge to accepted psychoanalytic thought, contain something of that other aspect of late works that Said addresses. And might we also be able to use this idea of associated meanings of lateness to register something of another idea of lateness with all its associations of regret in this failed fraternal connection?

By 1967, Winnicott had long left behind his Kleinian origins though always acknowledging their importance; these letters, fragments from an attempted working relationship, began well before the last decade of Winnicott's life and his growing preoccupations, but that last letter to Bion takes for granted their wider shared cultural milieu as well as their status as siblings in the narrower world of British psychoanalysis. Bion was perhaps on a similar journey in that where he goes in the last years of his own life also contains something of this perspective of pushing further, of challenging taken-for-granted assumptions, of confronting the ineffable to which psychoanalysis can lead. Much of our current interest in these two men regards those journeys, their respective destinations and the strangely similar routes they may have taken, the potentially similar places they sometimes arrived at.

In 1956, Winnicott wrote,

> I think we must reckon that there is in being from the first a crude form of what we later call the imagination. This enables us to say the infant takes in with the hands and with the sensitive skin of the face as well as of the mouth. The imaginative feeding experience is much wider than the purely physical experience.
>
> (CW 5:2:1,115-1186)

In his last paper, 'Making the Best of a Bad Job' (1979) Bion speaks of the body and communication, I now turn to the problem of communication within the Self. (I dislike terms that imply 'the body' and 'the mind,' therefore I use 'self' to include what I call body or mind, and 'a mental space' for further ideas which may be developed.... When we are engaged in psychoanalysis in which observation must play an extremely important part – as has always been recognised in a scientific inquiry – we should not be restricting our observation to too narrow a sphere.

When the patient comes into the consulting room the analyst needs to be sensitive to the totality of that person.... [He quotes Donne's poem, The Second Anniversary] 'Her pure and eloquent blood Spoke in her cheeks, and so distinctly wrought, That one might almost say, her body thought.' Or, putting it differently, the analyst needs to be able to listen not only to the words but also to the music, so that he can hear a remark which is not easily translated into black marks on paper ... ...So we must consider what is the method of communication of Self with Self. We are familiar with using free associations for purposes of interpretation; I wonder whether it is also possible to use or to tap these communications before they reach the cerebral spheres, before they reach the area which we regard as conscious or rational thought. Can any part be played in all this by what I have called 'imaginative conjectures'?

The resonance of these two descriptions written almost thirty years apart again evokes similar associations in their foregrounding of the imagination and though Winnicott and Bion would almost certainly have understood that imaginative feeding experience differently it forms a compelling basis for discussion and exchange.

Chris Mawson argued for Bion's last period as concerned with questions of being and becoming, a significant conjunction of interests between two eminent analysts who were frequent attenders and active participants at the same scientific meetings, the same discussions, in the same place, over many years, who were thinking about the same things in the same period, and yet it is only recently through clinicians and scholars who now think of them together as a matter of course, that more sustained research can be attempted about their respective ideas of being and becoming and the extent to which they lay the foundations for what many of us now understand by an analysis.

As part of a research project at the Institute of Germanic and Romance studies of London University on Psychoanalysis and the Humanities across five languages, Jacqueline Amati Mehler, one of the authors of *The Babel of the Unconscious* (1993) and like me, part of the Italian group, raised just how much the vicissitudes of translating Freud's work into various languages have influenced the development of psychoanalytic thought in different national contexts (Amati Mehler, 2010; Amati-Mehler, Argentieri, Canestri, 1993).Translation places a heavy responsibility on the translator in working to make available to different readers the language in which a creative act took place. Its dangers are captured in the Italian warning 'traduttore-traditore' equating translators with traitors. Reading and rereading participates in this caution especially when, as in Winnicott's letters to Bion, we have only one side of a correspondence, five unresponded to attempts at dialogue. Caution also forms part of our contemporary interest in the similarities and differences in their work and in the different psychoanalytic languages that emerged from the same psychoanalytic and socio-cultural context, inside the same institution. At times I think that coming to terms with the peculiarities of Winnicott and Bion's related but different languages in scientific meetings in their shared psychoanalytic home must have seemed as gargantuan a task as that of translating Freud. Certainly it was one, rarely, if ever, undertaken.

References

Amati-Mehler, J, Argentieri, S & Canestri, J (1993). *The Babel of the Unconscious*. International Universities Press Inc.

Amati-Mehler, J (2010). Translation and multi-lingualism in the psychoanalytic dimension. *Journal of Romance Studies*, 10(3): 89–100.

Bion, W (1951/1967). The imaginary twin. In: *Second Thoughts*. London: Routledge.

Bion, W (1955/1957). Differentiation of the psychotic from the non-psychotic personalities. *International Journal of Psycho-analysis*, 38: 266–275.

Bion, W (1976). Penetrating silence. In: C. Mawson (Ed.) *The Complete Works of W R Bion (CW)*. London: Karnac, 31–44.

Bion, W (1979). Making the best of a bad job. In: *The Complete Works of W R Bion*. London: Karnac.

Bion, WR (1962). The psycho-analytic study of thinking. *IJP*, 43: 306–310.

Caldwell, L & Taylor Robinson, H (2016). *The Collected Works of Donald Winnicott*. NYC: Oxford University Press.

Mawson, C (2015). *The Complete Works of W R Bion*. London: Karnac.

Mawson, C. (2019). Personal communication.

Mawson, C (2019). *Psychoanalysis and Anxiety From Knowing to Being*. London: Routledge.

Rodman, R (1987). *The Spontaneous Gesture. Selected Letters of D. W. Winnicott*. Cambridge, MA: Harvard University Press.

Said, E (2006). *Late Style*. New York: Pantheon Books.

Winnicott, DW (1951). Letter to Wilfred Bion. In: CW 3:6:2.

Winnicott, DW (1952, 17 November). Letter to Melanie Klein in Rodman, 33–38 and in CW 4:1:13.

Winnicott, DW (1955, 7 October). Letter to Wilfred Bion in Rodman, 89–93 and in CW 5:1:16.

Winnicott, DW (1956) What Do We Know About Babies as Cloth Suckers? CW5:2:1 115–118.

Winnicott, DW (1960, 17 November). Letter to Wilfred Bion in Rodman, p. 133 and in CW 6:1:18.

Winnicott, DW (1963/1965). Communicating and not communicating leading to a study of certain opposites. In: *The Maturational Processes and the Facilitating Environment*. London: Hogarth; 1965; reprinted London: Karnac, 1990, pp. 179–192; and in *The Collected Works of DW Winnicott*, 6:4:8. New York: Oxford University Press, 2016.

Winnicott, DW (1964). Letter to John Wisdom. In: Rodman, N. 142–4 and in CW, vol. 7:1:11. Oxford: Oxford University Press.

Winnicott, DW (1965). *The Maturational Processes and the Facilitating Environment: Studies in the Theory of Emotional Development*. London: Hogarth.

Winnicott, DW (1966, 25 October). Letter to Donald Meltzer. In: F. Robert Rodman (Ed.), 157–161 and in CW 7:3:24411–414, 2016.

Winnicott, DW (1967, 5 October). Letter to Wilfred Bion in Rodman, 169–170 and in CW 8:1:23.

3 Melanie Klein Absolutely Would Not Allow This

Winnicott's Shadowboxing in His Letter to Bion, October 5, 1967

Giuseppe Civitarese

> Now, when I listen to Dr Bion, I get drunk with a kind of delight because everything he says is so new, and so exciting, and I want to really express my resentment at this sort of drunkenness that he induces in me, and complain about how he does it, and why I think he shouldn't …
>
> D. Meltzer, in Mawson (2014, p. 22)

> if someone is playing squash, or tennis, it is not felt to be advisable that they should play static ball games such as golf.
>
> Bion, Memory & desire (2014 [1965], p. 11)

The letter that Winnicott wrote to Bion on October 5, 1967, is brief, consisting of only three paragraphs, and is clearly divided into two parts. The first part contains a comment on the work "Negative Capability" (NC), while the second part focuses on the essay "Catastrophic Change" (CC), which had been read and published the previous year. However, I argue that this division is only superficial and that, in reality, there is a more or less hidden continuity between the two parts, both on a manifest and latent level.

The explicit theme that connects the two texts is change. I am referring to change within the analytic setting and, consequently, to the question of what technique is most effective in promoting it; in the background, there is also the change in psychoanalytic theory, with the related differences between various models; and finally, change in society.

The implicit theme running through both comments is the polemic with Kleinian psychoanalysis. Let's take a closer look.

Bion presented the work that inspired Winnicott to write the letter during a meeting of the British Psychoanalytic Society in London. The text, initially known as "Negative Capability," was later published under the title "Notes on Memory and Desire" in the *Psychoanalytic Forum* (1967). It was subsequently reprinted in the collective volume edited by Bott Spillius, *Melanie Klein Today* (1988), and in *Cogitations* (1992). However, it is actually a reworking of an oral presentation, given without notes, that Bion had made two years earlier, on June 16, 1965. The transcript of that presentation, obtained from a recording of the meeting, is available in the *Complete Works* (CW).

DOI: 10.4324/9781003502067-3

For our purposes, it is relevant to note how Mawson (2014) highlights the emphatic and dogmatic tone of the text, arguing that this contributed to the frequent misunderstandings it generated. However, the 1965 text appears significantly less dogmatic and *authoritarian* than the 1967 version, likely due to its nature as an improvised speech. This aspect is also evident from the difference in length between the two writings: over five thousand words in the first, compared to just nine hundred in the second (with an additional similar word count for Bion's response to various questions and comments from the participants).

On the Topic of Memory and Desire

The first part of "Negative Capability" (NC) reflects Winnicott's reaction to the evening when Bion presented the essay in which he argued that the analyst should listen to the patient while renouncing memory, desire, and understanding (–MDC). In his letter, Winnicott expresses a superficial appreciation, but his disagreement is deep and substantial. He proposes replacing the term "desire" with "intention." Winnicott believes that the concept of desire is not the most appropriate to describe the attitude the analyst should adopt during the session. His critique implies that talking about desire represents yet another devaluation by Kleinian analysts of the role of external reality in the therapeutic relationship.

Winnicott's aim is to highlight the aspect of intentionality, an element that Bion, fond of ambiguity, tends to leave in the shadows. This detail is by no means secondary but rather crucial, as it encapsulates an entire conception of what the best attitude should be for the analyst in listening to the analysand. The term "intention" is connected to the idea of activity, even when it manifests in a negative form; "desire," on the other hand, is intrinsically linked to an idea of passivity.

Winnicott clarifies that regarding memory and desire, he "cannot accept that they are one hundred percent subjective." The issue becomes clearer when he writes that it is necessary to allow the patient "to be a separate person." This observation is a direct critique of the Kleinians' excessive emphasis on the internal world and unconscious fantasy, which, according to him, leads them to overlook the influence of the environment. It is possible that Winnicott sees Bion's extreme focus on the here and now as another way, albeit different, of neglecting the importance of the environment.

Winnicott remains faithful to the classical idea of interpretation as a tool for translating the unconscious into the conscious, unlike Bion, who instead focuses more on developing the capacity for independent thinking. However, in substance, there would be no divergence. Winnicott also often emphasizes the importance of not rushing to interpret, considering it essential to give the patient the necessary time to formulate their own interpretation of events. Naturally, Winnicott plays with children and is the author of the "snack bar therapy" formula (quoted in Abram & Hinshelwood, 2023, p. 55), aspects that converge with the post-Bionian concept of unsaturated interpretation.

The formula amended by Winnicott would read: the analyst must listen without memory, without intention, and without understanding. Corrected in this way, it would express the idea that the analyst can desire as much as they want, but what will emerge and constitute an analytical fact will be outside the analyst's subjective sphere and brought forth by the patient. In this way, Winnicott seems to assert the role of objective observation over subjective intuition. From a certain perspective, this appears paradoxical, as it is also Bion's stated goal: to improve the theory of observation in analysis, although Bion bases it on the intuition of experiences that cannot be grasped by the senses.

The problem is that Bion asserts that the analyst must renounce memory and desire, while Winnicott seems to accuse him of wanting instead to rely on them. The sentence is convoluted: Winnicott's point is that even if the analyst had desires, they would not be effective in the therapeutic process. Winnicott seems to overlook the fact that, although Bion is not a pediatrician, his "objectivity" derives from familiarity with extreme situations, such as war experiences and work with psychotic patients. And isn't it true that, for Klein, there is an equivalence between child and psychotic?

For Winnicott, speaking of "intention" might be a way to emphasize the importance of the real relationship. The term evokes the concept of intentionality, a Husserlian idea that asserts the mind cannot be empty but is always directed toward something, thereby implying a notion of objectivity. Husserl's approach, which draws on the concept of intentionality from Brentano—a shared mentor with Freud—aims to overcome Cartesian solipsism, although it initially seems to adopt an idealistic perspective.

We are, therefore, dealing with a possible misunderstanding. Bion does not propose anything fundamentally different but rather invites us to free ourselves from the preconceptions of militant Kleinianism. His suggestion to listen without memory, desire, and understanding (–MDC) is clearly a way to value the current relationship. More than a divergence, their respective views could be interpreted as convergent, though expressed in different ways.

However, the difference lies in what the analyst should renounce. It is as if what is being distanced from still continues, in a negative sense, to exert an influence, reflecting in the two authors a different approach. Indeed, this becomes evident if we consider, for example, the central role that Bion assigns to the concept of rêverie, which is clearly a positive expression of the analyst's subjectivity—that is, of memory and desire—although it paradoxically ends up being interpreted as a field phenomenon.

Bion's essay is often misunderstood. Could an analyst ever truly or completely renounce memory, desire, and understanding? No, it would be impossible; it would mean nullifying oneself as a subject, reducing oneself to a state similar to that of a severe Alzheimer's patient. There must be something else at play. And what is it? Winnicott's critique of the Kleinians now coincides with that of Bion: it is aimed at the mechanical, obsessive, and sterile use of concepts and interpretative formulas.

From another perspective, –MDC represents a re-presentation of the deconstructive attitude toward the discourse of abstract rationality, which is Freud's great innovation. The so-called evenly suspended attention is nothing more than the method by which the analyst interprets the patient's dream with their own dream. This leads Merleau-Ponty[1] to define analysis as a hermeneutic rêverie.

To understand the meaning of –MDC, which represents the practical externalization of the principle of evenly suspended attention, we must consider it as a call to the essence of the psychoanalytic method, which is embodied in the centrality of the dream. Bion asks us to renounce voluntary memory, desire, and understanding, but not the involuntary ones. This distinction lies at the heart of Proust's literary masterpiece and in Walter Benjamin's conception regarding the difference between chronicle and history. For a chronicle to become history, it must be immersed in the living subjectivity of the analyst.

Compared to intention, desire is more closely tied to emotion and affect. The term "intention" implies a conscious and planned decision to act toward a specific goal, whereas desire is rooted in a less rational substrate: you can decide whether to indulge a desire, but you cannot decide to desire something. Desire is spontaneous and uncontrollable: you either feel it or you don't. Ultimately, compared to Winnicott, it seems that Bion grounds his thinking more in the state of passivity that favors dreaming, and therefore more in the paradigm of the dream itself.

This implies that Winnicott's criticism is somewhat off-target when he prefers the term "intention" over "desire," considering it more precise and less subjective. In reality, it is not this type of precision or objectivity that Bion aspires to. On the contrary, it is quite the opposite. Winnicott could have instead highlighted a fruitful convergence with his own ideas of transitionality and the potential space, where individual subjectivities are enhanced in the creation of a third dimension that fosters the growth of both parties involved.

Winnicott also fails to recognize the possible link between the deconstruction inherent in renouncing voluntary MDC to rely on involuntary MDC (or –MDC) and his own concept of "destruction". For instance, he could have noted the analogy between the concept of the object's "survival" and Bion's idea of the "selected fact," understood as an element that imposes itself on the analyst's inattentive mind in –MDC and, so to speak, resists destruction/deconstruction.

The point is that, again, more than in Winnicott, it is in Bion that we find the unprecedented centrality given to the dream by Freud, a contribution that I consider both ingenious and enduring. –MDC means turning off the light and closing doors and windows to create the ideal environment for dreaming the session. Would we say that intention drives the dream? No, we would rather say that it is desire (subjective) that represents the true engine of the dream.

In this regard, Bion is crystal clear: "I think that the term Desire is also—and I wish to include in it—something which Freud speaks of as wish-fulfillment and the expression of wishes in dreams; it is similar to that" ([1965] 2014, p. 8). When Bion wrote this in *Transformations* in 1965, he was working on refining the theory of observation in psychoanalysis, where the key concept is "intuition" (Civitarese, 2024a). The memory that "possesses" the recollection is not the same as the memory embodied in the subject or from which the subject allows themselves to be possessed; similarly, the desire to possess a given thing is not the same as the latent desire that inspires the work of dreams.

This concept is reiterated in the work that Winnicott heard and was published in *Psychoanalytic Forum*:

> In any session, evolution takes place. Out of the darkness and form-lessness something evolves. That evolution can bear a superficial resemblance to memory, but once it has been experienced, it can never be confounded with memory. It shares with dreams the quality of being wholly present or unaccountably and suddenly absent. This evolution is what the psychoanalyst must be ready to interpret.
>
> (1967, p. 206, my italics)

But it is not enough to just assert this. The issue, rather, is having a sufficiently sophisticated understanding of what constitutes the fabric of human subjectivity, and thus of human desire. I am referring to its simultaneous and paradoxical nature: both subjective (individual or singular) and intersubjective (social or plural). The two components, which intertwine dialectically to form the subject, are distinct and distinguishable but never separate or separable.

This is a point that, despite the theorization of the middle realm of transitionality, does not seem to be entirely clear to Winnicott nor to his contemporary, prominent followers. On an ontological level, there is no separation between subjects, nor could there be, because otherwise, subjects would not exist. The very term "subject" indicates a condition in which the individual becomes themselves only through the necessary, structural, and permanent subjection to the Other (Civitarese, 2021).

Evolution

"Evolution" is not a concept to be underestimated, as it reflects an entire theory of the psyche, indicating that the issue is not so much whether desire or intention is preferable, but rather the complex network of concepts to which each of these terms refers. Bion's idea of the unconscious is closely related to the concept of evolution. How can we define it? Let's see in what contexts Bion discusses it.

Evolution is when a working group manages to reach internal consensus; it is what the analyst should facilitate during the session; it is the involuntary memory that "swims into view," "the experience of the dream in which it seems to float into the mind as it were a whole which was at one moment absent and at the next present"; it is the sudden appearance of a "selected fact" that gives coherence to the experience, "the coming together, by a sudden precipitating intuition, of a mass of apparently unrelated incoherent phenomena which are thereby given coherence and meaning not previously possessed"; it is the unexpected emergence of a configuration "like a pattern from a kaleidoscope"; evolution is the factor that resolves disharmony ("disharmony is resolved by 'evolution'").

There is a clear connection between evolution, rêverie, and involuntary memory. "Out of darkness and formlessness something evolves." To recognize that an evolution is taking place, the analyst must not be distracted by memory. Evolution can only be grasped at the moment it occurs. We see how the concept of evolution complements that of intuition: intuition targets evolution, and developing intuitive technique allows the analyst to more easily intercept evolution.

Thus, evolution is synonymous with catastrophic change, transformation, and growth. The main factor that stimulates evolution is intuition. It is not surprising that a term like this refers to Darwin. Bion invokes Darwinian ideas, particularly the notion that judgment is the enemy of observation ("Darwin expressed the view..."). Later in the same paragraph, Bion reiterates that, for him, "evolution" is the opposite of voluntary memory.

When Bion introduces the concept of O in *Transformations*, he immediately links it to evolution. For the analyst, being one with O, becoming O, means that "he is able to know the events that are evolutions of O." O cannot be known but only become. Only after becoming O—that is, fully opening oneself to the experience—can O manifest in K through the emergence of a real fact, allowing the analyst to formulate an interpretation. The interpretation itself can be considered nothing more than the evolution of O.

On Catastrophic Change

In the second part of the letter, Winnicott begins by noting that the topic shifts to "something completely different," but this statement almost seems like a *negation* in the Freudian sense. Winnicott expresses his interest in the reference Bion makes, in the essay "The Catastrophic Change," to the Bible to illustrate the container-contained configuration (♀♂). The idea is that a happy relationship (C/C) can lead to a catastrophic change (CC) either positively (C/C→+CC) or negatively (C/C→–CC). This represents a model (not yet a theory) with which Bion replaces the concept of projective identification, drawing on a 1952 Jungian work and Nietzsche's idea of genius as what society is tasked with generating.

In that essay, Bion writes, "The conflict between the mystic and his group is exhibited in its most exaggerated and therefore most easily studied form in the accounts of Jesus' relationship with his group" (1966, p. 22). For this reason, he mentions the Gospels and addresses the theme of religion. Curiously, Winnicott picks up the term "desire," expressing his intention to renounce it (almost as if he were unwittingly following Bion's controversial precept) and writes: "I have no desire to cast aside everything I have heard endlessly and have tried to assimilate by making a choice" (my emphasis), which evidently seems suitable to him in this context. He declares his intention to remain true to his religion, while recognizing the existence of people who consider themselves religious and believe in miracles.

However, his faith does not prevent him from continuing to see himself as an analyst. Subsequently, he advises Bion to read *The Nazarene Gospel Restored* by Robert Graves and Joshua Podro (1953), a book that, in his opinion, might shed light on the topics addressed in *The Catastrophic Change*. Given that Bion uses the story of Jesus, this book could offer him a "reconstruction of the original story." However, he warns that the book is difficult to find because it is "out of print"—a text in which the negative (i.e., theoretical ghosts) is prominent. Like the Cheshire Cat, the book seems to be both present and absent at the same time. Winnicott would gladly give him a copy, but he does not have one. He does suggest that the volume should be easily available in libraries.

All this invites the reader to indulge in the game of interpretation. In my view, a possible reading of the latent text might be as follows: Winnicott reiterates his incredulity toward "Kleinian miracles." His ambivalence toward Bion becomes evident, and perhaps for this reason, Bion does not respond to him. Essentially, when Bion exhibits Kleinian tendencies, Winnicott does not appreciate it, seeing Kleinianism as a "church," whereas his own psychoanalysis is a "book," "disapproved by all Christian churches." However, filled with resentment, he would not be satisfied if Bion stopped being Kleinian, because in that case, Bion should—or rather, would already have to—recognize that it was Winnicott who emphasized the idea that "there is no child" (except in relation to the mother and the environment). Currently, restoring this historical truth seems difficult, as evidenced by the limited accessibility of Robert Graves and Joshua Podro's *The Nazarene Gospel Restored*. But the possibility still exists.

One might wonder if, in his critique of those who believe in miracles, there is also a subtle poison directed at Bion, who, in a nearly mystical way, insists that the analyst must have the ability to intuit the evolution of the session; that is, "the experience where some idea or pictorial impression floats into the mind unbidden and as a whole" (Bion, 1967a, p. 208): as if to say, rêverie as a means to explore the emotional experience of the session.[2]

Naturally, we might ask whether instead of entering a different domain, this is rather a matter of hindsight, meaning that even the first paragraph dealt with religion, but of a different kind of religion. The initial point is a positive comment on Bion's use of biblical references in the essay on catastrophic change. Winnicott thus seems to blur the dissent expressed in the first paragraph. However, considering the underlying controversy, this part of the text might be interpreted as an implicit message to Bion: "I know you can't entirely or easily free yourself from Kleinian religion, and you don't even need to, just as I can't free myself from my education, even if I no longer believe in miracles."

In other words, it seems to suggest: "Stop believing in Klein's miracles, like the idea that the child is already a subject at birth, or that primary envy and similar concepts exist." The way Winnicott proposes for Bion to save himself is through heresy, just as one gathers data on the original history of the Gospels, or, in the case of psychoanalysis, on the history of the origins of subjectivity.

The suggestion is paradoxical, because Bion, for at least five years, has been trying to escape the suffocating grip of the orthodoxy/heresy dichotomy that burdens psychoanalysis. It is a difficult journey, which will lead him to an ideal endpoint in the mature reflections of *Cogitations* from July 1971 (see further). Winnicott's letter thus stands exactly halfway through this troubled path, a moment when Bion is engaged in freeing himself from the yoke of the Kleinian group and becoming fully himself.

It is clear that, through authors and books, Winnicott presents himself as the one who wants to correct the myth of the origins of the psyche. However, the endeavor is not simple. The "book" cannot be found, and he is unable to give it to him. In this way, Winnicott expresses the difficulty of direct dialogue, and indeed it seems that Bion never replies to him. But even if he had, we do not have the letters and would still be justified in considering this gap symptomatic.

The "book," or the possibility of modifying the theory of origins, can be found in libraries. It's as if he is saying: "If you visit libraries, if you read what I've been writing for decades, you too will be able to access the book by Graves and Podro."

Melanie Klein Would Never Allow This

Let's recap. In the letter dated October 5, Winnicott makes numerous references to classic texts such as Eliot, the Bible, and Graves. What is the significance of these references? Personally, I find them ironic. Winnicott wants to gift Bion a text on the Gospels that is unattainable for two reasons: (a) because it is "heretical" and (b) because it is out of print; but, paradoxically, it is available in libraries. In other words, a text that exists and does not exist simultaneously. The letter undoubtedly has a Borges-like flavor. The central theme is faith in miracles, which seems like a bizarre continuation of the first paragraph, which instead deals with the content of the scientific evening.

If we expand our view to other letters, the picture becomes clearer. Generally, Winnicott reproaches Bion for not citing him, for not recognizing him as a "classic" in the field. According to him, the role of the environment in psychic development is something that, he believes, Kleinians fail to truly consider.

Not so with Bion. For this reason, Winnicott writes that "Bion goes deeper than Melanie," but then why does he not mention his work? According to Winnicott, Bion "ought to say: this is what D.WW. has been trying to get us to see for two or three decades" (Rodman, 1987, p. 214). In a letter to John O. Wisdom from three years earlier (October 26, 1964), he writes:

> It is important to me that Bion states (obscurely of course) what I have been trying to state for 2Y2 decades but against the terrific opposition of Melanie. Bion uses the word reverie to cover the idea that I have stated in the complex way that it deserves that the infant is ready to create something, and in good-enough mothering *the mother lets the baby know what is being created*–of Sechehaye's term symbolic realization, i.e. in therapy. Bion says (half-way down page 36): "What happens will depend….." Melanie Klein absolutely would not allow this, and my relation to her was (though always warm and good) impaired by her adamant objection to "what happens depends …." …. You should have mentioned this fact, that Bion goes deeper than Melanie here, or finds a way of stating what Melanie would not allow.
>
> (Rodman, 1987, p. 145)

In essence, to reproach Bion for not citing him, Winnicott cites him himself, teaching him how it should be done. He then continues with another critique: "In a way, all that Bion has done is to divert our attention from the central theme and focus it on alpha and beta functions" (emphasis mine). But this is by no means a trivial detail. For Bion, it is a way to definitively emancipate psychoanalysis from the risk of becoming, as it was in part with Freud and Klein, a religion in disguise. Freud's and Klein's views are not only pessimistic or tragic but also have an ecclesial or theological character.

Even in this letter, the difference between the classical conception of the human being, based on a one-person psychology, and the view that Winnicott shares with Bion, is clearly evident. The latter is based rather on the Aristotelian definition of man as a social animal, the Hegelian dialectic of recognition as the royal road to self-consciousness, Spinoza's idea of freedom as a fruit of relationship, and finally the value that the concept of community holds in Eastern cultures. All these perspectives highlight the intersubjective essence of the individual.

For a Secular Psychoanalysis

The letter to Bion is quite striking, as it reveals how difficult it is for Winnicott to understand that Bion has profoundly changed from his Kleinian phase. By 1967, after having written three of the four books that mark Bion's mature phase, has Winnicott truly recognized his revolutionary merits, or does he simply appreciate him because he seems like a more reasonable Kleinian compared to others? His criticism comes across as rather belated, as if he were fighting against shadows. The adversaries, the "barbarians," have already left. 1967 is the year Bion publishes *Second Thoughts*. In this critical revisitation of his Kleinian-era papers, Bion seems to have embarked on a path that moves him away from old certainties and closer to a deeper and more autonomous reflection, as if he were freeing himself from the necessity to adhere to a specific "will to know."

By 1967, Bion is no longer Kleinian. Perhaps even today, we are not fully aware of the enormous impact that the introduction of the concept of "function" has on his work.[3] In my view, this novelty addresses several simultaneous needs, but most notably, the need to definitively secularize psychoanalysis. Psychoanalysis should be desacralized, in the sense of removing or revoking its sacred status, much like how former churches become gyms, concert halls, or lecture auditoriums: a kind of change of use.

In some countries, this process is already underway, but the backlash against the old theory presented as dogma may be so strong that it could lead to discarding even what is valid and valuable in the works of Freud and Klein. In some psychoanalytically oriented schools, they are simply no longer part of the curriculum. This shows us that those who turn their thoughts (or any thoughts) into catechism do a disservice to their idols.

Freud and Klein see the unconscious as the place of evil or envy, perhaps even more so the latter than the former. It's as if a biologist were to claim that transaminases are good and hemoglobin is bad. In characterizing the unconscious, Freud and Klein use not only scientific but also moral categories. This choice has had negative consequences for psychoanalysis and seems to be at the root of the well-known and recurring fideistic, dogmatic, intolerant, and uncritical attitudes among analysts, always ready to hunt for heresies to excommunicate and to maintain a pervasive suspicion towards colleagues and patients.

If psychoanalysis truly wants to be "scientific," it should limit itself to describing and explaining, not judging. Instead, for a long time, and still today, the idea has prevailed that the unconscious represents the worst of each person. Bion finally allows us to open our eyes to this absurd claim. Perhaps no one has better highlighted the alienating aspect of psychoanalysis when it becomes ideology than Foucault. This is evident in certain accounts from Kleinian authors who enthusiastically and with lethal determination engage in what Bion would call the "penetrating, sadistic, X-ray gaze" (1967a, p. 17).

For the sake of truth, it should be acknowledged that in the extremely broad and complex work of both Freud and Klein, there are theoretical hints of another nature, not moralistic or, to use a positive term from Nietzsche, *im-moralistic*, in the sense of a critical theory. For example, when Freud describes dream activity as a work of transformation in *Beyond the Pleasure Principle*, and Klein invents the technique of play in child analysis.

The fact remains, however, that both Winnicott and Bion reject the metapsychologies of Freud and Klein. As Abram and Hinshelwood remind us, "Winnicott proposed that the core problem for the human being is not primarily psychosexuality, as Freud held; nor is it the death instinct or aggression, as was suggested by Klein and Bion; rather it is the 'fact of dependency'" (2023, p. 4), which can indeed be seen as an extension of Freud's concept of helplessness (*Hilflosigkeit*).

Winnicott and Bion are, without a doubt, among the main architects of this shift, the consequences of which have yet to be fully assimilated in contemporary psychoanalysis. The crucial point lies in the element identified by Winnicott: the role of the other or the environment in psychic development. Now, if in 1964 he writes that he was saying the same things that Bion asserts, but already twenty or thirty years earlier, we arrive at 1934 or 1944. However, in 1943, Bion publishes with Rickman his brilliant essay on group psychology.[4] This cannot but be seen as the autonomous and original inauguration of a radical intersubjective shift (Civitarese, 2021). After all, Winnicott was a pediatrician working with children, while Bion had experience with groups of soldiers.

So, Winnicott is both right and wrong at the same time. The two authors are closer than they themselves would admit. When Winnicott writes the letter, the "middle group" has not yet formed, and he has not yet found a home. He would like to take refuge in the "Kleinian contingent" (p. 233), but knows he could not endure it due to the fanaticism it entails; moreover, he is actively excluded: "Mrs. Klein, however, does not seem able to see that her disciples are destroying the Society, as they are forming a block and there is no way to join this block" (p. 154).

Bion, while being part of the Kleinian group, is no longer in agreement with the dogmas of Kleinism and is exiting in what, using his term, is somewhat of a catastrophic manner. Not by chance, he ends up abandoning the concept of projective identification after attempting to make it less "religious," transforming it from an invariably aggressive relationship and emanation of primary envy into a normal mode of communication, and finally reinventing it in the "neutral" model concept of container/contained (Civitarese, 2024b).

But there are two other significant and dramatic breaks: (a) he leaves London, and one wonders if the real reason is that he could no longer tolerate the closed atmosphere of the Psychoanalytic Society, of which he was president from 1962 to 1965; (b) he is considered mad by some of his London colleagues for having written the mocking prose of *A Memoir of the Future*, a sort of spiritual testament, where one of the key aspects is certainly the struggle against the clerical, moralistic, and bigoted degradation of psychoanalysis.

In conclusion, Winnicott and Bion, despite beginning from different perspectives, appear to share a common goal: to liberate psychoanalysis from the dogmatic and religious constraints that risk stifling it. Winnicott, even as he critiques Bion, implicitly acknowledges the value of his contributions, while Bion strives to reinterpret Kleinian concepts in a less rigid and more open-minded way. Their correspondence and individual journeys highlight the complexity and delicacy of evolving psychoanalytic thought, which continually balances between tradition and innovation.

Shadowboxing

In the letter, Winnicott appears extremely human and vulnerable when he bluntly admits: "I do not accept being scotomized [...] I like to do a bit of boxing" (p. 215). Indeed, throughout his work, Bion cites Winnicott only six times (and Winnicott is not generous with references to Bion either; in the complete works, I have counted only a few mentions of Bion). It seems that a deep rift must have developed between them. Winnicott's words convey a strong sense of regret, almost like a boxer who has been knocked down with an unfair blow. But now, as he tries to convince Bion of the value of replacing "intention" with "desire," he is engaging in "shadowboxing": fighting against an opponent who is no longer present, who has already moved on.

Who is Bion when he receives Winnicott's letter? I repeat, by the autumn of 1967, Bion is a person profoundly different from the followers of Kleinian thought. That fall, he publishes *Notes on Memory and Desire*. More significantly, it is also the year of *Second Thoughts*, which, in its essay on arrogance and commentary, marks a dramatic departure from the classic conception of Oedipus. No longer is the focus on the grim vision centered on the two crimes of parricide and incest, but rather on the excess, or *hybris*, of the will to know.

To Klein's credit, she had anticipated the Oedipus complex in the primitive stages of the mind, thus mitigating the idea of the crimes. Moreover, her concept of epistemophilia perhaps paves the way for Bion to refocus the Oedipus around the scene with the Sphinx. However, the essence remains unchanged: both Freud and Klein maintain a view of humanity as intrinsically "evil."

If there were still any doubts about Bion's state of mind during those years, one needs only to reread the lecture given on April 20, 1967, at a joint meeting of the Los Angeles Psycho-Analytic Society and Institute and the

Southern California Psycho-Analytic Society, titled "Reverence and Awe." The summary can be found in *Cogitations* (1992, p. 284), just before the essay on memory and desire. I will not delve into the details of this text here, but it is sufficient to reflect on the title and implicit references, particularly regarding the concepts of *atonement/at-one-ment*—reconciliation with the "divine"—and those related to the aesthetics of the sublime (Civitarese, 2014), to understand that the issue extends beyond a simple debate on desire or intention.

Finally, in *Cogitations*, dated July 1971, we find a Bion who is already transformed, one who, a few years later, will note in his diary "A Fable for Our Time," a sort of spiritual testament where he tells the story of Mr. Smith (clearly an alias for himself). Bion[5] imagines a historical future, 300 years after the year 30070, attempting to reconstruct, from the "few remaining remains," a distant past in which…

> the practice of religion was regulated by a special hierarchy. *This organization was taken over, elaborated, but otherwise hardly changed, by the new religion, which was called a science* …. the word, 'ritual', was replaced by the term, 'scientific'. In those times it was the habit of the hierarchy to hunt out and destroy all evidence of potential growth. …. *the new religion had triumphed and was established as the 'science of psycho-analysis'*, with its hierarchy firmly in control and its ritual 'scientific method' codified and recognized as the hallmark of the New Era. …. the rules of psycho-analytic investigation—which were rigidly enforced so that there could be no breach in the solid foundation of what was already known and described as 'history'— began to be assailed by ominous and inexplicable attacks. One trouble-maker, called Smith, seems to have caused the authorities much difficulty.
>
> (Bion, 1992, pp. 328–329, my italics)

It's not that Winnicott doesn't see the change at all. In a letter to Meltzer, Winnicott reproaches him for neglecting the real, external mother in favor of the "internal" one:

> You shouldn't think that I am attacking the idea of the individual who has the delusion that ideas have an existence in his head or in his belly … I look forward to the day when someone in the Kleinian group will be able to say that the reliability of the internal mother has its history in the original real reliability; but Melanie Klein would not allow it. She would only say, 'Of course, I have always said that the environment is important … It seems to me that Bion is the only Kleinian who has used a phrase that has the same meaning as what I have now written
>
> (p. 234, my italics)

While this may not be another accusation of plagiarism, it does resonate with Bion's concept of "thought without a thinker." The paradox is that, by considering the role of the environment, the mother, the other, or the real object, Bion ends up surpassing Winnicott by giving unprecedented, almost absolute, emphasis to the relational experience in the session, in a way that remains unknown to Winnicott. In other words, Bion "outflanks" him. Writing to Meltzer (another non-fanatical Kleinian) on October 25, 1966, where he discusses the "Kleinian contingent," Winnicott says:

> To return to your paper: you do know, I suppose, that on page 3 when you use the word envy you are suddenly talking to a limited audience, namely the Kleinian group, and that the rest of the room is out of touch with you. This seems to me to be a great pity because one cannot always draw attention to these things which members of the Kleinian group tend to do as if they were determined to carry the point by propaganda, that is to say by repetition. You will agree, I think, that it is not possible for a Kleinian to use the word envy in the ordinary way that everyone uses the word unless this is specifically stated. If a Kleinian uses the word envy then this word carries the implication of acceptance of Melanie's Geneva paper (later her book), namely that the roots of aggression are linked with envy which accounts for the infant's impulse to destroy the good breast. It is the Kleinian group who feel that this makes sense and the whole of the rest of your audience feels irritated because for them *the introduction of the word envy at this point in the search for the origins of aggression does not add anything at all but confuses the issue by ascribing to the newborn infant this very complex thing that we mean by envy.* .... The same would be true if you were to use the words death instinct, taking for granted that this invention of Freud's has value. .... these things were thrown in in this way that irritates us beyond description. You know what I mean: a whole list of them *including projective identification.*
>
> (Rodman, 1987, pp. 159–160, my italics)

The passage clarifies why Winnicott, in his essay on the use of the object, speaks not of envy but of "destruction," a term that is equally strong and resonant but devoid of the moral connotation associated with envy. It is significant that Winnicott does not spare even the concept of projective identification. However, by 1967, Bion had already substantially abandoned the concept of projective identification, replacing it with that of container/contained.

A more systematic comparison between Winnicott and Bion still needs to be thoroughly explored. The real question to pose is: how effectively do Bion and Winnicott translate the centrality they each assign to the mother-child relationship into practical technical tools? To what extent does Winnicott, and those who are inspired by his thinking, manage to transform the principle of intersubjectivity inherent in the maternal-infant relationship as a model for the analytic process into new and effective technical instruments? And what contributions have they made in this regard compared to Bion on a metapsychological level, starting from the very definition of the concept of the unconscious?

My opinion is that, while Winnicott was the first to emphasize the mother-infant relationship, it is Bion who developed the more refined tools to intuit what actually happens on the unconscious level of the relationship in the here and now. This is made possible by his revolution in the concept of the unconscious and the radicalization of the centrality of dreaming in theory and practice, especially when considered alongside the fertile developments in the theory of the analytic field (Civitarese, 2023; Ferro & Civitarese, 2015).

Both adopt the mother-child model but use it in different ways: Bion uses it to understand what happens in the therapeutic relationship and to look toward the future, while Winnicott focuses on the past, using the model to explore the need to relive the original trauma through regression in analysis. Bion, with the basic assumption of the small group formed by the analytic pair, is concerned with developing the capacity to symbolize, whereas Winnicott concentrates on the need to relive the original trauma within the analytic context.

Notes

1 See Merleau-Ponty (2003, p. 155): "It is necessary to conceive all of what Freud has described …. not as the dogmatic explication of the human …. but as hermeneutical reverie [*rêverie hermeneutique*], introducing [some] unknown but not exclusive factors." And further: "Method proper to the understanding of dreams: reverie over dreams, hermeneutical reverie. Because it is not something said, but an echo through totality. It is this system of echoes which also constitutes the oneirism of wakefulness" (Merleau-Ponty, 2003, p. 154).

2 Consistent with these Bionian assumptions are the concepts and techniques of transformation into dreams (Ferro, 2009) and transformation into hallucinosis (Civitarese, 2015).

3 In the entry on projective identification in IRED, the authors correctly assert that the container-contained model conceptually derives from the Klein's concept of projective identification. However, they fail to address the dramatic paradigm shift that this implies, treating it as if it were merely an expansion or integration. Perhaps even Winnicott does not fully grasp its actual significance (Civitarese, 2024b).

4 It's true that as early as 1942, Winnicott asserts that there is no child without the mother. However, Bion's pioneering work on groups, which carries a similarly intersubjective imprint, dates back to the same years. In 1941, Bion, along with Rickman, created the Leaderless Group Project, *a method that truly anticipated –MDC*, and in 1942–43, at Northfield, he developed the small group therapy approach.

5 Cf. Abram e Hinshelwood (2023, p. 53): although Bion's change in his late work may well have departed from the Kleinian technique we know today. Most London Kleinians reject Bion's late work.

References

Abram, J., & Hinshelwood, R. (2023). *The Clinical Paradigms of Donald Winnicott and Wilfred Bion*. London: Routledge.

Bion, W. R. (1965). *Transformations: Change from Learning to Growth*. London: Tavistock.

Bion, W. R. (1966). The catastrophic change. In *The Complete Works of W. R. Bion*, vol. VI. London: Karnac, pp. 19–43.

Bion, W. R. (1967a). *Second Thoughts: Selected Papers on Psycho-Analysis*. London: Heinemann.

Bion, W. R. (1967b). Notes on memory and desire. In *The Complete Works of W. R. Bion*, vol. VI. London: Karnac, pp. 203–210; also in Bott Spillius, E. (Ed.). (1988). *Melanie Klein Today: Developments in Theory and Practice. Volume 2 Developments in Theory and Practice. Volume 2 Mainly Practice*. London: Routledge, pp. 15–18.

Bion, W. R. (1992). *Cogitations*. London: Karnac.

Bion, W. R. (2014 [1965]). Memory and desire. In *The Complete Works of W. R. Bion*, vol. VI. London: Karnac, pp. 1–17.

Bion, W. R. (2014). *The Complete Works of W. R. Bion*. London: Routledge.

Civitarese, G. (2014). Bion and the sublime: The origins of an aesthetic paradigm. *International Journal of Psychoanalysis*, 95, 1059–1086.

Civitarese, G. (2015). Transformations in hallucinosis and the receptivity of the analyst. *International Journal of Psychoanalysis*, 96, 1091–1116.

Civitarese, G. (2021). Intersubjectivity and the analytic field. *Journal of the American Psychoanalytic Association*, 69, 853–894.

Civitarese, G. (2023). *Psychoanalytic Field Theory: A Contemporary Introduction*. London: Routledge.

Civitarese, G. (2024a). Intuition and we-ness in Bion and post-Bionian field theory. *International Journal of Psychoanalysis*, 105, 13–39.

Civitarese, G. (2024b). Upgrade to PI.4, or rethinking projective identification from the vertex of the analytic field. *International Journal of Psychoanalysis*, in press.

Ferro, A. (2009). Transformations in dreaming and characters in the psychoanalytic field. *International Journal of Psychoanalysis*, 90, 209–230.

Ferro, A., & Civitarese, G. (2015). *The Analytic Field and Its Transformations*. London: Karnac.

Graves, R., & Podro, J. (1953). *The Nazareno Gospel Restored*. London: Cassell.

Mawson, C. (2014). Editor's introduction. In Bion, W. R. (Ed.) *The Complete Works of W. R. Bion*, vol. VI. London: Karnac, pp. 21–26.

Merleau-Ponty, M. (2003). *Institution and Passivity. Course Notes from the Collège de France (1954–1955)*. Evanston, IL: Northwestern University Press, 2010.

Rodman, F. R. (Ed.) (1987). *The Spontaneous Gesture ~ Selected Letters of D. W. Winnicott*. Cambridge: MA: Harvard University Press.

4 Winnicott's Paradox

Being with and without Memory and Desire

Steven H. Cooper

Winnicott's letter to Bion stimulates a few questions about important areas of overlap and difference between the two theorists. If anything, I'm surprised that Winnicott's objections to the paper were not stronger, raising the question of whether he was writing a courteous, collegial letter that belied some significant objections. It is possible that Winnicott was actually referring as much to Bion's paper, *Notes on Memory and Desire* (Bion, 1967, 1970) paper than the lecture on negative capability which immediately preceded the letter.

My reading of Winnicott's letter to Bion leads me to an assemblage of foci in Winnicott's writing about maternal preoccupation, being the guardian of play and the analytic setting, surviving the infant's and patient's destruction, and being both an actual and symbolic object in the analytic process. Each of these areas involves the analyst and mother holding a particular position of being with and without desire in their actions. To wit, the capacity to hold paradox is at the center of Winnicott's writings about interpretive stance, one that he felt promoted individuals' ability to live a creative life (Winnicott,1967; 1968a, 1968b).

To state my thesis as succinctly as possible, albeit a speculative one, Winnicott's differences with Bion's statement that the analyst should be without memory and desire revolve around Winnicott holding on to a paradox which requires that the analyst will hold that he will be both with and without memory and desire. I address how his views on the areas of maternal preoccupation, playing, temporality, and creative aggression contributed to Winnicott's reflections on Bion's suggestion to listen without memory and desire.

One notion that informs my thinking about Winnicott's letter to Bion, is the belief that throughout his writing, Winnicott is deeply interested in both the actuality and symbolic value of the object as they contribute to development and the therapeutic action of psychoanalysis. In the transitional object paper, he underscores the value of the transitional object as related to it being an actual object, not simply symbolic. He emphasizes in The Use of the Object that the subject destroys the object "because the object is placed outside the area of omnipotent control," but also that it is the destruction

DOI: 10.4324/9781003502067-4

of the object "that places the object outside the area of omnipotent control" (Winnicott, 1969, p. 90). I have argued (e.g., 2018) in agreement with many other authors (e.g., Bromberg, 1998; Ogden, 2016; Bonaminio, 2012) that the patient's experience of the analyst's actuality such as the fear of being destroyed is a part of the movement from relating to usage. I believe that the kind of actual object that Winnicott described is a different kind of actual object than the one Bion described.

Similarly, in his two major papers on play (Winnicott, 1967, 1968b), he is not especially concerned with who initiates play. For example, in his theoretical paper about play, the analyst became a wellspring of motivation for play (Winnicott, 1968b). Winnicott is more interested in whether play or any form of interpretation is getting ahead of the patient's ability to integrate what is occurring between patient and analyst, what he referred to as the patient's transference confidence than whether the analyst's motivations initiate play.

The Letter

I will quote only the first part of the letter which is the part related to Bion's lecture and the focus of my paper:

Dear Bion,
First, to thank you for a very interesting evening.

I am not quite settled in my mind about the idea of memory and desire or intention. When I got home, Clare reminded me again that the phrase memory and desire, which you have used before, is a quotation from T. S. Eliot, and she was able to give me the whole poem, and for some reason or other I accept memory and desire as naturally interrelated in the poem. At the same time, in the application of the same idea to psycho-analytic work I cannot help finding myself using the word intention and not feeling desire to be correct. As you said, we each have to find the word that fits for oneself. For me, memory and desire is all right in a poem because it refers to an experience that is 100% subjective. In the application of psycho-analytic work I find I cannot allow that this is 100% subjective. The memory includes memories of phenomena from external reality and certainly what is likely to turn up tomorrow in my analytic work cannot be covered by what I have in my own mind to want, precisely because I have to be able to allow the patient to be a separate person, as the patient has to come to be able to allow me to be outside his or her omnipotent control.

So you see why is that I find myself unhappy with your word desire in this context.

As you can see, Winnicott found the concept of without memory and desire quite intriguing but preferred the word, "intention" over "desire" because analytic work is not purely subjective in the way that poetry is. For Winnicott, the notion of the analyst's intentions were more applicable to the ways he wished to work with his memories of phenomena from external reality that he had already formed, "because I have to be able to allow the patient to be a separate person, as the patient has to come to be able to allow me to be outside his or her omnipotent control" (p. 158).

Let's address the implications of desire versus intention along several different dimensions.

The Actuality of the Object and the Paradox of Being With and Without Desire

Winnicott's response to Bion, captures the ethic of working with our intentions in order to use, construct, and destroy our affective and cognitive sketches along the way in knowing our patients and ourselves with our patients. It is an arduous process, one that Bion elaborated perhaps more than any other analyst. Winnicott ends his note to Bion, reminding him that Bion himself had stated in this and many other writings that, it is important for us each to find our own ways of referring to this process including our own language.

Winnicott's primary objection to the words, "without memory and desire" involves the fact that as an actual person and analyst, Winnicott knows that he has many desires and memories. He cannot be without them through fiat.

Part of the analyst's experience of the analytic process and of himself involves a kind of unlearning or maybe we could even say parricide toward elements of the analytic process with each patient. If we think of working as a psychoanalyst as always involving a tension between applying a body of learned technique (received wisdom) and our own individual sensibilities applied to the unique person with whom we are working, there is always a process of destruction that is occurring.

Winnicott's notion of the actuality of the object suggests that he is describing himself in the analytic process as real to himself and to some extent the patient. He is not wanting to push away too much of what makes him real such as memory and desire. Having said that, I imagine that Winnicott must have been aware of Bion's interest in the analyst's own disturbed attention in listening.

Both Winnicott and Bion were in their own revolutionary ways, working with the actuality of the object (mother and analyst) in ways that were at odds with their Kleinian training. They were each struggling with this fact both in their theory development and likely in the political climate in which they toiled.

Each were addressing the ways that the analyst will become an impediment to the analytic process, either in their own wishes to cure the patient or other related matters. Each were concerned with the problems of prosaic, over-formulated varieties of responsiveness to their patient. They were looking for fresh, creative forms of responsiveness that involved waiting and resisting obvious and more accessible types of interpretation. Each in their unique ways were developing Freud's discovery of free-floating attention.

Hinshelwood has suggested that Bion's (1967) statement of "without memory and desire" was in some ways indelicate since Bion was using the Eliot quote in a somewhat general, unnuanced manner. Bion had always considered that the analyst's attitudes and ideas are evolving during the analytic process. Thus, the analyst is striving toward "without memory and desire" but is by no means easily ever to be without it.

It is also possible that Winnicott (e.g., 1951, 1945, 1956, 1971), who had written extensively about the mother and analyst as actual objects, took exception to some of Bion's later writing about reverie which seems to lay claim to ideas about the analyst's actual function as a receptor-organ during the process of reverie. Aguayo (2018) has discussed Winnicott's abundant frustration with Wisdom's (1964) presentation of Bion's work on reverie and the actuality of the object analyst/mother. Winnicott was upset that Bion's work was presented as if it was original, a claim that is apparent in an angry letter that Winnicott wrote to Wisdom in 1964. In the letter, Winnicott states

> Bion uses the word reverie to cover the idea that I have stated in the complex way that it deserves that the infant is ready to create something, and in "good enough: mothering, the mother lets the baby know what is being created. I don't mind being shown to be wrong or criticized or banged about. But I have done some important work out of the sweat of my psycho-analytic brow (i.e. Clinically) and I refuse to be scotomized.
>
> (Rodman, 1987, p. 146)

Naturally, the tone of this letter as early as 1964 suggests that Winnicott was already prepared to greet Bion's ideas about "without memory and desire," with potential resentment. It seems that Winnicott was already upset that Bion was receiving attention for his discussion of the analyst as an actual object, a level of attention that Winnicott felt he had not received for his earlier work. Now, in his without memory and desire paper, whether Winnicott was correct or not, it may have seemed to Winnicott that Bion was less oriented to the actuality of the object and more toward a more dispassionate object. Bion went to some length to describe how for the analyst's responsiveness to be useful to the patient, it must hold different elements of the analyst's inner life. Still, it may have been a bit dizzying for Winnicott. Further, as Aguayo (2018) repeatedly noted in relation to a number of Bion's writings, Winnicott may have felt that Bion appropriated some of Winnicott's ideas about environmental influence without attributing credit to him for these ideas. This appropriation may have been further confounding for Winnicott given that at times Bion (e.g., 1949) may have noted the presence of the actual object but focused more on the "patient's phantasmic experience of the external object." While Winnicott was not insensitive to how this process might occur, it was not his focus on the external object in a number of papers that focused on the actuality of the object (e.g., Winnicott, 1945, 1951, 1956).

I now briefly touch on a few other areas that might shed light on Winnicott's reactions to Bion's lecture, namely his view of maternal preoccupation; his view of playing and creative aggression related to the use of the object and the object's survival; and finally his view of interpretation.

The Relevance of Maternal Preoccupation, Holding, and the Actuality of the Object

Winnicott (1945, 1956) argues that maternal preoccupation is based on the notion that the mother, "for the time being" is devoted to the care of her infant. At one level, the mother must recognize "absolute dependence on the mother and of her capacity for primary maternal preoccupation, or whatever it is called, is something which belongs to extreme sophistication, and to a stage not always reached by adults" (p. 304). Yet Winnicott repeatedly emphasized in his writing the need for the mother to be aware of her own limits and for the analyst to do so as well. I have suggested elsewhere that even the phrase, "for the time being" suggests the mother's limits in her ability to be preoccupied (e.g., Cooper, 2025).

To the extent that we can extrapolate the mother's attention to the interpretive focus of the analyst, the kind of attention that Winnicott is emphasizing both regarding preoccupation and to her own limits is driven by, and I don't believe well characterized by being without memory and desire. Put another way, for Winnicott limit is continually constitutive of play as is all interpretive responsiveness, and is driven by the need for survival (e.g., Cooper, 2019).

Winnicott's uses the phrase, "for the time being," in relation to the mother's fastened attention in both the maternal preoccupation paper and in his paper, Primitive Emotional Development. It is a beautifully condensed linguistic turn about how desire is temporally arriving and disappearing in the context of parenting and analytic work. The notion of the maternal preoccupation being held for the time being is to some extent at odds with an ideal of being without memory and desire, paradoxically so since the mother's conscious attention to her infant preoccupies as her own attention to any other conscious desires recede. His phrase "for the time being" reveals the impossibility of this stance as an ongoing position. Winnicott views limit as intrinsic to the guardianship of the setting and constitutive of play as evidenced in his two-part opus on play (Winnicott, 1967, 1968b) as well as in his writing about hate in the countertransference (Winnicott, 1949).

Similarly, during transitional object development the parent needs to be aware of the child's need for the transitional object, protecting that the child will have access to it, but too perfect an attunement to the child's need for the transitional object may interfere with the child's ability to parse the different between reality and hallucination (Winnicott, 1951). The good enough parent is devoted to honoring the illusory elements of an object that is both me and not/me; of understanding the need to contain ambivalence about separation both within the child and within the parent's affective experience; and appreciating that the child needs to understand the difference between hallucination and reality. The parent's desire, like the analyst's desire may involve wishes to provide awareness of these needs by the child, while holding the inevitability of failure along the way.

Playing With and Without Memory and Desire

In play, one of Winnicott's version of paradox related to how the analyst's mandate (is this desire?) is that he is to find play, initiated by the patient or analyst, but not search too much for it. Also, the analyst is both the guardian/supervisor of play but also a participant.

One of Winnicott's greatest contributions to psychoanalysis was his ability to view illusion so positively, as a generative force. For example, the analyst's ability to occupy a state where linear time is of no consequence involves an extraordinarily compassionate and creative capacity to work with illusion and wish (Winnicott,1967; Cooper, 2023a, 2023b, 2025). Winnicott is profoundly interested in reality, but illusion is required to more deeply interrogate what reality is all about. We can't exclusively understand reality by commenting on it through interpretation. Instead, living in illusory places in life and in analysis can help us see and experience reality in new ways.

I have been quite interested in playing in analytic work with adult patients as the theoretical undergirding for analytic process for a few reasons. Winnicott's genius regarding play, lay in his understanding of the relationship between the actuality of objects and experience interacting with fantasy and potential space. As I have defined it, playing in analysis with adults involves making use of reverie in particular ways that enter more deeply elements of transference and intersubjective engagement and enactment. This occurs through idiomatic expressions of unconscious fantasy, defense and conflict expressed by the patient or analyst through their associations and reverie. At the same time, playing is ordinary, a part of the associative process.

The play model rests on more overlapping assumptions with that of a focus on reverie and dreaming than not. In my view, in both playing and reverie, both patient and analyst have been changed by the experience and process of being inside an undergirded psychic reality. As Reis (2020) put it, the joined unconscious relation between analyst and patient, "subtends the content of any conscious exchange and provides the basis for a non-rational production of knowledge through non-interpretive mutual intervention, the operation of which represents the very heart of the treatment" (p. 3). Yet in my view, play makes use of reverie, including irreverent, subversive activity that at times rests less on at least the immediate goals of metabolization and integration. At times play grows out of paradoxically disruptive forays into unhappy stasis (e.g., repetitive patterns, defenses, and entrenched unconscious fantasy). Green (1993) pointed out, the analyst transforms into "a potential object including transformations" (p. 276). As Corbett (2023) put it, in play "the analyst plays the object and becomes the future; the capacity of the analyst to hold this paradox as they play is the foundation of analysis" (p. 277).

At times, in playing, there are elements of role-responsiveness (Sandler, 1976) or even projective identification that are being expressed and taken up by patient or analyst. When this occurs, playing mobilizes various feelings in the transference that are in transit (Cooper, 2023a, 2023b; Corbett, 2023) from manipulation of the object (attempts at omnipotent control) to allowing for the analyst to be seen as a separate object. This overlaps with Roussillon's (2011, p. 184) statement that in play, "the object is freed of the burden of the use of the object in the process of symbolization."

Both the reverie and playing models aim to promote self-observation, but they may each have different purposes at play related to metabolization. Both playing and reverie involve the goals of promoting equipoise related to holding sovereign states. I would suggest, however, that the analyst oriented toward play, waits in Winnicott's sense of waiting (Winnicott, 1968b) but he or she waits with and without memory and desire. In the remainder of this chapter, I try to shed light on the nature of this waiting and the paradox of being with and without memory and desire.

Creative Aggression, the Use of the Object, and Proceeding Without Memory and Desire

Archeologists understood before psychoanalysts that the act of understanding, locating, and piecing together how people lived in other times is intrinsically a destructive act. Bion and Winnicott in their own ways regarding examination of psychic phenomena revolutionized our sense of how destroying what exists can yield new levels of experience, and in the process brought us two overlapping and very distinct views of creative aggression.

Bion's (1967) quote of T. S. Eliot's Four Quartets, without "memory and desire," seen from the framework of creative aggression, was his statement that selected facts and overvalued ideas need to be questioned and often destroyed on the way to yielding something fresh for patient and analyst. He follows Shelley's (1840) trenchant remark about desire in "A Defense of Poetry" that "We want the creative faculty to imagine that which we know."

Regarding Winnicott's own notions of what efforts the analyst makes toward listening, there is merit to argue that Winnicott's (1969) main work on creative aggression was his view of psychoanalysis as a form of playing and his contribution to understanding the use of the object.

I view Winnicott's contribution to the understanding of how play is the logical undergirding of psychoanalytic process as a major contribution regarding the creative elements of destruction. In play, the "rules" that constitute transference-countertransference engagement are in some way in interpretive transit. Play manifested in the analysis of adult patients arrives through idiomatic language, an ordinary language that nevertheless creatively finds unconscious fantasy, defense, and transference phenomena, providing metacommentary on the repetitive and stagnant rules that govern these phenomena.

In his work on the use of the object, Winnicott described how destroying the object and the object's survival creates a more genuine capacity to appraise an actual object. In light of Winnicott's letter to Bion, I suggest that the object desires to survive. In object usage, the patient attempts to destroy the analyst but must find an analyst who is dedicated to his or her own survival. The analyst desires to survive both intrinsically for his own survival, but also to facilitate the patient's movement from destruction to object usage. This process is predicated on Winnicott's (1969, p. 1244) statement that: "the object, if it is to be used must necessarily be real in the sense of being part of shared reality, not a bundle of projections."

The analyst's desire to survive rest on his actual existence as an object. In Winnicott's (1951) paper on transitional objects, he offered an intriguing statement, namely that the importance of the transitional object lies in its "actuality" as an object more than it's symbolic value. He was stating that while the object's symbolic linkage to the maternal figure is important, the actuality of the object as an object outside the subjective self is essential to the actual negotiation of separation. Symbolically the transitional object serves to mitigate separation anxiety, but the second part of the transitional object is its function to shepherd the child's exploration with the object world. What better object with which to explore actual objects than an object that at the very least holds a dual function – to mitigate separation as an object outside the child's control, but an object that also exists in fantasy as an object that is partly in the child's possession.

For our purposes of considering Winnicott's reservations about Bion's use of the phrase, "without memory and desire," I think it is essential to consider a paradox that Winnicott (1969) holds regarding the simultaneity of the object as actual and symbolic in transitional object development. As an actual object, Winnicott cannot quite promise to be without memory and desire beyond intention. In this view then, the word intention is meant to capture a way that he persists in the importance of the interaction between the analyst as an actual and symbolic object, holding each side in paradoxical tension with one another.

In their unique ways, both Winnicott's and Bion were contributing to creative versions of the concept of destruction in post-WWII England. The use of creative destruction in development for Winnicott was crucial to his development of the concept of the use of the object and to his theory of playing as the underlying logic for psychoanalysis. The object only becomes real if destroyed. One can speculate that Bion's recommendation to be without memory and desire is a kind of destruction of the object (memory and desire). However in his letter to Bion, Winnicott, might be suggesting that his experience of himself as an analytic object includes some elements of his memory and desire and of course his patient's memory and desire are necessary in the process of living experiences together in the analytic process. We also know, thanks to Aguayo's (2014, 2018) nuanced reading of Bion (1974) that Bion's notion of "without memory and desire" points to Bion's (1967) appreciation that there is an evolution of the analyst's memory that includes realistically necessary and often helpful retention of what has happened in prior sessions. The notion of a constantly evolving position of without memory and desire in Bion's clinical listening, may in fact be consistent with Winnicott's description of his own stance.

For Bion, we can derive a kind of creative destruction in the analyst's efforts to strive toward being without memory and desire. The questioning of certainty and the view that the "answer is the question's misfortune" (Blanchot, 1969) led to a view of the creative elements of tearing down particularly easily arrived at insights. This includes the analyst's receptivity to his or her disruptions in the capacity to think and disturbances in attunement.

We see how in both Winnicott and Bion's version of the destruction of the object through playing and reverie, each were searching for frontiers that went beyond what was more accessible through formulation. They are each discovering their idioms of playing and reverie for learning from their patients' unconscious experiences. They each hold the analyst responsible for finding playing and dreaming when the patient is unable to play and dream.

While we see some of the roots of ontological analysis here, I hasten to add that I increasingly question the value of distinguishing between the epistemological and ontological axes. For example, Freud cannot be clearly specified as an epistemologically oriented analyst. Consider that when he discovered free floating attention, he was trying to accompany his patients in a new way, albeit to arrive at new insights. Still, his efforts to unlearn his training that had asked of him to fix and solve symptoms involved a great deal of work to be present with his patients in a different way. Further still, his views on mourning as continuous rather than discrete, suggest his burgeoning attunement to psychoanalysis and living as a process that could not always demarcate definite goals and ending points.

Winnicott's Interpretive Stance: Where Is the Analyst's Desire Located?

The texts I refer to here include the enigmatic Chapter 4 in Playing and Reality, "Playing, Creativity, and the Search for the Self" written in 1967 (1967), one part of his two-piece opus on play: his tour de force paper on interpretation (Winnicott, 1968b); and The Use of the Object (Winnicott, 1969).

On the face of it, Winnicott's approach to interpretation, one that gathered over the course of his career was to avoid anything that hinted at indoctrination of the patient. He is very aligned with Bion's concern about over developed formulations and the possibility that interpretations are pseudo-integrative rather than honoring the particular state of disintegration that any patient might be in at any given moment.

In his paper on playing and creativity (Winnicott,1967), he is in a sense living in an illusory world of a patient who wishes for a session of indefinite length. He offers his patient a once-a-week treatment of three hours ("the best that I could manage" that is eventually modified into a two-hour session. One could say that his desire is expressed in the construction of the setting. He is giving himself over to the illusion that there is a session of indefinite length when in reality, it is decidedly a session of defined length. His desire is to not interrupt the me/not me possession of the patient's view of the setting, particularly by interpreting it in all of the obvious ways that we as psychoanalysts are trained to do.

Winnicott's desire is to gather up the patient's bits and pieces and to not get ahead of what he refers to as the patient's "transference confidence" (Winnicott, 1968a). Put succinctly, his desire is to promote the patient's discovery of elements of her creativity. We could say that his desire is in the waiting. Waiting here relates to a degree of trust that the patient will make her own discoveries, perhaps Winnicott's own version of faith.

In some ways, I believe that Winnicott's waiting is related to what the French philosopher, Bernard Stiegler (2019) referred to as taking care. He plays on the French word attendre, to wait, but it includes attending. Stiegler refers to waiting as a waiting for the disclosure of webs of connectedness in oneself or in the other. It is a kind of mirroring. I see this as very similar to the very active waiting that Winnicott was describing.

Winnicott's waiting also relates to his notion that the analyst's job when patients are unable to play to help find play. Here it seems to me is another element of the analyst's desire, not just a job description. Playing involves an openness to the kind of leap that Erikson and Plato associated with play. If nothing else, it is a usage of reverie and a different stage of interpretation that includes the analyst's registration of transference history with the patient in what often feels new.

If we think of Winnicott's waiting as related to Bion's trust in listening without memory and desire, here I would ask how or whether playing and reverie diverge a bit. Playing makes constant use of the analyst's reverie (e.g., Parsons, 1999; Cooper, 2018, 2019). Does playing involve an openness to the kind of leap that Erikson and Plato associated with play? If nothing else, playing involves a preliminary usage of reverie that leads to a different stage of interpretation, one that includes the analyst's registration of transference history with the patient in what often feels new.

It is my sense that play enters a listening position slightly less devoted to metabolization than that of reverie. Perhaps it could also be said that the aims of playing and reverie are overlapping and different. Winnicott's version of playing asks the patient and analyst to try to hold incompatible parts of self in an ongoing state of good enough unintegration. For Winnicott, the bits and pieces are searching less for equanimity but instead a sense of real and alive conversation with one another. I am not sure that metabolization is the most useful way to describe the function of play, even though play does help us to parse what is inside and outside.

Having described this particular state of unintegratedness in playing, I believe that this new state of responsiveness in playing is often mistakenly referred to as spontaneity. Spontaneity itself includes illusory experiences in the transference-countertransference because it builds on the evolving intersubjective history between patient and analyst. We could say that it builds on a history of memory and desire that has been held in abeyance as the analyst waits.

Regardless of the complex set of personal circumstances that prompted this letter, I am reminded of the importance that each analyst find their own idiom to describe their responsiveness and participation in clinical analysis. I have emphasized a series of paradoxes in Winnicott's clinical stance that illuminate his objection to "without memory and desire," Winnicott's waiting is likely highly overlapping with Bion's instruction to listen without memory and desire. In that particular way, Winnicott's letter expresses the irrepressible need for each of us to be our own analyst.

References

Aguayo, J. (2014) Bion's notes on memory and desire – Its initial clinical reception in the United States: A note on archival material. *Int. J. Psycho-Anal.* 95: 889–910.

Aguayo, J. (2018) Winnicott, Melanie Klein, and W. R. Bion: The controversy over the nature of the external object-holding and container/contained (1941–1967). *Psychoanal. Q.* 87: 767–807.

Bion, W. (1967) Notes on memory and desire. *Psychoanal. Forum.* 2: 272–280.

Bion, W. (1970) *Attention and Interpretation.* London: Karnac Books.

Bonaminio, V. (2012) On Winnicott's clinical innovations in the analysis of adults. *Int. J Psycho-Anal.* 93: 1475–1485.

Bromberg, P. (1998) *Standing in the Spaces: Essays on Clinical Process, Trauma, and Dissociation.* New Jersey: Analytic Press.

Cooper, S. H. (2019) Playing in the darkness: The use of the object and use of the subject. *J. Amer. Psychoanal. Assn.* 66: 743–765.

Cooper, S. H. (2023a) *Playing and Becoming in Psychoanalysis.* London: Routledge.

Cooper, S. H. (2023b) The play of mourning. *J. Am. Psychoanal. Assoc.* 71: 61–82.

Cooper, S. H. (2025) *Psychoanalysis in Play. Expanding Psychoanalytic Concepts from a Play Perspective.* London: Routledge.

Corbett, K. (2023) Playing the object, becoming the analyst. *J Am. Psychoanal. Assoc.* 70: 1967; 263–282.

Fabazzi, P. (2016) The use of the analyst and the sense of being real: The clinical meaning of Winnicott's "The use of an object." *Psychoanal Q.* 85(1):1–34.

Green, A. (1993) *On Primitive Madness*. Madison, CT: Internation Universities Press.

Ogden, T. H. (2016) Destruction reconceived: On Winnicott's 'The use of an object and relating through identifications'. *Int. Psychoanal.* 97(5):1243–1262.

Ogden, T. H. (2019) Ontological psychoanalysis or "What do you want to be when you grow up?. *Psycho. Q.* 88: 661–684.

Ogden, T. H. (2022) *Coming to Life in the Consulting Room: Toward a New Analytic Sensibility*. London: Routledge.

Reis, B. (2020) *Creative Repetition and Inersubjectivity: Contemporary Freudian Explorations of Trauma, Memory, and Clinical Process*. New York: Routledge.

Rodman, R. (1987) *The Spontaneous Gesture: Selected Letters of D. W. Winnicott*, ed. F. R. Rodman. Cambridge: Harvard University Press.

Roussillon, R. (2011) Primitive Agony and Symbolization. London: Routledge.

Sandler, J. (1976) Countertransference and role-responsiveness. *Int. Rev. Psychoanal.* 3:43–47.

Scarfone, D. (2015) *The Unpast*. New York: The Unconscious in Translation.

Shelley, P. B. (1840) *A Defense of Poetry and Other Essays*. London: Edward Moxen.

Stiegler, B. (2019) *The Age of Disruption: Technology and Madness in Computational Capitalism*. Cambridge: Polity Press.

Winnicott, D. W. (1945) Primitive emotional development. *Int. J. Psychoanal.* 26: 137–143.

Winnicott, D. W. (1949) Hate in the countertransference. *Int. J. Psychoanal.* 30: 69–74.

Winnicott, D. W. (1951) L. Caldwell, and H. T. Robinson. *The Collected Works of D.W. Winnicott: Volume 3 1967*. Oxford, p. 447–462.

Winnicott, D. W. (1956) Primary maternal preoccupation, eds. C. Winnicott, R. Shepherd, M. Davis. *Psychoanalytic Explorations*. Cambridge: Harvard University Press.

Winnicott, D. W. (1967a) Letter to W. Bion, eds. L. Caldwell, and H. T. Robinson. *The Collected Works of D.W. Winnicott: Volume 8, 1967*. Oxford.

Winnicott, D. W. (1967b) Creativity activity and the search for the self, eds. L. Caldwell, and D. W. Winnicott, *Playing and Reality*. London: Tavistock.

Winnicott, D. W. (1968a) Interpretation in psycho-analysis, eds. L. Caldwell, H. T. Robinson, *The Collected Works of D.W. Winnicott: Volume 8, 1967*. Oxford: Oxford University Press.

Winnicott, D. W. (1968b) Playing: A theoretical statement, eds. L. Caldwell, H. T. Robinson, *The Collected Works of D.W. Winnicott: Volume 8, 1967*. Oxford: Oxford University Press..

Winnicott, D. W. (1969) The use of the object. *Int. J. Psycho-Anal.* 50: 711–716.

Winnicott, D. W. (1971) *Playing and Reality*. London: Tavistock.

5 Winnicott's Research

Between Parallel Convergences and Uniqueness

Paolo Fabozzi

"11 October 1967

Dear Dr. Winnicott,
Thank you for the attention you have given to my presentations at our Society. I am afraid I may not have fully understood your point. You appear to disagree with what I have been suggesting, yet I have the unpleasant feeling – perhaps one you share – that on this occasion we are both attempting to say something quite similar, albeit in our own respective languages. That is, I speak of the suspension of memory, desire, and understanding, and of the importance of remaining in a state of uncertainty, while you refer to the fact that the patient you will meet tomorrow cannot match what you have in mind, as he will need to place you outside of his own omnipotence. In other words, we are both addressing the necessity of preserving the patient's need to evolve beyond our arrogant omniscience.

Perhaps, however, you are gently pointing out that you anticipated, by several years, the positions I have been putting forward in my recent lectures. You see, I try to listen to my patients rather than to read and cite psychoanalytic papers…

I hope that in the future we will not have to find further points of unpleasant contact and irritating overlap in our perspectives.

Yours sincerely,
W. R. Bion".

Unfortunately, no, this is not an unpublished letter from Bion to Winnicott, unearthed from some basement or private archive; it is merely an "imaginative conjectures", akin to the exercise we are invited to engage in when reading Yehoshua's masterpiece, *Mr. Mani* (1989). The novel unfolds through dialogues in which the other's response is entirely absent, a structure that reminds us of the "exchanges" between Winnicott and Bion. To date, we have five letters from Winnicott to Bion, but none of Bion's replies, if any exist, have been published. We know of the citations Winnicott makes of Bion's work in his published works, but Bion never reciprocated

DOI: 10.4324/9781003502067-5

with any citations or bibliographical references to Winnicott's work, except for a brief mention of regression in *Cogitations*. In fact, in a letter to his wife Bion mentioned that it might be wise not to cite somebody else's works, so as to avoid giving them undue prominence ....

In the first part, I attempt to reconstruct the context immediately preceding Winnicott's letter, namely Bion's two lectures, "Memory and Desire" and "Negative Capability". In the second part, I draw a map – in part inevitably hypothetical – of a possible connection between the two authors. In the final part, I focus on the research programme that surfaces in Winnicott's letter, which he contrasted with Bion's technical developments.

Prelude

Winnicott's letter, dated 5 October 1967, has an enigmatic quality, as it makes no mention of the main theme of the previous evening's lecture – Negative Capability. Instead, it focuses on the concepts of memory and desire, which, though referenced in the lecture, were the subject of Bion's earlier presentation on 16 June 1965. That year marked a fundamental "shift of emphasis in Bion's psychoanalytical attitude" (Mawson, 2018, p. 43), which could be summarised as a move from K to O. Bion transitioned from an analysis deeply rooted in transference, the dynamics of internal partial objects, and the impact these dynamics have on the patient's mind and capacity to think – an analysis primarily characterised by understanding and knowledge, and based on the communication of that understanding to the patient – to an approach where the focus is on the here-and-now experience, the becoming (of both patient and analyst), and the attainment in the session of a state of atonement between the ultimate reality or truth of the patient and that of the analyst (Bion, 1965b, 1970; Blass et al., 2011; Ogden, 2015). While the knowledge/understanding was not completely displaced, we witness a powerful downsizing of it, in favour of the "intuition" factor (Hinshelwood, 2018).

Here are the key points of Bion's 1965 lecture, "Memory and Desire":

- A technique is required that facilitates becoming O and contact with the patient's psychic reality; one that does not place obstacles between analyst and patient by inhibiting emotional experiences or turning analysis into an endless conversation.
- The stripping away of memory and desire – described as a "positive discipline", extremely difficult and "inherently improbable" to achieve – aims to permit that a real object "emerges, evolves, and becomes possible for us to be aware of" (1965a, p. 6) during the session.
- Sensuous experiences saturate the analyst's mind and obstruct the movement from K to O. It is necessary to exclude our senses through a kind of blindness, as they hinder the emergence of the analytic object, which is "formless".

- Memory and desire are obstacles because they collude with the analyst's need to retain a concrete image of the patient, making static what must be understood in its dynamic nature.
- In every session, a "dynamic emotional experience" is occurring.
- Memory is called upon when the session reaches a critical point. The suspension of memory and desire is, therefore, a "frightening" discipline (p. 7), generating anxiety in the analyst. It fosters a sense of estrangement, disorienting both analyst and patient.
- The suspension of memory, desire, and understanding intensifies and enhances the connection between analyst and patient by maximising the expression and awareness of emotions in the analytic situation: the focus is not on the past or the future, but the here and now.
- We may know something about the patient, but we cannot fully know *the* patient. What we can engage with, however, is "the actual emotional reality of the situation" (p. 9).

  A year later, Bion clarified that memory and desire "got between oneself and the patient" preventing the analyst from intuiting what is happening in the session (Maslow, 2018, p. 14). With the suspension of memory and desire, the analyst loses any "anchorage", as we are always seeking what is known and familiar in order to protect ourselves from "what is really an unpleasant situation, a situation in which *anything may happen*" (p. 14; italics mine).

  The 1967 lecture "Negative Capability" represents an evolution and extension of the earlier seminar "Memory and Desire".

- In the session, we are burdened by too much knowledge, too many theories, too much light:

For this particular search in which we are engaged, I do not think of a *bright* light, if I can use this model, as to get the situation so *obscure* that the dimmest object, the faintest scrap of light, will show up. Therefore the important thing is to be able to exclude as much as you can, in order to bring a penetrating shaft of darkness to bear on the obscure spot.

(1967a, p. 23)[1]

- The clue is "the capacity to tolerate half-truth, uncertainties, mysteries, doubts, without any irritable reaching after fact and reason" (p. 24).
- Negative Capability is not "a state, but a characteristic" (p. 27).
- The overall effect of this approach

is to intensify the analytic experience very much. So much indeed, that the psychoanalysis of patients moves into the centre of the analyst's life. And you get an effect which is rather similar to being analysed, in the same way that one's analyst is always a very important person.

(p. 26)

- In the session, we encounter numerous isolated, seemingly meaningless episodes: "Now that is difficult to tolerate, it requires Negative Capability. Otherwise one will rush in with an interpretation to get out of the dilemma of tolerating mysteries, half-truths, and so on" (p. 26).

This summary does not fully capture the essence of the two lectures, not so much in terms of content, but in terms of style, which reflects an open, fluid, confident, and non-rigid quality of thought. When comparing these lectures with the version Bion (1967b) published on *Psychoanalytic Forum* and the chapters of *Attention and Interpretation* that explore these concepts, one is struck by his difficulty to implement what he proposed in the lectures. Paradoxically, the invitation to remain in doubt and uncertainty, at first cautious and judicious, becomes in the printed texts a series of dogmatic, apodictic, and prescriptive assertions.[2]

As Winnicott, chair of the 1967 evening session, remarked immediately after Bion's speech, "We seem to be in the process of learning new techniques" (Maslow, 2018, p. 33). Indeed, both works reflect a radical shift in how Bion conceives the analyst's role in the consulting room. I say "conceives" because we lack specific clinical examples directly illustrating these concepts – we are, in fact, well aware of Bion's dissatisfaction with session reports – which could help us better understand how the technical principles suggested in these two texts might be applied.[3]

The stripping away of memory, desire, and the pursuit of understanding is aimed at minimising preconceptions and theories as much as possible. This technical approach results in an increased reality of the phenomena and objects that need to be interpreted, a heightened awareness of the uniqueness of each psychoanalytic experience and of psychoanalysis itself, and a clear emergence of O (Bion, 1992).

It seeks to eliminate a "dirty" element of interfering subjectivity in order to foster the state Bion refers to as *becoming O*. This process aims at legitimising – circularly, in a sense – the idea that in a session we can only engage with the present, not as a static moment, but as something in constant becoming ("evolution"). It seeks to create a state akin to a *tabula rasa*: the zero point of the analyst-patient encounter. Ultimately, through the suspension of memory and desire, and with the aid of negative capability, a specific ecology of the mind is cultivated: an expansion of emotional resonance, an intuitive grasp of the patient's psychic reality, and a facilitation of *becoming O*.

This is the framework within which Winnicott's letter must be situated.

Parallel Convergences[4]

"It is important to me that Bion states (obscurely of course) what I have been trying to state for 2½ decades but against the terrific opposition of Melanie" (Letter to Wisdom, 10-26-1964, in Winnicott [1987]). There is no doubt about the absolute and unquestionable precedence of Winnicott's discoveries and insights in relation to the significant extensions Bion later made to Kleinian theory, which shaped his unique approach to psychoanalysis from the early 1960s onwards. Winnicott was the first to articulate clearly and coherently, both in theory and clinical practice, the role played by the psyche-soma of the mother and the analyst. I would like to emphasise how misleading it is to claim that he introduced into psychoanalysis the so-called "external object", a term that creates ambiguity. This notion erroneously sets the external object in contrast to the internal object, implying a diminished role and importance for the latter. Winnicott (and, nearly fifteen years later, Bion, through the concepts of containment, alpha function, and rêverie) liberated the object from being merely the target of drives and highlighted its essential psychic functions for the infans (and the patient) in their process of becoming a subject. It is not merely the existence of the real mother, but the vital functions performed by the psyche-soma of the mother and the analyst – their unconscious, body, emotions, as well as their higher functions – that influence the development and growth of the infans and the patient in analysis. Winnicott demonstrated that the matter is not merely one of tolerating and containing the emotions solicited by the other, but of *elaborating* what from the other's unconscious reaches the subject's unconscious (Fabozzi, 2012).

There are broad factors that bring Winnicott and Bion closer together, such as their strong intellectual lineage with M. Klein. However, when comparing their writings, we inevitably see a different writing style, a different lexicon, and a different way of thinking and practising psychoanalysis. Winnicott had no interest whatsoever in metapsychological pursuits, being focused primarily on clinical practice, with a vast wealth of experience working with children of all ages. Bion, by contrast, was passionate about method, theory, and the effort to "mathematise" psychoanalysis and make it more scientific. Both were protective and proud of their individual research paths, and for each, it was vital to develop their own language and style of thinking. Winnicott allowed the clinical material to speak for itself, often without theorising it in an organised way. Bion favoured a more abstract approach, even when discussing technique, and did not concern himself with "illustrating" what he theorised. In the close interplay between form and content, one might suggest that Winnicott's theoretical nonchalance and late Bion's renunciation of a purely scientific approach enabled them both to achieve a fertile creativity.

What most strongly characterises any comparison between Bion and Winnicott is their irreducibility and incomparability. Bion employs the concept of the death drive, which Winnicott rejects outright. Hatred of reality is a central theme in Bion's study of psychosis in the 1950s, drawing on Freud's essay on the two principles of mental functioning as a key theoretical reference. Winnicott, by contrast, places at the heart of his research on psychosis the impingement the environment can have on the infans, and he stresses the need "of examining the reality principle under high power"

(1968a, p. 91). He has always maintained that the relationship with external reality is an extremely fragile achievement for both the child and the patient. While Bion (1962) highlights the role of the absent breast in structuring the apparatus for thinking, Winnicott argues that symbolic functions are established primarily through a presence that adapts to the infant's needs.[5]

Both, however, leave room for unformulated ideas, and at times it seems that one complements the other's formulations, even beyond their own intentions. Moreover, we can observe numerous subtle and subterranean exchanges – terms, concepts, and intuitions that oscillate and flow between them. The critique of abstract interpretations, and ten years later a reference to the abstract nature of interpretation; the rejection of psychopathological terms to describe physiological phenomena, again a decade later; the "formlessness" of the analytic object, and the allowance for formlessness in the patient. Paradoxically, it is these resonances that accentuate the originality and incomparability of their respective ways of thinking and practising psychoanalysis. As Winnicott remarked,

> Bion uses the word reverie to cover the idea that I have stated in the complex way that it deserves that the infant is ready to create something, and in good-enough mothering the mother lets the baby know what is being created.
> (Letter to Wisdom, 10-26-1964, in Winnicott [1987])[6]

Their mutual incomparability softens somewhat, revealing areas of partial convergence, when we consider their later work, particularly the three lectures Winnicott's 1967 letter briefly touched upon. By this time, the cultural and scientific context had shifted from the positivist remnants that characterised Freud and Klein, and both Winnicott and Bion aligned in their aim of letting the patient be "free" to mature and evolve in their own way. Both likely reacted against the omni-explanatory tendencies of Kleinian technique: Winnicott interpreted "mainly to let the patient know the limits of my understanding" (1968a, pp. 86–87), while Bion, with negative capability and active blindness, sought to rid the analyst's mind of overbearing knowledge.

A key turning point in Bion's clinical approach came with "On Arrogance" (1958), where he had a pivotal insight: the risk that the analyst could become an obstructing object, unable to be receptive to the patient's non-verbal forms of communication. This clinical impasse was rooted partly in the idea that analysis should unfold exclusively through verbal language, partly in the one-person conception of development and clinical work, and perhaps also in Bion's initial reluctance to allow himself to be influenced and, to some extent, transformed by the patient's projective identifications. This insight was later developed and expanded upon in the 1960s, significantly shaping the theorisation of containment, alpha function, and rêverie, as well as the expansion of projective identification and the concepts of suspending memory and desire, and negative capability. Along this path, Bion gradually introduced the need to explore the functions of the analyst, emphasising the importance of the analyst's presence (no longer limited to interpreting) and, to some extent, subjectivity, while strengthening the significance of the impact between patient and analyst.

Might echoes of Winnicott's contributions have resonated in Bion's reflections? It is difficult not to think of the letter Winnicott wrote to him on 7 October 1955, immediately after Bion's presentation of "Differentiation of the Psychotic from the Non-Psychotic Personalities", in which Winnicott offered his own personal reading of the case:

> [...] I would say that if a patient of mine lay on the couch moving to and fro in the way your patient did and then said: "I ought to have telephoned my mother" I would know that he was talking about communication and his incapacity for making communication. Should it interest you to know, I will say what I would have interpreted: I would have said: "A mother properly oriented to her baby would know from your movements what you need. There would be a communication because of this knowledge which belongs to her devotion and she would do something which would show that the communication had taken place. I am not sensitive enough or orientated in that way to be able to act well enough and therefore I in this present analytic situation fall into the category of the mother who failed to make communication possible. In the present relationship therefore there is given a sample of the original failure from the environment which contributed to your difficulty in communication. Of course you could always cry and so draw attention to need. In the same way you could telephone your mother and get a reply but this represents a failure of the more subtle communication which is the only basis for communication that does not violate the fact of the essential isolation of each individual." You will see that from my point of view you were talking about the environment.
>
> (Winnicott, 1987)

Perhaps this letter, along with some irritation, also created fertile ground, and that clinical impasse became an opportunity for a realization – one in line with Winnicott's observations – emerging from the intersection of analytic experience and the theory of projective identification, as well as future insights into the functions of the object. A few years later, Keats' and Freud's letters and a passage from St. John of the Cross – remarkably similar to Bion's reflections on memory and desire (see Mawson, 2018) – allowed the "logical-mathematical" Bion to develop a new way of thinking about the analytic function and the analyst's mental stance.

It seems reasonable to suggest that the suspension of memory and desire was also a significant critical response and alternative to both the explanatory and mechanically reconstructive tendencies of the Freudian group, which focused on the "there and then", and the concrete, explicative language of the Kleinian group, which risked interpreting transference in a circular, self-confirming manner. Bion strongly emphasises the need to focus on what is happening *now* in the session to engage with the "dynamic emotional experience" and access the patient's unconscious psychic reality. He achieves this by "forgetting" the patient's history, though paradoxically he is still concerned with ensuring that the fact is present to both patient and analyst, without feeling the need to offer examples of becoming O or atonement.

Winnicott takes a markedly different approach to placing experience at the centre of analysis: a key example is how he expanded and extended the concept of transference, stating that while, for neurotic patients, transference represents the past, for psychotic patients "the present goes back into the past and *is* the past" (1955, p. 298). These patients experience a temporal collapse where the "as if" dimension cannot appear, and instead of functioning on the level of representation, the analytic exchange is imbued with acting out (1954). The pressure exerted by the patient affects the analyst's functioning and challenges the reliability of their technique. In the present of the session, this recreates the traumatic nature of the patient's prehistory, turning the patient's history and the data gathered during analysis from abstract and artificial matter into living and pulsating matter. Winnicott is not guided by the abstract imposition of the patient's history or anamnesis onto the clinical material but rather by the "here and now", made meaningful through the transference-countertransference dynamic, or more precisely, through the changes that their psyche-soma undergoes. Moreover, while Bion (1967a, p. 27), through the suspension of memory and desire, seeks to reduce the overstimulation of reality in the session to reach the unconscious, Winnicott focuses on how to process traumatic reality in the session, that is "to deal with the environmental factor in terms of the transference" (1968–1969, p. 189).

Both thinkers transform the analyst's role, in a sense, uniquely challenging. With negative capability, the analyst becomes psychoanalysed, and the patient takes centre stage in the analyst's life. Furthermore, the concept of container-contained and the transformations of the analyst place far greater importance on the analyst's mental functioning compared to Kleinian technique. However, as early as the 1940s, Winnicott's clinical research had emphasised the importance of the analyst's functions and subjectivity in the analytic process: the role of hate in countertransference (1947); linking the patient's resistances to errors by the analyst that require self-analysis (1954); theorising the need for active holding in situations of regression to dependence; and his thoughts on the role of subjective mirroring by the mother and analyst towards the infant and patient (1967b). Every stage of Winnicott's work highlights the vital role of the analyst's subjectivity, which never overshadows nor negates the patient's needs. Ultimately, in both Bion and Winnicott, the effectiveness of analysis is rooted in a necessary and profound transformation of the analyst, and it is reasonable to suggest that echoes of Winnicott's way of thinking about the analyst's position subtly influenced Bion's reflections.

Moreover, within a context marked by incomparability and parallel convergences, we can sometimes identify significant points of contact between Winnicott's clinical practice and certain Bionian theories, suggesting possible intersections reached via different, independent paths. For example, Bion emphasised the irrelevance of the patient's biographical and objective data, as it might obscure contact with their psychic truth. Winnicott takes a markedly similar approach when he tells a fifty-year-old male patient that, while he knows a man is lying on the couch, it feels as though he is listening to and speaking with a girl – a girl to whom he interprets penis envy. And, in passing, he adds: "For my part, I have needed to live through a deep personal experience in order to arrive at the understanding I feel I now have reached" (1966, p. 74), illustrating the necessity for the analyst to undergo a transformation of their own being to reach an interpretation. This also demonstrates Winnicott's capacity to facilitate the evolution of the session while engaging with the patient beyond reliance on their objective data.

Another example can be found in the squiggle technique, often used in single sessions, typically without knowing the child's or adolescent's history. This technique, involving the joint creation of drawings, allows the subject's dominant unconscious issue to emerge while also facilitating some embryonic transformation.

When Bion asserts the need for *every* possible emotional evolution to unfold in the session, we are reminded of the central role Winnicott attributes to the mother's active adaptation to the infant's needs, his work with deprived children, and his psychological and technical receptivity in situations of regression to dependency. It is evident how important the psyche-soma of the analyst was to him, as well as the analyst's emotional response and the need to accommodate any manifestation from the patient.

Perhaps what most unites these two authors – Winnicott demonstrates this clinically, while Bion only theorises it – is their approach to thinking and using technique: it is no longer merely an implicit constraint or a necessary limit but becomes a potential, a tool that above all allows emotional experiences to emerge in the session without leading to manipulation. It is a technique that inherently amplifies the role of the non-verbal, emotions, and the body. Winnicott was driven by his work with very young children, Bion by his analyses of psychotic patients and thought disorders. In both thinkers, there is a fertile, heuristically circular connection between this stance and the idea that much exists beyond the repressed and split-off: for Winnicott, there are traumatic impingements, dissociated and inscribed in the psyche-soma in forms not yet symbolised or fully psychical; for Bion, there are transformations into hallucinosis and protomental dimensions. The late Bion explores the unknown and the unexpressed, focusing his investigation on the psychic stance of the analyst that might facilitate their transformation. Winnicott, meanwhile, seeks what has not yet been able to emerge or what remains in a state of non-life. Sutters? Babbling?

Although Bion repeatedly stated he was not a poet, he felt compelled to seek expression in narrative form, as seen in *A Memoir of the Future* and in the Language of Achievement, inspired by Keats. Winnicott, recognising the limits of scientific knowledge on adaptation, argued that psychoanalysts must work like artists, wondering "what patient wants to be someone else's poem or picture?" (1954, p. 291). Both inclined towards poetry, though – they knew it – neither was a poet, they have left us the task of seeking and finding words that can touch the patient, and of using a language that is neither petrified nor laden with jargon to express ourselves.

What emerges is a spatial-temporal map where Winnicottian "settlements" precede Bion's, with regions where entirely different languages are spoken. We discern neighbouring areas, subterranean encounters, and echoes of one author reverberating through the other; convergences developed in original, unintentional ways; and then divergences and departures on related themes.

The Uniqueness of Winnicottian Research

In a passage from his letter dated 5 October 1967, Winnicott briefly touches on two issues that had shaped his clinical research throughout his life and found significant development in the second half of the 1960s: the infans' access to reality and the sense of being real, and the relationship between what is objective and what is subjective:

> In the application to psycho-analytic work I find I cannot allow that [memory and desire are] 100% subjective [as in a poem]. The memory includes memories of phenomena from external reality and certainly what is likely to turn up tomorrow in my analytic work cannot be covered by what I have in my own mind to want, precisely because I have to be able to allow the patient to be a separate person, as the patient has to come to be able to allow me to be outside his or her omnipotent control.

Here, Winnicott sets aside the distinction Bion makes between memory and "evolution", offering an apparently simple statement that implicitly contains his own research agenda. This statement, however, points to the highly complex analytic work required to make two distinct processes possible: one concerning the search for and discovery of the self, and the other involving the use of an object.

3.1 Subjectivity and objectivity

How did Winnicott conceptualise the relationship between objectivity and subjectivity? In some areas of his thinking, he considered it possible, helpful, and necessary to keep them distinct: for example, when distinguishing between objective and subjective countertransference; when stressing the difference between a father's death in early childhood versus adolescence; or when addressing the (objective) error made by an experienced and well-analysed analyst. In other, more numerous and significant areas, he theorised a fruitful and indispensable interconnection, seen as the basis of living and experiencing: the newborn's illusion of creating the breast (the subjective object), an expression of the primal fusion between mother and infant.

> [...] the baby has instinctual urges and predatory ideas. The mother has [...] the idea that she would like to be attacked by a hungry baby. These two phenomena do not come into relation with each other till the mother and child *live an experience together*. [...] I think of the process as if two lines came from opposite directions, liable to come near each other. If they overlap there is a moment of *illusion* – a bit of experience which the infant can take as *either* his hallucination *or* a thing belonging to external reality.
>
> (Winnicott, 1945, p. 152)

The birth of that fundamental psychic function that is the relationship with external reality is located in the possibility that an *overlap* may be created between something that stems from the mother's psyche and something that originates from the baby's (*in fieri*) psyche. To suggest that Winnicott is a naïve realist is an ideological and unfounded interpretation. On the contrary, throughout his work, he moves beyond a simple assertion about the interaction between the objective and subjective; he subordinates the meaning, richness, and function of external reality to what is specifically subjective – that is, creative. As early as 1945, he grounds this in the dimension of experience.

At the heart of the concept of the subjective object, we find a fruitful interplay, rather than a static opposition, between perception and hallucination. Moreover, we find a paradox: the *necessary* condition for an individual to establish a meaningful relationship with external reality, one in which they can feel real, lies precisely in the illusion of creating the world. In other words, to develop the capacity to relate to an objectively perceived object, the child must – over and over again – have an experience where they can pause and fully enjoy their subjectivity, experiencing the sensation of creating the breast.

A failure of the processes associated with the created/found prevents the development of a healthy experience of omnipotence and, more significantly, distorts it, since the original encounter with the other is marked by intrusions, impingements, and unpredictability. What we initially observe in analysis, then, will not be a healthy fusion experience, but rather an omnipotent functioning aimed at tightly controlling the other, both in internal and external reality. This control inevitably rebounds onto the subject's self, imprisoning it in a state that restricts every psychic movement and stunts its development. In this space, what emerges is a distortion of the encounter with the object: the dimensions of presence and absence become persecutory; symbolisation processes remain atrophied; the concreteness of reality becomes the universal key to all relationships; and the internal world and external reality are confined to two impermeable compartments. A critical clinical issue is, therefore, the need to transform the patient's omnipotent control into a creative experience of omnipotence, and then to allow the analyst to be placed outside the patient's sphere of omnipotence.

There are two key concepts in Winnicott's work that help us navigate in analysing patients with these characteristics: *playing*, a process linked to creativity and thus the discovery of the patient's self, and the *use of an object*, which refers to the capacity to establish the object's full autonomy and the sense of being real. Both are the result of a long analytic work and cannot be assumed to exist by default, nor can they be seen as models that explain every phenomenon in the analytic relationship. Both require psychic achievements and allow for the construction of missing psychic functions. Both ground the analysis in the experience generated between patient and analyst.[7]

3.2 Playing

I briefly touch on a few fundamental aspects of playing (see Fabozzi, 2024). It involves the body, but not the instincts. Winnicott describes a particular mode of personality functioning, using a concept derived from bodily experience: *relaxation*, a state free from anxiety and tension that allows for rest after a period of work and restores balance after disturbance. Anxiety, defensive structures, lack of trust, and implicit demands from the analyst often prompt the patient to organise free associations and give them a sense of direction, meaning, and intention. Recognising the reliability of the analytic situation and a growing sense of trust will allow the patient to reach a state of psychic relaxation, which enables them to "communicate a succession of ideas, thoughts, sensations that are not linked except in some way that is neurological or physiological and perhaps beyond detection" (1971, p. 55). These are "unrelated thought sequences which the analyst will do well to accept as such, not assuming the existence of a significant thread" (1971, p. 55). Communication can only occur within the experience of playing: it arises from a state of calm, not driven by instincts. Its origins lie in *"nonsense"*, and this communication would be wasted if the analyst insisted on finding meaning, rather than acknowledging and accepting its absence. In this state, *the personality can function at its minimal level of integration*, a condition Winnicott refers to as *formlessness*. Formlessness is, above all, the state that allows form to emerge without having to adapt compliantly to the environment through dissociation or the construction of a false self defensive organisation.

The "immensely exciting" nature of playing does not stem from the involvement of instincts, but rather from a second defining characteristic: its *precariousness*. This characteristic arises from the space in which play takes place, as it exists "on the theoretical line between the subjective and that which is objectively perceived" (1971, p. 50). More specifically, precariousness comes from the reciprocal influence, in the child's mind, between "that which is subjective (near-hallucination) and that which is objectively perceived (actual, or shared reality)" (1971, p. 52). The term "precarious" refers to what is uncertain and subject to chance, akin to "the precariousness of magic itself, magic that arises in intimacy, in a relationship that is being found to be reliable" (1971, p. 47). This is something we must handle with great care, since we are in the realm of trust and reliability, and since intimacy is fragile and fleeting.

Finally, a third defining characteristic of playing is that it "is neither dream nor object-relating. At the same time that it is neither the one nor the other of these two it is also both" (1968b, p. 204). In what sense is playing both real and dream-like? Here, the idea of playing emerges as both reciprocal to and the inverse of the formation of dreams:

> Into this play area the child gathers objects or phenomena from external reality and uses these in the service of some sample derived from inner or personal reality. Without hallucinating the child puts out a sample of dream potential and lives with this sample in a chosen setting of fragments from external reality.
>
> (Winnicott, 1971, p. 51)

This is not the Kleinian notion of personalising the unconscious through play in the consulting room, and it would be inaccurate to compare it to Bion's concept of waking dream thoughts. Rather, it is as if playing was the equivalent of dreaming in the waking state. If dreams are the highway to the unconscious, playing is the highway that leads the child – and sometimes the patient – to experience an area of living where they can engage with both internal and external reality.

Playing, a paradoxical experience in itself, takes place in a space that is similarly marked by paradox. Potential space – which "only comes to have significance as a result of a baby's living experience" (1968b, p. 205) – does not coincide with, nor is it realised within, the interpersonal relationship, but rather within the reciprocal influence between the intrapsychic and the intersubjective. That is "the only place where play can start, a place that is at the continuity-contiguity moment, where transitional phenomena originate" (1967a, p. 103). This space becomes "potential" when, through a separation that is *about to be achieved*, the child can bridge the distance from the mother by introducing an experience that symbolically allows for a new union with her. It is potential because its realisation consists in the possibility it offers the child to generate a creative act, a game, a movement towards the formation of a symbol, which fills and shapes the space itself. What is achieved, then, is the coexistence of two states of being, the movement between a state of separateness and a state of union, which starts from continuity and moves towards contiguity.

I personally see potential space and playing in terms of a developmental dimension of transference. Transference is primarily about repetition, whereas an experience in the potential space makes self-exploration and discovery possible. In other words, while transference tends to involve finding the known in the unknown, in potential space the patient has the opportunity to explore, seek, and discover the unknown within the known. Playing is that which transcends transference – though transference retains its function as the motor of the cure – and if we choose to "inhabit" this particular vision of the analytic situation, then playing should be considered the territory of *the search for the self*.

3.3 Making the reality

The development of the capacity to use an object is a function that allows an individual to recognise that the other has a life outside their own omnipotence. We might hypothesise – though this oversimplifies what is, in reality, a complex, multilayered, and dynamic process – that the analyst first creates a situation of trust and reliability, which supports and fosters moments of healthy fusion. Then, within this situation, the analyst's presence and contributions gradually introduce subtle elements of difference and separateness. Following this, the patient begins to test the analyst, probing their availability, and at this point, movements of provocation may start to take shape.

I see this final phase as being divided into two stages, marked by the sequence of provocation and destruction. If the analyst unconsciously demands the patient to be spared or protected, and if the patient, in their history, has experienced an unstable, depressed, or disorienting parent (Winnicott, 1948, 1962), it becomes extremely difficult for what is an indispensable characteristic of this process to unfold: the experience of maximum provocation and destructiveness. This experience can only occur if the patient and analyst avoid colluding in repeating the unconscious pact of protection that marked the patient's primary relationships. Then we will reach the second, vital stage: the analyst's response, that is, "the nature and the behaviour of the object" (1968a, p. 88).

When Winnicott describes the processes that lead to the capacity to use an object, he uses terms such as "destructive attacks", "survival", "retaliation", "delusion", "manipulation", and "suicide" – terms that are neither neutral nor rhetorical. These words vividly evoke the burden of tensions and turbulence which the analytic couple can be subjected to, and the risk that both analyst and patient may go through potentially disruptive experiences. If the analyst reacts and retaliates, they die for the patient. More accurately, they "remain dead", or suspended in a limbo, as they remain trapped within the patient's omnipotent sphere. The patient, in turn, will be forced to continue protecting the analyst, idealising or denigrating them, while being pushed back into a dissociated state of self and experience.

Since his work in the 1940s, Winnicott emphasised the importance of the analyst's response, and in his theorisation of the processes that lead to the use of an object, this perspective takes on a decisive role: the patient's movements *become* destructive if the analyst does not survive. The survival of the analyst, the setting, and the technique, I believe, should primarily be understood as the analyst's capacity to *keep their subjectivity and creative functions alive*. Survival, ultimately, involves restoring and maintaining our trust in the analytic process and the patient's capacity for growth, and this trust is fuelled by the patient's developmental achievements and our own creativity.

One outcome of the process that leads to the capacity to use an object is that the object "is *in fantasy* always being destroyed" (1968a, p. 93). If we consider that Winnicott links the impulse to destroy to the life force, that destruction is a function of the object's response – thus it remains merely potential – and lastly, that if we are not referring to either anger or hatred, then the idea that the object is always constantly being destroyed reflects the subject's capacity to establish a relationship unburdened by the paralysing need to protect the object at all costs. Thus, it is only after having intensely provoked the object, and accepting the risk that it may not survive, that one can develop genuine love and concern for the object, leading to an emotionally vital relationship with the other.

What is at stake here is not merely the acceptance of reality, as in Freud or M. Klein, which is achieved through frustration and object loss. Instead, "In this way [through the acquisition of the capacity to use an object] a world of shared reality is created" (1968a, p. 94). Reality is not simply acknowledged, accepted, or found. Rather, it is an active process of establishing the object as external to the self: "[…] my thesis is that the destruction plays its part in making the reality, placing the object outside the self" (1968a, p. 91). The intentional act of provocation greatly contributes to the construction of reality. This (potential) destruction, which is not actual destruction, is what creates. *Even objectively shared reality is constructed* (see Fabozzi, 2016, 2024).

Conclusion

We have examined a complex and nuanced theoretical formulation that addresses constructive processes – which are rooted on the concept of illusion and of the created-found – alongside destructive processes that enable the object to be situated in external reality and the construction of a sense of being real. This formulation is inseparably tied to the experiential dimension of analysis and the functions performed by the analyst. When it comes to creative processes and playing, the analyst must bring the patient "into a state of being able to play" (Winnicott, 1968c, p. 38). In the processes of using an object, the analyst's task is to survive the potential destruction brought on by the patient. Bion (1976) embraces the turbulence within the patient and the analytic situation, stressing the necessity of analysing these dynamics. By contrast, in situations marked by delusional transference and heightened tensions, Winnicott turns to the nature and behaviour of the analyst, urging a suspension of interpretation and trusting in the analyst's capacity to survive, thereby highlighting once again the distinctly experiential nature of analysis – though still accompanied by the search for and attribution of meaning.

Unlike the more abstract – and perhaps unsaturated – formulations of at-one-ment and becoming O, playing and the use of an object are, to some degree, observable and describable experiences, even with the challenges they present, within the dynamics of the "here and now". These are not abstract or mystical concepts, but rather descriptions of processes that we can identify, modify, and use in our clinical practice – processes we are tasked with clarifying, expanding, and deploying.

Referring to the "basic forces of individual living", Winnicott once stated: "[…] to me it is certain that if the real basis is creativiness the very next thing is destruction" (1964, p. 491). I believe that the concept of using an object and the continuous destruction in unconscious fantasy should be seen as a necessary extension of Winnicott's idea of creative play.

If creative illusion is the foundation of a life worth living, then the capacity to use an object is what allows the subject to create a *fertile oscillation* and *vital redeployment* between what is subjective and what is objective. In other words, the constant destruction that is always at work in unconscious fantasy ensures one of the essential functions that makes possible the dialogue and mutual enrichment between creative imagination and what can now be found in shared, communicable reality. It is a continuous cycle of creation and destruction, a fertile exchange that enables human beings to derive meaning from their existence. The ability to establish a dialectical tension, or oscillation, between creative and destructive processes offers, in my opinion, a vital and developmental alternative that allows us to avoid, on the one hand, the ever-present risk of being confused and hallucinating, and on the other hand, the opposite risk of becoming trapped in a fixed and lifeless reality.

Notes

1 This notion was already present in 1965: Freud's letter to Lou Andreas-Salomé refers to it, although in the context of writing rather than the analytic session itself.

2 Bion's thinking regains an open nature when, years later, he describes his position in terms of "trying to dismiss memory and desire […] trying to start a

session with as nearly blank a mind as one can get – *which is not altogether very near because one has such an enormous past history between the time that one is born and the present day"* (Bion, 1976, p. 241; italics mine).

3 Aguayo (2018) believes that the clinical cases reported in Bion's Los Angeles seminars "provided a clinical counterpoint to the purely theoretical aphorisms adduced in the enigmatic 'Notes on memory and desire'" and in "Negative capability". In my opinion, this deserves a separate study. Moreover, Bion's account, given in Buenos Aires in 1968, of a patient who would scream, frequently leave for the bathroom during sessions, and on one occasion, even threatened him with her handbag, as well as Bion's subsequent decision to terminate the analysis, is striking (see Aguayo, 2024). It is doubtful that this could be considered an example of negative capability.

4 *Parallel convergences:*

1 In Euclidean geometry, this term denotes an oxymoron, a paradox, given that two parallel lines can never intersect.
2 In kinematics, it refers to the movement of two points along separate lines at the same speed, such that they can be connected by parallel lines.
3 In Italian political history, the expression is attributed to Aldo Moro to describe and advocate for an alliance between two ideologically distant and irreconcilable political parties – an alliance that was ultimately thwarted by his kidnapping and assassination.

5 I am not interested in focusing on the similarities and divergences between holding and containment, and the question of the external object, issues that are, in a sense, plain and have already been debated (among others, see Ogden, 2004; Hinshelwood, 2015; Aguayo, 2018).
6 I find Hinshelwood's (2018) hypothesis convincing when he suggests that in the 1950s Bion "was responding to Winnicott, and was loyally trying to show that Klein's new theory could encompass what Winnicott was trying to describe" (p. 203). I disagree, however, with his assertion that Bion "moved into a field of intuitive and subjective thinking, which was not that of Winnicott" (p. 210), since much of Winnicott's work focuses on the role and significance of the analyst's subjectivity.
7 The authors who have significantly investigated these two processes include Benjamin (2016), Cooper (2018), Elkins (2017), Ogden (2016), Rappaport (1998), and Slochower (1994).

References

Aguayo, J. (2018). "D.W. Winnicott, Melanie Klein, and W.R. Bion: The controversy over the nature of the external object—holding and container/contained (1941–1967)". *The Psychoanalytic Quarterly*, 87:4, 767–807.

Aguayo, J. (2024). "Contextualizing Bion's Clinical Practices during his Career as a Psychoanalyst: (1950–1979)". Paper delivered to the *Società Psicoanalitica Italiana*, Rome, September 26.

Benjamin, J. (2016). "From enactment to play: Metacomunication, acknowledgment and the third of paradox". *Rivista di Psicoanalisi*, 565–593.

Bion, W.R. (1958). "On arrogance". *The International Journal of Psychoanalysis*, 39, 144–146.

Bion, W.R. (1962). "The psychoanalytic theory of thinking". *The International Journal of Psychoanalysis*, 43, 306–310.

Bion, W.R. (1965a). "Memory and desire". Maslow, C. (ed) (2018). *Three Papers of W. R. Bion*. London: Routledge, pp. 1–10.

Bion, W.R. (1965b). *Transformations*. London: Heinemann.

Bion, W.R. (1967a). "Negative capability". Maslow, C. (ed) (2018). *Three Papers of W. R. Bion*. London: Routledge, pp. 19–28.

Bion, W.R. (1967b). "Notes on memory and desire". *Psychoanalytic Forum*, 2, 272–280.

Bion, W.R. (1970). *Attention and Interpretation*. London: Heinemann.

Bion, W.R. (1976). "Evidence". In *Clinical Seminars and Other Works*. London: Karnac, 2008, pp. 312–320.

Bion, W.R. (1992). *Cogitations*. London: Karnac.

Blass, R., Vermote, R. & Taylor, D. (2011). "Psychoanalytic controversies: Introduction to 'On the value of 'late Bion' to analytic theory and practice". *International Journal of Psychoanalysis*, 92, 1081–1116.

Cooper, S.H. (2018). "Playing in the darkness: use of the object and use of the subject". *Journal of the American Psychoanalytic Association*, 743–765.

Elkins, J. (2017). "Revisiting destruction in 'The use of an object". *The Psychoanalytic Quarterly*, 109–148.

Fabozzi, P. (2012). "A silent yet radical future revolution: Winnicott's innovative perspective". *The Psychoanalytic Quarterly*, 601–626.

Fabozzi, P. (2016). "The use of the analyst and the sense of being real: The clinical meaning of Winnicott's 'The use of an object". *The Psychoanalytic Quarterly*, 1–34.

Fabozzi, P. (2024). *Dispiegando margini. Nei dintorni di D.W.Winnicott. E oltre*. Milano: FrancoAngeli.

Hinshelwood, R.D. (2015). "Winnicott and Bion: Claiming alternate legacies". In: Spellman, M. & Salo, F. (eds), *The Winnicott Tradition: Lines of Development – Evolution of Theory and Practice Over the Decades*. London: Karnac, 61–68.

Hinshelwood, R.D. (2018). "Intuition from beginning to end? Bion's clinical approaches". *British Journal of Psychotherapy*, 34:2, 198–213.

Mawson, C. (2018). *Three Papers of W. R. Bion*. London: Routledge.

Ogden, T.H. (2004). "On holding and containing, being and dreaming". *International Journal of Psychoanalysis*, 85, 1349–1364.

Ogden, T.H. (2015). "Intuiting the truth of what's happening: On Bion's 'Notes on memory and desire". *Psychoanalytic Quarterly*, 84:2, 285–306.

Ogden, T.H. (2016). "Destruction reconceived: On Winnicott's 'The use of an object and relating through identifications". *The International Journal of Psychoanalysis*, 1243–1262.

Rappaport, D. (1998). "Destruction and gratitude. Some thoughts on 'The use of an object". *Contemporary Psychoanalysis*, 369–378.

Slochower, J. (1994). "The evolution of object usage and the holding environment". *Contemporary Psychoanalysis*, 135–151.

Winnicott, D.W. (1945). "Primitive emotional development". *Collected Papers: Through Paediatrics to Psycho-Analysis*, London: Tavistock Publications, 1958, pp. 145–156.

Winnicott, D.W. (1947). "Hate in the countertransference". *Collected Papers*, London: Tavistock Publications, 1958, pp. 194–203.

Winnicott, D.W. (1948). "Reparation in respect of mother's organized defence against depression". *Collected Papers*, London: Tavistock Publications, 1958, pp. 91–96.

Winnicott, D.W. (1954). "Metapsychological and clinical aspects of regression within the psycho-analytical set-up". In *Collected Papers*, London: Tavistock Publications, pp. 278–294.

Winnicott, D.W. (1955). "Clinical varieties of transference". In *Collected Papers*, London: Tavistock Publications, pp. 295–299.

Winnicott, D.W. (1962). "Ego integration in child development". In *The Maturational Processes and the Facilitating Environment*, The Hogarth Press and the Institute of Psycho-analysis, London, pp. 56–63.

Winnicott, D.W. (1964). "Review of *memories, dreams, reflections* by C. G. Jung". In *Psycho-Analytic Explorations*, Cambridge, Massachusetts: Harvard University Press, pp. 482–492.

Winnicott, D.W. (1966). "The split-off male and female elements to be found in men and women". In *Playing and Reality*, Tavistock Publications, London, 1971, pp. 65–85.

Winnicott, D.W. (1967a). "The location of cultural experience". In *Playing and Reality*, Tavistock Publications, London, pp. 95–103.

Winnicott, D.W. (1967b). "Mirror-role of mother and family in child development". In *Playing and Reality*, Tavistock Publications, London, pp. 111–118.

Winnicott, D.W. (1968–69). "On the split-off male and female elements. III. Answer to comments". In *Psycho-Analytic Explorations*, Cambridge, Massachusetts: Harvard University Press, pp. 189–192.

Winnicott, D.W. (1968a). "The use of an object and relating through identifications". In *Psycho-Analytic Explorations*, Cambridge, Massachusetts: Harvard University Press, pp. 218–227.

Winnicott, D.W. (1968b) "Playing and culture". In *Psycho-Analytic Explorations*, Cambridge, Massachusetts: Harvard University Press, pp. 203–206.

Winnicott, D.W. (1968c). "Playing: A theoretical statement". In *Playing and Reality*, Tavistock Publications, London, pp. 38–52.

Winnicott, D.W. (1987). *The Spontaneous Gesture. Selected Letters of D. W. Winnicott*. Rodman, F.R. (ed). Cambridge, MA: Harvard University Press.

Yehoshua, A. (1989). *Mr. Mani*. San Diego: Harcourt, 1993.

6 Pluperfect Errands in the Controversial Discussions of Bion and Winnicott

Jack Foehl

What are we to make of the fact that none of the five published letters written over more than a decade (1951–1967) by Donald Winnicott to Wilfred Bion seem to be favored with a reply? Is this simply a quirk of character? Winnicott wrote letters to many fellow psychoanalysts following their presentations over the course of his career (his published letters total over eight hundred). At the same time, we have no record of Bion's correspondence apart from his tender letters to his wife, Francesca, and to his analyst-turned-colleague and friend, John Rickman. I argue that rather than a quirk or slight, this one-sided correspondence is evidence of an "errand" (Apprey, 2024), where "[i]n a transgenerational haunting, … a contemporary generation is unwittingly possessed by an earlier generation. The possession preserves history, but in a poisonous, un-metabolized version" (Apprey, 2003, p. 12). The recent literature on the emergence of Bion and Winnicott as ambassadors of a new psychoanalytic paradigm of "ontology" offers the beginning of recovery from a "hauntology." But is this indeed the case?

On February 17, 1943, attendees of the British Psychoanalytic Society's second meeting of the year were deep into their continued (Controversial) Discussion around Susan Isaacs's crucial paper, "The Nature and Function of Phantasy." Isaacs directed a critique at Anna Freud for her remarks at the previous meeting regarding Klein's view that object relations began soon after birth, claiming that indeed Anna's father supported Klein's contention about the early life of the infant and the range of near-birth object relations, both libidinal and aggressive. Several responses were made to this claim by supporters of both Klein and Freud, and in the midst of this,

> …an air raid started, but the members were so absorbed in their own battle that they remained glued to their seats. Indeed, Winnicott had to draw their attention to the uproar outdoors: 'I would like to point out that there is an air raid going on.'
>
> (Grosskurth, 1986, p. 321)

Edward Glover suggested in the next meeting that during air raids, members should pause, carry their chairs to the basement, and resume the

DOI: 10.4324/9781003502067-6

meeting there. In this well-known scene, of course it was Winnicott calling attention to the environment, the surround (the bombardment both in
the room and outdoors!), and this would be a continued strain that can be
found in Winnicott's letters over the history of his life as an analyst. I argue
that it is also a strain found in psychoanalysis as a whole, a strain regarding
the role of reality in psychoanalytic thought and praxis.

Bion was conducting his studies at the Northfield Hospital at that time,
and would subsequently become a member of the British Society in 1950.
But the divisive trajectory of the Society, the stark lines drawn in the several
years of the Controversial Discussions, continued to ramify in the work of
Winnicott and Bion long after the deaths of Klein and Anna Freud. As we
know, Klein named Winnicott one of the first five "Kleinian" analysts. He
was a pediatrician and the first male child psychoanalyst. Klein selected
him to treat her son; he was supervised by Klein and was analyzed (for
his second analysis after James Strachey) by Klein's close confidant, Joan
Riviere. And then, in the early 1940s, he was dropped by Klein and her
followers, never to be cited or seriously taken up by them again. This is
often seen in relation to his early disagreement with Klein over the role of
aggression, the death instinct, and constitutional envy. Around this time,
his Transitional Object paper (1953) was rejected for publication in a book
for Klein's 70th birthday Festschrift.

Bion entered psychoanalysis as a staunch Kleinian. He joined them in
the study of aggression in the etiology of psychosis and, following his short
analysis with John Rickman, was analyzed by Klein. He began a series of
papers on projective identification and its evolution as a primitive form
of communication (container-contained), developed his theory of thinking (alpha function) and his evolving ideas on the intersubjective nature
of therapeutic action (reverie, atonement, O). Although his work evolved
far beyond his Kleinian brethren, he was never rejected by Kleinian thinkers and is very much embraced as one of their own (he continues to be
included as an esteemed writer in the Melanie Klein Trust: https://mela-
nie-klein-trust.org.uk/writers/).

Jan Abram has suggested, in her conversation with Bob Hinshelwood
(2023), that both thinkers were "released" after 1960 and the death of Klein
(p. 75). This is clearly the case in the evolution of Bion's phases, but I would
argue that Winnicott had always pushed against a kind of theoretical fore-
closure and defensive exclusivity in the presentation of Klein's concepts
and ideas. He commented about this defensiveness over the many years of
his career seen in his letters, sometimes in strenuous terms (which is very
much part of the "errand" I wish to convey). Take Winnicott's letter to his
junior colleague, Hanna Segal, on 21 February 1952 (CW 4:1:3):

> I do think that just at times for a few minutes you are tremen-
> dously cocksure of yourself, and if you happen to be speaking just
> then it shows. Perhaps what I am afraid of is that there is terrible

disillusionment inherent in all this and I would much rather you knew about it before you come to it. The fact is that you are capable of failing just as other analysts are, because there is so much that we do not yet know. When you talk at these moments of cocksureness you give no indication whatever that you believe that there could be anything that you do not understand.

(pp. 29–30)

Winnicott followed with a hearty compliment about her work and aptitude but continued in a way that addressed his main concern:

I am very genuinely concerned with Melanie Klein's contribution to psychoanalysis. This contribution of hers is steadily being made unacceptable because of the propaganda indulged in at every meeting … There is a saying that good wine needs no bush. In a similar way the good in Melanie's contribution need not be pushed forward … it can be expressed and discussed. At present it is seldom discussed because it is put forward aggressively and then defended in a way which can only be called paranoid

(ibid., p., 30)

So many of Winnicott's letters to colleagues echo this thread, conveying an analyst deeply dismayed with the direction of discourse in the British Society. He expressed this to Melanie Klein in his well-known letter on 17 November 1952 (CW 4:1:12) concerning the reception of one of his own papers, in a way that begins to show his theoretical sensibility:

What I was wanting on Friday undoubtedly was that there should be some move from your direction towards the gesture that I make in this paper. It is a creative gesture and I cannot make any relationship through this gesture except if someone come to meet it. I think that I was wanting something which I have no right to expect from your group, and it is really of the nature of a therapeutic act, something which I could not get in either of my two long analyses, although I got so much else. … I personally think that it is very important that your work should be restated by people discovering in their own way and presenting what they discover in their own language. It is only in this way that the language will be kept alive. If you make the stipulation that in the future only your language shall be used for the statement of other people's discoveries then the language becomes a dead language, as it has already become in the Society.

(p. 60)

Far from simply making a political statement about the struggles within the British Society, Winnicott brought his evolving psychoanalytic vision to this letter. In 1960, he published his ideas on the infant's "creative gesture," facilitated by good enough maternal care and holding (1960, p. 593). He held that active spontaneity and the quality of aliveness in human related-ness entails being met by another in a manner that does not initially chal-lenge the infant's early omnipotence. Such challenges engage a reactivity that deadens spontaneity.

Winnicott carried aspects of this tone in all of his letters to Bion, where he integrates his challenges regarding presentation in the Society, his concep-tual innovations, with questions regarding Bion's thinking and style, and his wish for an engagement. We see this in his last letter, which offers the topic of this entire book, where he questions Bion on his use of the phrase "memory and desire" from the Eliot poem. It also comes up in earlier letters where Winnicott melds a combination of flattery and challenge in response to Bion's presentations. It is tempting to hear in Winnicott's questions a prodding forth of something from Bion, taking him into spheres that they were both expanding beyond their Kleinian roots. How can we not hear this in Winnicott's questions in his letter on November 17, 1960. He won-ders following Bion's talk on "A Theory of Functions," whether psychotics have lost the capacity to dream?

> [...or] have [they] never achieved this elbow room between the con-crete and abstract, or between psychic reality and external reality? ... Another way of getting at this point would be to ask you what it is in the analysis that may possibly enable a patient who cannot dream and who cannot sleep or wake to achieve at last the dream?
>
> (CW 6:1:18, p. 125)

Winnicott continues (possibly disingenuously) by suggesting

> ...that I am not expecting you to write a letter answering these ques-tions ... I wanted to write you and put into question form (sic.) [from] the place where I was able to come into contact with your paper last night.
>
> (ibid., pp. 125–126)

We hear Winnicott engaging Bion on their respective concerns with "ex-ternal reality," also addressed in his final letter. Winnicott indicates the *be-tween* of the psychic and the real. And he brings into his description his special phrasing of a *place*, offered as a conceptual tool a decade later, in *Playing and Reality* (1971), *The Place where we Live* (CW 8:21). "Place" has the early connotation of potential space in which cultural experience (playing) can take place, with an emphasis on *living*, on *being alive*. Winnicott pulls for a reflection from Bion on the nature of what's mutative in the work on dreaming at a time when Bion was at the heart of his epistemology papers, at a point when he would develop his conception of dreaming and reverie through the next decade.

A similar movement might be found in Winnicott's letter of October 7, 1955 (CW 5:1:16). Without elaborating the detail of the entire letter, it centers around Winnicott's reaction to Bion's clinical material in his presentation of a paper entitled "Personalities," published as "Differentiation of the Psychotic from the Non-Psychotic Personalities" (1957). For my purposes, it is significant that Winnicott emphasizes his difficulty with Bion being "cluttered around by the organisation of the Klein group" (p. 84), and the disruption of the Society that this causes. Winnicott's main thrust is in noting that Bion's clinical material "...cried out for an interpretation about communication" (p. 84), when his patient began by saying: I ought to have called my mother." Winnicott would have noted to this patient:

> a mother properly oriented to her baby would know from your movements what you need. There would be a communication because of this knowledge which belongs to her devotion and she would do something which would show that the communication had taken place. I in this present analytic situation fall into the category of the mother who failed to make communication possible. In the present relationship there is given a sample of the original failure from the environment which contributed to your difficulty in communication.
>
> (pp. 84–85)

This fails to convey the contrast with Bion's process, and I'm afraid such detail lies outside the range of my current interest. My point is that Winnicott engaged Bion regarding the maternal environment (in his letter, he continues: "You will see that from my point of view you were talking about the environment although you said you were not going to do so...") at a point when Bion was beginning to deepen his crucial investigations into his own theory of communication (alpha function). Winnicott's interpretation offered a shift of recognition to the immediate movement of the clinical scene, contextualized in relation to the "original failure" as interpreted by Winnicott. In this letter, he further critiques the "group behavior" of the Society and the "plugging of theme songs" (p. 85) in the familiar deadened use of Kleinian concepts.

Mauro Manica (2023) has offered a detailed "conjecture" regarding Winnicott's influence in a paradigm shift for both thinkers. But my emphasis is on the one-sided nature of this discourse, the absence of a dialogue between these two influential thinkers and subsequently between those who have elucidated and built upon their work. A notable early exception is Green (1975, 1998), who found compelling intersections in their work, and then more contemporary integrations that are part of the recognition of the profound paradigm shift that is part of a theoretical *après coup*, a reconsideration of both thinkers in their role of the shift in our thought and practice from *being* to *knowing* (Eshel, 2017; Ogden, 2019, 2020; Mawson, 2019; Abram and Hinshelwood, 2023).

There are a number of basic similarities in the focus of Winnicott and Bion, starting with the profound influence of Klein from which each of them diverges. There is the fundamental importance of infantile dependency and intolerable anxiety, the centrality of an intersubjective process for developmental growth and change as a model for the processes of change in treatment. There is also the crucial role of the analyst's sensitivity to their experience of being with the patient. Although both Winnicott and Bion recognize the infant's dependency, for Winnicott, the mother sustains the infant's initial "illusion of omnipotence" in an undifferentiated state with the gradual disillusionment of separation. For Bion, the infant is exposed to the awareness of its intolerable helplessness and dependence since for him, infant and mother are separate from the start. Like Klein, Bion sees the infant as capable of aggression/hate as well as desire/love, relying exclusively on projective mechanisms in the paranoid-schizoid position. For Winnicott, the paranoid-schizoid experience is occasioned by the catastrophic traumatic failure of good enough mothering. The infant is not capable of feeling murderous hate because this or any organized affects have not yet developed. These differences lead to differences in the nature of interpretation and the kind of communication offered by the patient to be worked with and through by means of interpretation or otherwise.

This is a dialogue never to be had between these two thinkers. But further, much like the foreclosures with Klein and her group, Bion never referred to Winnicott in his publications. Interestingly, Winnicott was sparing in citations to Bion as well. This is where the issue of an "errand" is relevant. What errand is unconsciously transmitted in a family, organization, or tradition where certain ways of thinking and experiencing are traumatically foreclosed?

There is a larger literature that addresses this kind of transmission, including Nicolas Abraham's (1975) "notes on the phantom," Kestenberg's (1982) "transgenerational transposition," Schützenberger's (1998) "ancestor syndrome," and Faimberg's (2005) "telescoping of generations," but Apprey's "pluperfect errand" is apt in addressing the psychoanalytic enterprise. Apprey asks: "What implications present themselves when we use existing psychoanalytic theories in inflexible ways as points of entry into psychoanalytic exploration" (2017, p. 16)? What is the haunting of a preserved traumatic past, that continued unresolved in the foreclosed relations between Winnicott and Bion? What kind of psychoanalysis remains when traumatic effects of past generations find their expression through exclusion, through rendering parts of our tradition outside the established cannon?

The great challenge and traumatic thread in the psychoanalytic tradition is found in its relation to external traumatic reality. What was the role of traumatic reality in psychoanalytic theorizing and practice? What was its connection to the individual's internal world? This is a long dispute starting with Freud's rejection of the seduction theory onward, finding expression in repeated exclusions and foreclosures of thought and exploration, the isolation of thinkers (such as Ferenczi, Reich) in the service of "othering" aspects of experience. Melanie Klein (1961) treated her young patient Richard with no mention of the raging bombardments outside their intrapsychic explorations. Winnicott announces at a Society meeting: "I would like to point out that there is an air raid going on!" This is a call to external reality, something that he developed with great nuance in situating his focus on the role of the actual mother in the generation of an essential illusory space paradoxically connecting inside and outside in a new way of configuring "reality." Winnicott's appeal to Bion and other analysts in his circle was to open this haunted discourse, but it is left to current generations to bring the dialogue of these two great thinkers to life.

References

Abraham, N. (1975). Notes on the phantom: A complement to Freud's metapsychology. In: N. Abraham and M. Torok (1994) *The Shell and the Kernel: Renewals of Psychoanalysis* (N. Rand, Ed.). Chicago: University of Chicago Press.

Abram, J. and Hinshelwood, R. D. (2023). *The Clinical Paradigms of Donald Winnicott and Wilfred Bion: Comparisons and Dialogues*. London: Routledge.

Apprey, M. (2003). Repairing history: Reworking transgenerational trauma. In: *Hating in the First Person Plural* (D. Moss, Ed.). New York: The Other Press.

Apprey, M. (2017). Representing, theorizing and reconfiguring the concept of transgenerational haunting on order to facilitate healing. In: *Transgenerational Trauma and the Other: Dialogues Across History and Difference* (S. Grand and J. Salberg, Eds.). New York: Routledge.

Apprey, M. (2024). *Transgenerational Haunting in Psychoanalysis: Toxic Errands* (W. F. Cornell, Ed.). London: Routledge.

Bion, W. R. (1957). Differentiation of the psychotic from the non-psychotic personalities. *International Journal of Psychoanalysis*, 38: 266–275.

Eshel, O. (2017). From extension to revolutionary change in clinical psychoanalysis: The radical influence of Bion and Winnicott. *Psychoanalytic Quarterly*, 86: 753–794.

Faimberg, H. (2005). *The Telescoping of Generations: Listening the Narcissistic Links Between Generations*. London: Routledge.

Green, A. (1975). The analyst, symbolization and absence in the analytic setting (on changes in analytic practice and analytic experience): In memory of D. W. Winnicott. *International Journal of Psychoanalysis*, 56: 1–22.

Green, A. (1998). The primordial mind and the work of the negative. *International Journal of Psychoanalysis*, 79: 649–665.

Grosskurth, P. (1986). *Melanie Klein: Her World and Her Work*. Cambridge, MA: Harvard University Press.

Kestenberg, J. S. (1982). A psychological assessment based on analysis of a survivor's child. In: *Generations of the Holocaust* (M. S. Bergman and M. E. Jucovy, Eds.). New York: Columbia University Press.

Klein, M. (1961). *Narrative of a Child Analysis: The Conduct of the Psychoanalysis of Children as Seen in the Treatment of a Ten-Year-Old Boy*. London: Hogarth Press.

Manica, M. (2023). A letter from Winnicott to Bion: An imaginative conjecture to illustrate a paradigm transformation. *Psychoanalytic Quarterly*, 92(2): 263–288.

Mawson, C. (2019). *Psychoanalysis and Anxiety: From Knowing to Being*. New York: Routledge.

Ogden, T. (2019). Ontological psychoanalysis or "what do you want to be when you grow up?". *Psychoanalytic Quarterly*, 88: 661–684.

Ogden, T. (2020). Toward a revised form of analytic thinking and practice: The evolution of analytic theory of mind. *Psychoanalytic Quarterly*, 89: 219–243.

Schützenberger, A. A. (1998). *The Ancestor Syndrom: Transgenerational Psychotherapy and the Hidden Links in the Family Tree*. New York: Routledge.

Winnicott, D. W. (1953). Transitional objects and transitional phenomena—A study of the first not-me possession. *International Journal of Psychoanalysis*, 34: 89–97.

Winnicott, D. W. (1960). The theory of the parent-infant relationship. *International Journal of Psychoanalysis*, 41: 585–595.

Winnicott, D. W. (1971). *Playing and Reality*. London: Tavistock.

7   On the Question of the Sensuous in Winnicott/Bion

Peter Goldberg

Part One

Winnicott and Bion, so different in their manner of thinking and idiosyncrasies, nevertheless address strikingly similar concerns about the human condition, and in my view are highly complimentary in their effects on clinical theory. Yet the contrast between them is both instructive and important for our current modes of analytic practice. They certainly come at things from different vantage points, which I am tempted to describe rather globally – and surely too simplistically – in this way: that for Winnicott, the essential thing is that we can feel while thinking, while for Bion, it is that we can think while feeling. Winnicott wants to be sure that thinking should not usurp sensory affective experience (hence the importance, for him, of being embodied – or what he calls *in-dwelling of mind in psyche-soma*). Bion, for his part, wants to be sure that sensation does not crowd out the thinking self's experience of psychical truth (hence the importance of what his conception of alpha function transformation). But common to both, there is always the question (largely absent from Freud and Klein) of whether an experiential sense of self can be found and maintained at all. In this regard both Winnicott and Bion were very much of their time: theorists who, in the wake of WWII, were undoubtedly affected by modern concerns about the human condition (with existentialism and phenomenology in the air), and affected more particularly by a discernable shift in how mental suffering was perceived in the clinical situation. Here the picture of the integrated individual suffering internal conflict, bequeathed by the Oedipal situation, was giving way to a newer perception of the fragile self, haunted by early loss and trauma, threatened by anxieties of annihilation, dissolution, erasure, and non-existence, and forced to resort to defenses of splintering and dissociation. In an effort to retrofit psychoanalysis for a new age, Bion and Winnicott set about searching, each in their own fashion, for new and more effective ways of *being with* the patient,[1] which I think is very much reflected in the letter under consideration. Both authors expanded the clinical description of existential suffering ("primitive agonies", "nameless dread"), while also bringing the function of the environment – as well as

DOI: 10.4324/9781003502067-7

the actuality of the analyst – into clinical theory. In re-centering the clinical method on *holding* and *containing*, Winnicott invented a new psychoanalysis for the deadened or dissociated self, while for his part, Bion provided a far-reaching model of the persecuted self lost to excessive splitting and fragmentation. In shifting focus to the building blocks of self-hood and our dependency on a humanizing environment, Winnicott and Bion instigated a paradigmatic shift in clinical psychoanalysis.

But what of their differences? The somewhat gnomic letter written to Bion on October 5, 1967, would seem to indicate some divergence of views, but it is far from clear what this disagreement might be. For all its oddness, the letter is very much characteristic of Winnicott. For one thing, it shows the peculiar, even slightly eccentric, way in which he would tackle differences. In his letters, talks, and papers, whenever expressing disagreement, he rarely did so in a conventionally coherent way. So it is in this letter to Bion is hard to discern whether he is quibbling over semantics ("desire" vs "intention"), or hiding a far more substantial disagreement behind a somewhat dissembling way of putting things. My impression is that he is neither quibbling nor dissembling, but is looking for a way to introduce what Bion would call an alternate *vertex*, another way of seeing.

The fact is that Winnicott's highly idiosyncratic way of expressing things has proved enduringly generative. Never resorting to lofty concepts or theory-heavy thinking, his experience-near mode of expression in his writing tends to have the rather special effect, as Ogden (2018) has noted, of inducing new thoughts in the reader. Indeed, Winnicott's unique way of seeding ideas as he goes along, rather than relying on a harvest of mature thoughts or established concepts, is perhaps the reason why, over half a century later, we find ourselves revisiting his papers and poring over various of his utterances.

This particular letter to Bion, however, is especially enigmatic, because it is hard to tell what he was hearing and reacting to in Bion's presentation. We know that the letter was written in response to a lecture that Bion gave on negative capability,[2] but it is clear that Winnicott is actually focused on the main assertion of Bion's (1967) short paper *Notes on Memory and Desire* (later elaborated in Chapter 4 of *Attention and Interpretation*), namely that the exercise of memory and desire is essentially at odds with the development of a capacity for negative capability.

Perhaps it is worth highlighting what is at stake for Bion in focusing on the twin phenomena of memory and desire, conjoined phenomena which he came to think of as something that we analysts should, as far as possible, be *without*, at least as we enter the analytic situation. His reasons for this are well known: because memory and desire are realized through sensory perception, because the sensory domain is implicated in the way we remember things and the way in which we desire things, it follows that *remembering* and *desiring* in the analytic situation will obstruct the work of analysis, by keeping us locked into familiar ways of seeing and sensing and knowing things, beholden to a familiar consciousness of the world. The essence of analysis, for Bion, involves creating the conditions in which this familiar sensuous consciousness of things can be interrupted or suspended, creating the potential for new experience and new registration of our psychical reality. Minimizing memory and desire, then, offers a way of optimizing negative capability, which entails the ability to intuit *psychical* facts rather than perceiving facts given by sensory perception. In other words, if the analyst is busy remembering or busy desiring, psychical reality will be elided or remain inaccessible to the analyst, which makes him useless to the patient. Having previously described a number of important processes associated with projective identification and the analyst's receptivity (conceptions such as reverie, metabolization, containment, transformations), Bion now brings the analyst's psychical posture, his negative capability (or empty mindedness, if you will), into the center of the clinical picture, and in so doing brings the function of intuition to the forefront of his clinical model. Bion's remarkably influential proposal regarding relinquishment of memory and desire is nothing if not a robust extension of Freud's conception of "evenly hovering attention".

This is the highly original new development in Bion's thought that stimulated Winnicott's response in the note he sent to Bion. From what we can discern from the letter, Winnicott seems to question Bion on two points: on *memory*, he suggests that we cannot really do without it because it is a main way that reality enters the clinical situation. On *desire*, the question seems possibly more pointed: there is a sense that we cannot relinquish desire due to its being somehow integral to the role of the analyst as an *objective* object, that is someone operating outside of the patient's omnipotence.

It seems difficult, however, to follow Winnicott's argument here; his point about the patient placing the analyst outside the area of omnipotence strikes me as a bit of a non-sequitur. When he explains that "what is likely to turn up tomorrow in my analytic work cannot be covered by what I have in my own mind to want, precisely because I have to be able to allow the patient to be a separate person", he seems to be saying that we do not operate entirely in the area of (omnipotently created) subjective objects and phenomena, that there is some important objective perception of objects. In other words, objects are never just what we desire (i.e., create) them to be. But what does the prevalence of omnipotence in the patient have to do with whether or not the analyst engages the patient with (or without) desire? Does my possession of desire as an analyst make it any less likely that the patient remain omnipotent? (Why wouldn't my being desirous make it *more* likely that the patient's omnipotence be reinforced?) The argument, such as it is, seems convoluted, and is puzzling, if not confounding. It could be that Winnicott is simply misunderstanding Bion – this is, after all, a brief "day after" note, probably written quickly, rather than a thoroughly thought-through commentary. Alternately, Winnicott may simply reckon that it is entirely impossible to relinquish memory and desire, that it is a fool's errand, so why propose it at all. Yet Winnicott does not seem dismissive. There is clearly something he is trying to get at, but what is it?

Winnicott's Conception of Omnipotence

Winnicott's puzzling reference to omnipotence – his specifying that it is somehow the relinquishment of omnipotence that is the important factor – seems ironic, since a distinctive and even unique part of his contribution lies in his conviction that omnipotence plays an essential and vitalizing role in psychical life. He is eloquent about the value of *illusion*, which is fueled by omnipotence – the importance of our creative apprehension of objects,[3] how we feel that the world is made by us and for us. Of course he also stressed the developmental necessity of *disillusion*, of recognizing the objective existence of things in the world, but clearly he felt that the sense of omnipotence persists in the paradoxical state of illusion that he famously described as key to the ongoing sense of self – the paradox, captured in the concept of transitional phenomena, wherein we both create our objects and recognize their independent existence at the same time. There seems little doubt that Winnicott saw the subjective way of relating as most essential for the feeling of being real and alive, and hence of primary importance in the therapy situation. Reading Winnicott, seeing how he works, one is left with the impression that for him it is not objective perception but subjective perception that needs cultivation, especially among those false-self personalities who were of such interest to him – those patients who had become dissociated from their subjective embodied experience and consequently struggled with depersonalization and deadness, and a sense of unreality. This conception of the vital role of subjective objects and what he called *creative apperception* of the world could be considered Winnicott's own version of the importance of a kind of *at-one-ment*, the vitalizing experience of unity with things. But this would be a kind of *at-one-ment* that is quite different from Bion's conception of O. To put it simply, at-one-ment for Bion becomes possible where sensuous experience is curtailed, whereas for Winnicott, at-one-ment would be something that occurs precisely through shared sensoriality, or what I refer to as "sensory symbiosis" (Goldberg, 2012).

I think it likely, then, that Winnicott's rather obtuse comments about omnipotence reflect his looking for a way to express his broader point of view, his own way of thinking about *being with* the patient, which is perhaps not well captured in the language of memory and desire and negative capability, but might be better represented in another language – for example, in terms of subjective objects, the spontaneous gesture, creative apperception, muscle eroticism, holding and handling – though he does not introduce his distinctive terminology into the letter. It seems to me that Winnicott is hinting at something about *his* way of *being-with* the patient that differs from Bion's, without actually articulating it.

Desire and Sensuous Engagement

It may be worth noting here that Winnicott's (1960) conception of the function of *holding*, both in the infant care setting and the analytic situation, captures something distinctive that is different from (though compatible with) Bion's (1962) landmark description of the analyst's reverie and deep receptivity entailed in the analyst's containment function. What is distinctive about "holding" is that it suggests something like a proprioceptive posture on the part of the analyst, a capacity and willingness to search for and experience sensory engagement. Holding requires embodied engagement, something perhaps akin to desire.

Is it possible, then, that *this* is what Winnicott is getting at in the letter, albeit cryptically – namely that we should not attempt to relinquish desire precisely because desire is necessary to ensure sensuous contact? Could it be that the play of the senses, which Bion views as obstructing our most profound experience of connectivity (O), is the very thing that Winnicott considers *key* to our connectivity with self and others? If so, then we have a very big difference indeed.

We get a clue along these lines from Winnicott's introducing a possible distinction between "intent" and "desire". The possible implication is this: whereas we might see the virtue of trying to relinquish *intent* in the clinical situation (e.g., to avoid imposing our agenda and expectations on the patient in the clinical hour), it might be a mistake to try to void ourselves of *desire*. This raises the question: what is the difference between intent and desire in this context? Intent, we can say, entails *wanting specific things to happen* in the clinical encounter; desire, on the other hand, is non-specific – it is a drive to engage, rather than to get something done. If this distinction holds water, then we can imagine Winnicott saying (without really saying it): *Bion, if you try to rid yourself of desire, you may think you are facilitating "negative capability" (i.e., making more room for "O" or truth of psychical reality), but in fact by relinquishing desire you actually court disengagement from the patient. By all means relinquish intent, but not desire.* Of course this would naturally raise the question of how it is that the analyst's desire is such an essential ingredient in the clinical encounter (Wilson, 2020); I have already suggested that our desire for something like psycho-sensory engagement might be an essential ingredient of our work in analysis.

My speculation, whatever its worth, about what Winnicott is getting at in his query about *desire* versus *intent*, reflects my perception of a broader difference in perspective. Bion's linking of memory and desire arises, as I have noted, within a particular context – his belief that sensuous states of mind are an impediment to analytic work and the analyst's intuition, and hence should be minimized in the analyst's clinical approach. But nowhere in Winnicott's work do we find a similar view on the relation of the sensuous and the psychical; certainly there is no equivalent idea that cultivation of the analyst's clinical intuition rests upon minimizing the sensuous, that relinquishing the sensuous will bring us potentially closer to psychical and emotional truth. On the contrary, Winnicott seems to find a kind of intuitive connection *through* the sensuous (though he does not elevate the notion of intuition the way Bion does). For Winnicott, the truth of emotional life lies in "the psychical elaboration of somatic experience". One of his most profound ideas is that what feels most meaningful and real in our thinking is rooted in psyche-soma experience (Winnicott, 1949). His whole evolving clinical approach may be viewed as facilitating the imaginative elaboration of psyche-soma experience, which gives the feeling of being real.

This divergence over the place of sensuous experience in the clinical situation highlights a significant difference of perspective on what constitutes the task of treatment: for Winnicott, the most germane problem is loss of the somatic-sensory basis of experience (which connects us sensuously to things); for Bion, it is the loss of dream-work-alpha, which is the way we can know ourselves and the world. Another way of describing the difference is that Winnicott's interest was always primarily in psyche-soma dissociation, while Bion's *metier* is the exploration of splitting and projective identification.

Part Two

Winnicott introduces the second half of the letter by saying that it has "to do with something quite separate". This may be so, but is it possible that the two parts are somehow linked? There is no clue as to why Winnicott is urging Bion to read the book he is so strongly recommending, a book about the reinterpretation of the gospels in light of newly unearthed historical documents, wielding a challenge to established church doctrine at the time. Winnicott's somewhat dismissive comments about how organized religion relies on the invention of "miracles" suggest his own preference for a demystified religious doctrine; but could he be trying to get Bion to see something about this too?

As I have noted, when Bion makes the case for the suspension of memory and desire in the clinical situation, he is doing so in the context of his conception of O, the domain of psychical experience *in itself*, which he increasingly believes is the proper terrain for psychoanalytic transformations: analysis works not by increasing *knowledge* of self (K), but by expanding the area of psychical experience itself (O), which defies easy description. Bion tries to capture the nature of O by reference to the experience of *at-one-ment*, of the *God-head*, of the "formless infinite". It is easy to see why the conception of O subsequently lent itself to comparisons with mystical thought (though Bion himself disavowed saturating the idea of O in this way). The question of whether O is inherently a mystical concept, or whether it can be understood in more purely psychological terms, has been taken up by Civitarese (2020). I have argued that *at-one-ment* may fruitfully be viewed from another (Winnicott inflected) vertex, in terms of shared psycho-sensory experience (Goldberg, 2020).

Realness and Truth

It is significant, I think, that both theorists find it important to place a sense of *realness* or of truth-of-experience at the center of their emergent models. Again, I suspect this reflects the mid-century *zeitgeist*, the struggle over the sense of alienation and inauthenticity, as reflected in the philosophy and art and music of the post-war period. But I assume that the focus on realness (Winnicott) and truth (Bion) arose, first and foremost, from observations made in the clinical situation – observations of the tenuousness and fragility of the self, reflecting perhaps the increasing tenuousness of psychosocial conditions of human existence in a global context (world war, nuclear armament, the beginnings of ecological consciousness). One gets the impression that these path-breaking psychoanalysts perceived in their patients not just a struggle with internal conflict, but an urgent need for a sense of realness or psychical truth. At the risk, once again, of oversimplification, we might say that for Bion, realness comes through thinking, for Winnicott through feeling. Neither of them are talking about *reality testing*; rather, it is a matter of feeling the reality of one's own being-in-the-world. Bion ties this to a kind of psychical registration of *truth*, which he ultimately denotes in terms of O. Winnicott's version of feeling real is something closer to registering somatic vitality as the basis for feeling truly alive. It is particularly striking that both envisioned the analytic "cure" in terms of providing the patient with a way to find what might called a renewable life, a way of finding existential viability, not by establishing objective truth or reality but by finding a personally creative psychical relation to self and the world, a *realness* or *truth-ness* of experiencing being in the world. Both explicitly moved away from the idea of cure, toward a vision of analysis as a framework for generativity or enlivenment: Winnicott viewed the therapeutic process as a means of finding a sense of aliveness; Bion, for his part, insisted that we set aside the question of cure in favor of *transformations in O*. Both viewed analysis, then, along the lines of finding a way to live; and in this regard they are the early protagonists of the ontological ethos that has come to feel so persuasive in our current-day clinical practice.

Notes

1 Winnicott especially intuited the importance of an ongoing sense of *being-with*, as it underwrites the development of being an individual, and the role of the analyst's active participation and cultivation of being-with where it has been disrupted, as is often the case in those who suffered premature loss. Bion grasped this in his own way, at least in his in his late phase.

2 This lecture became Chapter 13 of *Attention and Interpretation* (1970) (thanks to Nicola Abel-Herch for this information).
3 Winnicott (1960) speaks of omnipotence almost fondly, regretting its premature loss in children who are forced to adapt to the otherness of the world too soon. Using the term this way could not have been more at odds than the customary negative use of the term by Klein and her followers.

References

Bion, W.R. (1962) *Learning from Experience*. London: Tavistock.
Bion, W.R. (1967) Notes on memory and desire. In *Melanie Klein Today: Vol. 2. Mainly Practice*, ed. E.B. Spillius. London: Routledge, 1988, pp. 17–21.
Bion, W.R. (1970) *Attention and Interpretation*. New York: Basic Books.
Civitarese, G. (2020) Bion's O and his pseudo-mystical path. *Psychoanalytic Dialogues*, 29(4):388–403.
Goldberg, P. (2012) Active perception and the search for sensory symbiosis. *Journal of the American Psychoanalytic Association*: 60(4):791–812.
Goldberg, P. (2020) Where are we when we are at-one? Discussion of "Bion's O and his pseudo-mystical path" by Guiseppe Civitarese. *Psychoanalytic Dialogues*, 29(4):404–417.
Ogden, T. H. (2018) The feeling of real: On Winnicott's "Communicating and not communicating leading to a study of certain opposites." *International Journal of Psychoanalysis* 99:1288–1304.
Wilson, M. (2020) The Analyst's Desire: The Ethical Foundation of Clinical Practice. New York: Bloomsbury Academic.
Winnicott, D.W. (1949) Mind and its relation to the psyche-soma. In *Through Paediatrics to Psychoanalysis: Collected Papers*. New York: Basic Books, 1975, pp. 243–254.
Winnicott, D.W. (1960) The theory of the parent-infant relationship. *International Journal of Psychoanalysis* 41:585–595.

8 Winnicott to Bion

Reflections on Winnicott's Letter

R.D. Hinshelwood

There are quantities of Donald Winnicott's letters available that he wrote to a huge number of people available in Rodman (1987) as well as in the collected edition of Winnicott's work edited by Leslie Cauldwell and Helen Taylor Robinson (2016). The availability of these letters means that Winnicott kept copies of everything he sent, and suggests he had an alert eye to posterity. The letter we are considering is not a personal communication to a friend or even a collegial dispute. It reads like an instructive comment from a supervisor. There is a somewhat didactic quality about his gentle confiding to Bion that the phrase 'memory and desire' repeats from T.S. Eliot's poem 'The Wasteland' (1922) written as it happens about the devastation of the First World War. He then proceeds with advice to read Graves and Podro (1955) who rewrote the Gospels. Both references are actually wide of the mark in terms of Bion's intentions to discuss the problems and vagaries of psychoanalytic listening.

Debating with Each Other

Bion had given a paper titled 'On memory and desire' to the British Psychoanalytical Society in 1965 (not published until 2016) and a brief digest of that in Los Angeles in 1967a. The presentation Winnicott was responding to was titled 'Negative Capability' not published as such but is probably the substance of *Attention and Interpretation* (1970). It is tempting to consider that Winnicott's display of his wider knowledge of literature was provoked by Bion's reference to John Keat's letters to his brothers, George and Tom where the term 'negative capability' comes from (Keats 1818). It may be fanciful to suggest such a supervisory intent but Winnicott at this stage in 1967 had just left the role of President of the British Psychoanalytical Society after his second stint in that office.

Since the 1920s, Winnicott as a paediatrician had been an ardent follower of Melanie Klein who initiated the psychoanalytic play technique for children. However, he was a follower only until the mid-1940s, when Klein more or less substituted Wilfred Bion for Winnicott in her group, as Bion entered his analysis and training as a psychoanalyst. He was over 20 years

DOI: 10.4324/9781003502067-8

after Winnicott in starting his psychoanalytic training, although only one year younger in age. Klein's substitution appears to have originated in Winnicott's disagreement with Klein over her theorising of the schizoid mechanisms in her paper in 1946. Winnicott, it seems, must have been well acquainted with this development of her ideas, and published his own paper on the primitive levels of development, disagreeing with Klein – in 1945, one year *before*, and thus anticipating, Klein's paper. Was he making an attempt to pre-empt her views and relegate them from the outset to be dismissed? It is possible to read the history this way.

I have commenced with these rather personal biographical details to inform something of a more professional and academic kind. Psychoanalysis is not short of examples of intense rivalries going back to that of Freud and Jung in 1909 if not before. And my suggestion is that Winnicott's letter could be seen as a somewhat superior comment on a rival disguised as a helpful communication of informative references (T.S. Eliot and Robert Graves and Joshua Podro). It would be easy, and perhaps just, to dismiss my comments here as merely the one-sided prejudice of a Kleinian such as myself if it were not for an important issue we can see in the letter.

Bion's paper was conveying a specific message when referring to Keats' 'negative capability'. He considered that, as psychoanalysts, we can get our heads so full of memories of our theories and of all the preceding work done, as well as impelled by a desire to get everything right for the suffering patient (as well as for our reputation with colleagues), that we miss what is impelling our patient in the moment we are meeting. If we then carefully read the overall message of the letter, it seems to miss what was driving Bion at this moment in *his thinking* about psychoanalytic work. Bion is warning us about clogging our minds with our knowledge and hopes which can badly obstruct a receptive state of mind (the negative capability; or, he also uses the term 'reverie for that state of receptivity). And Winnicott, unhappily, demonstrates how his mind is filled with alternative literary references, and he is left with little to attend to Bion's actual thinking. Such an omission in listening to each other is a characteristic of much of psychoanalytic debate in the past and in the present.

I was recently invited to make publishable comments on a paper by a seasoned psychoanalytic writer who was commenting on Bion's work. The author I was supposed to comment on made reference to only one short paper by Bion's as if he were completely unaware of Bion's major works and phases in his thinking. The comment I wrote concentrated on our inability to appraise ourselves fully of the thinking of those we disagree with. My comment was rejected for publication, understandably perhaps.

Intentions and Responsibilities

I want now to turn to a serious professional, even philosophical, point that Winnicott makes. That point is about abolishing memory and desire.

Dealing with those faculties may be appropriate for writing poetry: "At the same time in the application of the same idea to psychoanalytic work, I cannot help finding myself using the word intention and not feeling desire to be correct' (Winnicott 1967, p. 157 [Vol 8]). This, in my view, is an important point. The psychoanalytic intention is to help suffering people; but Winnicott is suggesting that *desiring* to help suffering people is more an intention to satisfy oneself, one's professional self. It is not clear from Bion's work if he did mean it in this sense of a kind of professional narcissism. But it does seem to illuminate Bion's point, and Winnicott could be right. Winnicott says, in his criticism of subjectively desiring one's own satisfaction, 'I have to be able to allow the patient to be a separate person' (pp. 157–158).

Winnicott's rather tentative style of expressing his important contrast is typical as he frequently uses it to avoid how adamant he feels about what he is expressing. This contrast goes to the core of his dispute with Klein. He asserts:

> In the application to psychoanalytic work I find I cannot allow that this is 100% subjective.
>
> (p. 157)

His critique is that Bion's approach to a patient is entirely subjective; in other words, that it can deny the patient a 'separate existence'. However, from Bion's point of view this seems not quite relevant, since what Bion (1959) has been advocating for some ten years is that the analyst makes his mind available, as much as possible, for the patient's use as a container (however much the patient may be ambivalent about a containing link). Thus, the patient himself could deny the separateness of the two parties in this way. From this point of view, we allow the *patient* to decide not to be a separate person (although that would need to be interpreted in the process of the session).

Bion had explained at this time that containing was dependent on a second step – the ancillary function by which the container modifies the projected element of the ego and its experience, and then reprojects for the patent's re-introjection. He is in effect assuming the separation of container and contents when things go right; but they can go wrong when the patient attacks the link. Bion would also agree that Winnicott could be right at times, when the *analyst* does not use the container for the modifying function. The failure of this containing function may occur because of either party. What Winnicott ignores is that the patient may not intend to project for purposes of containing, but rather for evacuation (Klein 1955). So, it looks pretty clear that Winnicott's correction was based on only a partial reading of what Bion was trying to expose. Winnicott was adding the possibility that it is the analyst (the 'environmental object' in Winnicott's terms) could *also* attack the containing link, an addition that Bion would not have objected to, I guess.

This double step of Bion's container – its receptivity and its modifying function – is very explicit in Bion's accounts, and draws from a long way back to his pre-psychoanalytic experience as a therapist in wartime (Bion 1961). Then, soldiers who broke down on active service were admitted as passive patients to be rehabilitated for active service again. They were given active responsibility *in* the hospital. As he said of one meeting with his patients/soldiers on parade:

> I turned the discussion over at that point as a matter of communal responsibility and not something that concerned myself, as an officer, alone
>
> (Bion and Rickman 1943, pp. 109–110)

The soldiers, when passive as patients, gave up their initiative as active persons, and the officer had to try to push it back into the soldiers to induce them to take initiative again as active partners. The engagement of both sides of the relationship is a mutual responsibility. The intention to preserve the separate individuals would have been, for Bion, a shared one. This expectation of a joint responsibility was adhered to by Bion up to 1967 and beyond.

The dispute comes down to the relevance of the medical model – who knows best for the patient? For Winnicott, the necessary achievement of individual separateness devolves to the analyst who must take responsibility for 'allowing separation'. For Bion, it is more complex; it is a joint responsibility and a part of the dynamic situation to adjust to and reveal the distortion of the personalities. It is the analyst in collaboration with the patient's unconscious. The latter is the true partner in a psychoanalysis. It is not the analyst's role to impose his own theories and metapsychology, nor to conquer severe personality disorder or psychotic states. He must listen, unobstructed, to the patient's theories and the distortion of the mutuality of the work.

As I say the tendency to critique without fully understanding the model one is critiquing is widespread in psychoanalysis. It may be reprehensible but may be quite understandable considering that analysts spend their working day listening to patients and any critiquing of each other has to be rushed in the in-between slots of time. I don't think it is *only* time restraints that diminish a full understanding of what we criticise. And I'd like to devote a few lines on the stresses that also contribute to a not-listening and an urge-to-criticise between psychoanalytic schools of thought.

Stresses and Strains

Having worked therapeutically and psychoanalytically for over forty years, I draw again on personal experience. There are particular strains inherent in psychoanalytic practice, and they are not altogether dissimilar from those in a medical practice though we should keep the two strictly distinct. The

Table 8.1 The anxiety-defence dynamic in analysts and carers

Anxiety	Defence
Despair	Idealised hope from our correct theories
Obscure communication	The sense of mastery over the unconscious
Loss of control (madness and violence)	Secure confinement
A fear of being infected with madness	An emotional distance to sterilise the impact
A sense of meaninglessness	Our theories given meaning to everything

aim is to alleviate the suffering whether bodily or mental. And that leads to a set of specific anxieties, much of which may remain unconscious in both parties, despite analysts' belief in their own mastery of the unconscious.

Here I follow a line of thought I first encountered some time ago (Jaques 1955, Hinshelwood 1998). There are a number of specific anxieties that come from our work in mental health and demand an unruffled confidence in our own specific theories, a belief that they are powerful even omnipotent.

Table 8.1 sets out the several dynamics which I discern in the work we do. *Firstly*, patients come despairingly. They have suffered and battled with conflicts and anxieties without any enduring success for a long time, and they come to us feeling helpless about themselves and in despair. We are confronted with that despair and unfortunately aim for our own sakes as well as the patient's, to turn it into hope. We, *secondly*, are confronted by obscure communications, mostly in actions and in implicit influencing of our own feelings, rather than communicating in words. We need then to 'know' that we have the understanding needed and our theoretical model will suffice. *Third*, like everyone else we fear the outbreak of madness and the loss of control which has often led to physical confinement approaching a prison regime in mental health institutions. For an analyst there is a need to combat that threat with an understanding, and giving meaning and we then turn, obviously, to our theories which we have to believe will never let us down. *Fourthly*, there is another fear, mostly unconscious in us, that some madness in ourselves could be released, or that we become infected as it were by the contact with the craze-making conflicts and anxieties brought to us. We then need to believe that we know all about our own conflicts and anxieties which we have confronted in our personal analyses with the analyst of a particular school; that is, our theories need to be prized as supremely effective. *Finally*, like with madness, we are confronted with states of meaninglessness, even in our less severe cases. And so, again, we need our theories to be powerful enough to rescue us and our patients from drowning in incomprehensible actions and words.

Crucially, these and maybe other dynamics confront each other across the boundaries of the different schools of thought. And one of the threatening issues of such a confrontation is that the different schools have confidence in different theories. Such confident assumptions can be used as socially agreed defences against these stresses in the work (see Jaques 1955). Debate and engagement then threaten the customary defences on either side. So for each group, a weakening of their defensive use of theory risks a potential emergence of the conflicts and anxieties coming to the conscious surface. It is unconsciously much more relevant to use each other to keep one's own conscious models and unconscious defences intact through mutual distancing. Those other theories risk confounding ours, and therefore our own defensive use of our theories. Any failures can always be emphasised in other schools of thought. The example of the coming together of the early groups in Vienna and Zurich was addressed in a previous paper (Hinshelwood 2018). It is comparable to the coming together of commercial organisations which merge or one takes over another; this has been studied byJinette de Gooijer (2009), who found that usually no real merger takes place, only that one organisation takes over the other. Mergers are a threat to avoid.

Conclusions

I started with a personal perspective on the differences between Winnicott and Bion, and what seems only a partial reading of each other. In fact, there is no evidence that Bion responded or even took seriously Winnicott's points because any reply from Bion was neither kept by Winnicott or it never existed as a listening response. And I have come to the point of finishing on a personal note about the painful psychology of the working practice of psychoanalysts or those caring for mental disorders.

I am unashamed by this intertwining of the personal with the professional since psychoanalysis *is* personal. Psychoanalysis is not a material science like physics or chemistry. It does not deal with a physical entity made of a material substance, as medicine does. We deal with a non-material substance, the mind. Our practice is the 'science' of the subjective.

However, there is a tendency often to collapse the psychoanalysis of our individual patients into the analysis of the *inter*subjective. This creates the 'analytic third' as Thomas Ogden (2004) called it. However, I tend to agree with Winnicott that we do not wish to merge the two parties of the analytic setting and would view then separately until there is clear evidence of the patient seeking a merger (Mahler, Pine and Bergman 1975, Rosenfeld 1947). It is apparent as suggested above that we should also be in agreement with Bion's model of the container-contained as two separately functioning systems entwined with each other. In the definitive statement of Edna O'Shaughnessy:

> It is now widely held that instead of being about the patient's intra-psychic dynamics, interpretations should be about the interaction of patient and analyst at an *intrapsychic* level.
>
> (O'Shaughnessy, 1983, p. 281)

We are interested in the working together of the two systems, despite the anxieties that the result could be the possible dissolution of the anxiety-defence dynamics of either or both, if they were to merge.

Winnicott's diversion from the focus of Bion's paper in 1967b, is, I argue an instance of the more emotional unconscious of psychoanalysts' themselves which keeps distance from each other in order to protect ourselves from the unconscious stresses, anxieties, and conflicts in the nature of our work with despairing patients.

References

Bion, W.R. (1959) Attacks on linking *International Journal of Psychoanalysis 40*: 308–315. Republished 1967 in *Second Thoughts*: 93–109. London: Heinemann. In Elizabeth Bott Spillius (1988) *Melanie Klein, Today, Volume 1*. London: Routledge. Republished in *The Complete Works of W.R. Bion*, Vol VI: 138–152. London: Karnac.

Bion, W.R. (1965) On memory and desire. *The Complete Works of W.R. Bion*, Vol VI: 7–17. London: Karnac.

Bion, W.R. (1967a) Negative capability. Paper presented at the British Psychoanalytical Society, October 1967.

Bion, W.R. (1967b) Notes on memory and desire. *Psychoanalytic Forum*, 2: 271–280. Reprinted in Bott Spillius E (Ed) (1988) *Melanie Klein Today, Vol 2: Mainly Practice*. London: Routledge: 17–21. Reprinted in Aguayo, J. and Malin, B. (2013) *Los Angeles Seminars and Supervision*: 133–149. London: Karnac. Republished in *The Complete Works of W.R. Bion*, Vol VI: 205–210. London: Karnac Books.

Bion, W.R. (1970) *Attention and Interpretation*. London: Tavistock. In *The Complete Works of W.R. Bion*, Vol VI, 221–330. London: Karnac.

Bion, W.R. and Rickman, J. (1943) Intra-group tensions in therapy. *The Lancet*, 2: 678–681. Republished in W. R. Bion (1961) *Experiences in Groups and Other Papers*: 11–26. London: Routledge. Republished 2014 in *The Complete Works of W.R. Bion*, Vol IV: 106–117. London: Karnac.

de Gooijer, J. (2009) *The Murder in Merger*. London: Karnac/Routledge.

Eliot, T.S. (1922) The Wasteland. New York: Boni and Liveright.

Graves, R. and Podro, J. (1955) *The Nazarene Gospel Revisited*. London: Cassel.

Hinshelwood, R.D. (1998) Creatures of each other: Some historical considerations of responsibility and care and some present undercurrents. In Angela Foster and Vega Roberts (Eds) *Managing Mental Health in the Community: Chaos and Containment in Community Care*. London: Routledge.

Hinshelwood, R.D. (2018) Freud and/or Jung: A group dynamic approach. In Brown, R. (Ed.) *Re-Encountering Jung: Analytical Psychology and Psychoanalysis*: 20–30. London: Routledge.

Jaques, E. (1955) Social systems as a defence against persecutory and depressive anxiety. In: Klein, Heimann & Money-Kyrle (Eds) *New Directions in Psychoanalysis*: 478–498. London: Tavistock.

Keats, J. (1818) Letter 22 December, *Poems and Letters. John Keats*. London: Longman (1988).

Klein, M. (1946) Notes on some schizoid mechanisms. *International Journal of Psycho-Analysis 27*: 99–110; republished (1952) in Melanie Klein, Paula Heimann, Susan Isaacs and Joan Riviere, *Developments in Psycho-Analysis*: 292–320. London: Hogarth. Republished in *The Writings of Melanie Klein*, Vol 3: 1–24. London: Hogarth.

Klein, M. (1955) On identification. In *The Writings of Melanie Klein* Vol 3, 141–175. London: Hogarth. Republished (1975) in *The Writings of Melanie Klein*, Vol 2: 176–235. London: Hogarth.

Mahler, M, Pine F., and Bergman, A. (1975) *The Psychological Birth of the Human Infant*. London: Hutchison.

Ogden, T.H. (2004) The analytic third: Implications for psychoanalytic theory and technique. *Psychoanalytic Quarterly 73*: 167–195.

O'Shaughnessy, E. (1983) Words and working through. *International Journal of Psychoanalysis 64*: 281–289.

Rodman, F.R. (1987) *The Spontaneous Gesture: Selected Letters of D.W. Winnicott*. London: Routledge.

Rosenfeld, H. (1947). Analysis of a schizophrenic state with depersonalization. *International Journal of Psychoanalysis 28*:130–139. Republished (1965) in Herbert Rosenfeld *Psychotic States*. London: Hogarth.

Winnicott, D.W. (1945) Primitive emotional development. *International Journal of Psychoanalysis 26*: 137–143.

Winnicott, D.W. (1967) Letter to Bion, 5 October. In Rodman, F.R. (1987) *The Spontaneous Gesture*. Cambridge, MA: Harvard University Press.

Winnicott, D.W. (2016) *The Collected Works of D.W.* Winnicott. Oxford, Oxford University Press.

9   On Not Playing with Winnicott

A Not-So-Curious Case of Non-Communication

Christopher G. Lovett

> *Can access to any true dimension of intersubjectivity be had without taking into account, within intersubjectivity itself, one specific feature specific to human beings: they have an unknown, shadowy area, their messages have dimension that eludes them, an unconscious that interacts from subject to subject.*
>
> Rene Roussillon (2011)

Over the course of several decades, Donald Winnicott and Wilfred Bion were engaged in a nearly parallel development in the advancement of psychoanalytic theory and technique, often crisscrossing one another's paths in the worlds of both the British Psychoanalytic Society and international psychoanalysis in general through their writing and speaking. Born only a little short of a year and a half apart at the close of the nineteenth century, through their combined influence they provided the groundwork for many of the most notable advances in contemporary analytic theory and practice, including intersubjectivity, analytic field theory, and the ontological aspects of the psychoanalytic process and experience. Between the years of 1951 and 1967 Winnicott wrote a series of five letters to Bion, in each instance following a presentation Bion had made at a scientific meeting of the British Psychoanalytic Society. It is the intriguing case that in response to every one of these instances of Winnicott's effort to engage Bion in some form of serious exchange, Bion did not respond to his colleague's overtures. It could be easily said, therefore, that, on the one hand, Bion chose not to play with Winnicott, the foremost authority on the subject of playing in the psychoanalytic world. On the other hand, it can also be argued that, while often encouraging and including various points of praise, Winnicott's letters to Bion were not necessarily playful in their tone or apparent intent. It remains, therefore, something of a mystery in the chronicles of psychoanalysis as to the reasons, first, as to why Bion chose not to respond to any of the letters, and second, why Winnicott and Bion could not experience some greater shared sense of mutual influence and recognition in relation to one another's work.

At the outset, in fairness, it is also important to note that Winnicott did engage in many efforts to recognize the importance of Bion's work. In fact,

DOI: 10.4324/9781003502067-9

it was during the meeting of the British Psychoanalytical Society on October 5, 1967, before the onset of the discussion of Bion's last paper before leaving for California, 'Negative Capability', that Winnicott spoke in praise of Bion, while also indirectly citing his introduction of the concept of negative capability that took on immense importance in Bion's thinking over that latter portion of his working life and in his conceptualization of analytic practice:

> We seem to be in the process of learning new techniques. Dr. Bion will I hope remember when he goes abroad that he is still a member of this Society and that we count on him to come back, and give papers of this kind, which is one of a series, and it is a tremendous loss to us to have Dr. Bion going, and he's just got to remember that we shan't forget him.
>
> (Mawson, 2018, p. 33)

In his writing about 'negative capability', a phrase he borrowed from the poet John Keats (1817/1931), Bion outlined a disciplined position in the matter of the analyst's attention, one that emphasized the analyst's need to eschew, as much as possible, the influence of memory and desire in his or her analytic attitude and practice in listening to the unconscious. Winnicott's note to Bion two days after the meeting, in contrast to his generous recognition of Bion's importance as chairman of the meeting two days earlier, expressed a different sort of feeling, one of discomfort with Bion's recommendations, 'I am not quite settled in my mind about the idea of memory and desire or intention, which you have used before'. It is intriguing that Winnicott focuses on the word 'desire' instead of 'memory', which is more often the focus of the contemporary analytic reader's misgivings in relation to Bion's seeming unorthodox, but carefully considered recommendations. Winnicott continued, 'I cannot help finding myself using the word intention and not feeling desire to be correct. As you said, we each have to find the word that fits oneself.'

The letter, the last to Bion recorded in the record of Winnicott's letters (Rodman, 1987), includes an intriguing twist. Winnicott appears to want to avoid, or perhaps even argue against, the use of the term 'desire', presumably a word that was not felt by Winnicott to be 'too subjective' to 'fit' his analytic sensibilities and methods properly. At the same time, he appears to make use of the term 'desire' in an ironic or wry sense, describing himself as without any feeling of desire that might hinder his freedom of thought or expression, such as in his writing to Bion. Winnicott's preferred choice of the term 'intention' in this passage seems, in effect, to pull his choice of operative term toward a more formal and less emotionally laden status, that is, 'intention' as it might be used in the realm of logic. In philosophical discourse the term 'intention' refers to the direction or application of the mind to an object, as matter of attention and intent, including the development of an understanding of other minds. It is clear, however, that Winnicott felt a very strong desire to be in contact with Bion and, in particular, in contact with his very fertile and highly innovative mind. This does not mean, however, that Winnicott did not on several occasions express a sense of difficulty in understanding and integrating into his own way of understanding the field of analysis and its practices what Bion had to say. In fact, he struggled to do so, often writing to Bion to express both his interest and admiration, but also his difficulty in understanding Bion's often highly condensed and sometimes ornately enigmatic style of expression, even while at the same time praising his talent and potential. For instance, as early as 1951, Winnicott wrote to Bion regarding his presentation of his paper 'The Imaginary Twin', his first paper presented to the British Psychoanalytical Society. In it Winnicott wrote:

> I read your paper immediately you gave it to me, but I had to keep it till now before I could read it again. I've just read it backwards.
>
> I think I understand what you are saying but I do find it very difficult. This is due mostly to me mostly. Whatever else I have got from the paper I get from it an insight into your doing analysis, and I feel very confident about the future of your analytic work. There is something essentially individual about whatever you do and write, and eventually your contribution to the Society will be a big one. It is for us to gradually find out how to understand what you say.
>
> (Winnicott, 2017, p. 433)

As was his habit in this correspondence, Bion did not reply, but in this context, it is interesting to note that a number of years later Bion (1963) recognized the special importance of the quality of the function of attention in the construction of his Grid, a graphically mapped out conceptual device intended to help the analyst to develop greater capacities for observation and intuition (Vermote, 2019). One of principal intentions of Bion's in constructing this sort of instrument was to categorize the various forms of thought, along with changing patterns of emotional experience, encountered in the process of analysis. Aguayo (2023) has pointed out that in using the Grid, recommended as a practice to be carried out after an analytic session, it can be employed as a means of exercising the analyst's intuition, in the form of, a sort of 'psychoanalytic game' (p. 109).

Bion himself excelled at games as a schoolboy and young sportsman, and so certain forms of playing held a special importance for him, as, of course, it did for Winnicott as well. The Grid itself, while modeled after Mendeleev's periodic table of elements, also resembles a sort of gameboard in which movements can be traced in the evolution of an experience in an analytic process, beginning from a mode of action, then to emotion, to thought, or the reverse. For instance, one of the games Bion suggested might be played by the analyst involves replacing all the columns and rows with different elements of the Oedipus myth. Thus, a fascinating question emerges from the correspondence between the Winnicott and Bion, that is, the themes of 'playing', the 'exercise of the analyst's intuition', and the idea of psychoanalytic games, all lead directly to the question as to why there seems to have occurred a failure to play, or even a refusal to do so, between the two. One clue may be found in the exception to the failure or, one might also wonder, apparent refusal on Bion's part to respond to Winnicott's notes and letters.

After Bion had visited Los Angeles in the spring of 1967, he was invited by members of the psychoanalytic community there to come work in Los Angeles. When his plans to relocate became generally known, Winnicott wrote to him on July 10th that year, nearly three months prior to the meeting on October 5th when Bion presented his paper 'Negative Capability' at the British Psychoanalytic Society that is the focus of this volume. In Winnicott's letter, included in only partial form in Rodman's biography of Winnicott, he wrote:

> I have been told, of course, about your proposal to leave England in the new year and to spend a few years in Los Angeles. This will be very good for Los Angles and I think you may do a really good job there. The trouble is, however, that we shall miss you a very great deal in this country. Your position here and your personality in what you stand for in the work is of the greatest importance to us and we can ill afford to lose you.
>
> (Rodman, 2003, p. 313)

Contrary to Bion's apparently usual non-response to Winnicott's communications, on this occasion he replied within days, though his reply is also only partially reproduced in Rodman:

> Dear Winnicott, many thanks for your kind letter and generous remarks. Francesca and I both look forward, with some trepidation … Naturally we hope good will come of it; what it costs to uproot from all our friends and associates here is painfully obvious but we shall have to wait and see what the compensating … may be—and hope. With all good wishes to Clare and yourself from Francesca and me.
>
> (Rodman, 2003, pp. 313–314)

In considering Bion's response to this different, more socially conventional and appreciative note from Winnicott, it is difficult not to wonder if Bion's previous failure to respond to Winnicott's more professional, but pointed communications might stem from a deep reluctance to engage in an open dialogue that might reveal, and thus threaten, newly emergent ideas and movements in his own analytic identity that felt too fragile and as yet unformed to introduce them into a dialogue with his very accomplished colleague. In this context, several possibilities quickly come to mind, including several that stem from the two psychoanalysts involved, including Winnicott's (1963) idea of an *incommunicado isolate/self* that is non-communicating. As Abram (1996) points out, at the center of Winnicott's theory of communication is a paradoxical notion that every individual is an isolate, and that, in keeping with this understanding, the right not to communicate must be respected. This point is most memorably expressed in one of Winnicott's paradoxical assertions, that is, 'It's a joy to be hidden and a disaster not to be found'. This central concept in Winnicott's model was certainly put to the test in his communications with Bion, who did not respond and, perhaps, pertinent to this tendency, his early life included at least two major separations, one to travel at age eight several thousand miles away from his home in India in order to attend boarding school in England, the other comprised by his experiences as a tank commander in World War I. This wartime ordeal included an immense experience of loss and terror that left him with a lasting feeling of distrust of authority and an abiding interest in the nature of the catastrophic dimension in life, both in its threatening and disruptive aspect and in the experience of transformative emergence and growth in the individual.

I would like to suggest, however, that Winnicott's line of thinking concerning the importance of the *incommunicado self* can be usefully conjoined to the idea of the analyst's *internal analytic setting* (Parsons, 2007) to illuminate the mostly one-sided communication that took place between Winnicott and Bion. Specifically, I think the process on Bion's side, while obviously multiple in its contributing dynamic factors, can be usefully employed in the service of exploring the questions that remain regarding Bion's seeming disinterest in a serious psychoanalytic dialogue with an esteemed colleague, despite Winnicott's repeated attempts to engage with him. To begin to answer this particular inquiry into Bion's frequent silences with a question, it seems relevant to ask, first, how does one create an internal analytic setting and, second and, perhaps, more important to the issue at hand, how does one preserve it, develop it, and continually recreate it in the face of various threats or disruptions. Parsons speaks of both internal and external aspects of psychoanalytic listening, but his initial paper that introduced the subject to the field included an exceptionally well-conceptualized depiction and exploration of the experience of the analyst's own internal listening, experienced in the mind's imagined internal space that features a structure or framework that ensures the maintenance of an analytic attitude and the reliable access to an interior psychoanalytic reality.

As described by Vermote (2011) Bion's later work provides a number of indications of important changes in his evolving theoretical orientation, beginning in the mid-1960s and expanding in their extent over the remaining years of his life. His shift from a focus on a theory of thinking, which, while developing a highly technical and original terminology, such as *'alpha-function'* and *'beta elements'* also attempted to capture the process of experience achieving a status of psychical and able to be thought about, led to a deepening interest in transformations in the patient's experience of *being*, as opposed to simply *knowing* in the classical mode of making the unconscious conscious and achieving psychoanalytic insight. His turn from what he termed transformations in K to transformations in O featured the cultivation of a radical openness to the undifferentiated levels of experience and the unknown.

Thus, it remains an ironic, but intriguing question as to why this shift in his analytic focus might have included an attitude of, perhaps, not being fully open to the influence of another in the person of Winnicott. It is likely, however, that Bion found this period of transformation and refashioning of his analytic orientation and clinical approach as too much in a transitional state to engage in the kind of exchange Winnicott appeared to pursue in his professional activities. At the same time, it is important to point out that during much of decade leading up to Melanie Klein's death, both Winnicott and Bion were attempting to separate themselves from the influence of Klein (Abram and Hinshelwood, 2023). Each were engaged in introducing new ideas into the theory of developmental and clinical psychoanalysis that would result in allowing some greater integration of the external and internal aspects of psychic life, but ironically, Bion was not especially receptive, nor responsive, to the entreaties from Winnicott. While much of Bion's work was deeply influenced by other people, his clear intent was to fashion out an independent line of thinking. His interest in some of Winnicott's ideas were usually translated into Kleinian terminology (Hinshelwood, 2023), yet Bion's creative output increased dramatically following Klein's passing, as did Winnicott's (Abram and Hinshelwood, 2023).

Returning to the matter raised at the beginning of this essay, it seems important to investigate further the question of Bion's rather consistent refusal to play in any intellectual or professional activity with his prominent contemporary in the person of Winnicott. It may be apposite to mention here that, while away during World War I, Bion did not write to his parents through his wartime service. Immediately following the war, he undertook to write an account of his experience that he planned to give to his parents in place of the letters he did not write during his time in combat, yet he somehow lost his writing before delivering it to his parents. So Bion had an important history of not writing, despite the fact that later in life he became a rather avid correspondent with his wife Francesca when they were separated for any reason. Ambivalence would seem a likely factor in this matter, because certainly his output in later life would tend to demonstrate no major inhibitions in writing, including his autobiographical works and his fictional work published near the end of his life, *A Memoir of the Future* (1977), as well as his many professional papers and books.

Winnicott, for his part, took issue with Bion and his seeming reluctance to both separate himself from the influence of Klein and the Klien group in the British Psychoanalytical Society. In one of his letters to Bion, written in 1955 after Bion had presented his paper 'Differentiation of the Psychotic from the Non-Psychotic Personalities', Winnicott took Bion to task in a manner that showed some significant measure of frustration of the sort that is expressed when a child's schoolmate claims that he is unable to come out and play.

> … at the meeting on Wednesday your relation to the society was completely spoiled by the fact that the first three or four speakers were Mrs. Klein and the pro-Kleinians. The impression was given that you were being protected from the Society and I really believe you must hate this sort of thing, as you are quite capable of defending yourself and of enjoying a contact with people who feel they want to challenge something you have said. After you had been insulated from the Society by the first four speakers there was no hope whatsoever that someone would get up to challenge you…In 10 years time I believe you will find yourself in contact with the whole Society but you have not yet started, being as you are cluttered about by the organisation of the Klein group…As I hope you will be president soon, I very much feel that I want to feel I have expressed my point of view clearly because you cannot emerge as president of the whole society until you have emerged from the Klein grouping.
>
> (Rodman, 1987, p. 90)

There is an emphasis here on Winnicott's part with respect to Bion's *'emergence'* out from under the wings of the 'Kleinian group', which comes across as more of a phalanx in Winnicott's view, in close ranks and with theoretical shields joined together. One can only wonder what Bion felt at it being suggested that he was 'insulated' and shielded by a band of Kleinian troops. The question seemed imperative to Winnicott—how eager to emerge was Bion? This emphasis on 'emergence', however, does provide a strong indication that Winnicott was not seeing Bion yet as his own man. Is it possible that Bion, sent away from home at a young age, then immersed in a war renowned for its devastating carnage, and, finally, a man whose first wife died in childbirth, was grateful for the shelter of the group at that point?

In addition, if Bion was not playing, how much might have this reluctance been in response to Winnicott's own seeming not fully playful, in fact, not showing the level of 'not knowing' that he wrote about and related to providing a facilitating presence in his analytic work (Winnicott, 1969). Instead, as Wilson (2020) has pointed out, it seems that Winnicott's desire in relation to Bion interfered in his capacity to simply be with him, or perhaps truly know him. He is, in this circumstance, enacting the role referred to

Lacan (1964/1981) as the *sujet supposé savoir*, or the subject who is supposed to know.

Later in his life Bion wrote in 1968:

> The capacity for doubt, the condition in which doubt can be entertained, has become central. The 'analytic situation' must be one in which two people can have a relationship in which neither is compelled to search 'irritably' for certainty as a method of sifting doubts, uncertainties, mysteries, half-truths and neither is compelled to assert anything as a means by which doubt and uncertainties are evaded.
>
> (2014, p. 70)

Was Winnicott in some way unable to reside in doubt, or uncertainties, as Bion writes about by way of his use of Keat's (1817/1958) term 'negative capability', in his correspondence with Bion? We will never know, but this capacity, to be in doubt or uncertainty, even mysteries, can be seen as closely related to what Winnicott wrote about in his paper on transitional objects. Ogden (2019) has written about Winnicott's (1971b) 'Transitional Object' paper, Winnicott, 'almost in passing … uses a phrase that I view as the process underlying successful psychoanalysis and every other form of psychic growth: 'we weave other-than-me objects into the personal pattern' (p. 665).

Elaborating on Winnicott's thought, this process of 'weaving' is described by Ogden, again quoting Winnicott, as the 'overlap of the two areas of playing'. Building on this line of thinking, it can be argued that the process of weaving with those objects experienced as 'other', or 'other than the self' is a form of (1) intersubjectivity, (2) a metabolization that takes place between container and contained, where both subject and object change by virtue of the 'overlap', a process of mutual metabolization; and (3) that the disruption or destabilization brought about by *'difference'*, as opposed to, but in combination with repetition, can be thought of in terms of a continual *'refitting'* of the breast and mouth of the mother and infant that changes the experience of each with every new *'re-orientation'* (Di Ceglie, 2013). Ogden writes in this regard, 'When the patient or analyst is unable to engage in playing, the analyst's attention must be directed to this problem, for it precludes the patient and analyst from experiencing 'the overlap of the two areas of playing'.

It is in this context that one can only feel unsure at best whether Winnicott and Bion really ever found a mutually satisfying 'overlap of the two areas of playing', and, instead, one can only wonder whether these two psychoanalytic contemporaries, each so important to the evolution of the analytic field, were instead more or less engaged in a form of parallel play, each of them propelling psychoanalysis forward into a new sensibility and an advanced set of clinical capabilities while keeping tabs on the other out of the respective corners of their eyes from adjacent corners of the British Psychoanalytic Society.

Mauro Manica, one of this volume's contributors, suggested in a 2023 article, 'A letter from Winnicott to Bion: An imaginative conjecture to illustrate a paradigm transformation', that Winnicott had a significant influence on Bion's work, so much that Winnicott, in a letter to the philosopher and psychoanalyst John O. Wisdom, complained that, 'Bion states (obscurely of course) what I have been trying to show for 21/2 decades but against the terrific opposition of Melanie' (Rodman, 1987, p. 145). Dr. Manica makes an excellent case in this regard, arguing that Winnicott's influence on Bion, through a process that Manica labels a form of 'imprinting', an unconscious process of influence in relation to early objects in infancy that gives rise to lasting behavioral patterns and attachments. The Bion in transition to what has been called the 'late Bion' phase of his work, if Manica is correct in his speculative hypothesis, if it was influenced by Winnicott, seems not to have been a 'shared' experience of influence, if Winnicott's letters are any indication.

To return to the question raised earlier regarding Bion's lack of response to Winnicott's often incisive and sometimes encouraging, sometimes subtly critical, and sometimes supervisory letters, Bion's reluctance to engage on a serious intellectual or clinical theoretical level of exchange seems in itself to express a reluctance, or flat refusal to engage with a learned colleague who was also under the heavy influence of Melanie Klein and immersed in his own efforts to emancipate himself from operating while under her influence. More importantly, it seems likely that, in keeping with Manica's speculation regarding Winnicott's unacknowledged influence on Bion's work, I would add the matter mentioned earlier in terms of Bion wanting to minimize outside influence on his own thinking while undergoing some evolution in the nature of his analytic self, or more specifically, in the character of his internal analytic frame. In his seminal article, Parsons (2007) describes well-functioning internal setting as one that is, 'genuinely free-floating' in relation to the analyst's own internal processes. He likens it to Bion's 'waking dream thought' as well as *'reverie'*, which, like Winnicott's (1971b) description of 'weaving other-than-me objects into the personal pattern', works by way of experiencing one's own internal process while, 'taking in the experience of the other' and allowing it to interact with the individual's own internal processes. During the transition from Bion's earlier 'epistemological' period, when he worked and thought in a way much more closely aligned with Klein and other British Kleinian analysts, such as Hanna Segal and Herbert Rosenfeld, it would seem likely that Bion tried to minimize outside influence on his own thinking while he was undertaking some transformation in his own way of processing his analytic experiences.

This returns this inquiry to the question of the re-formation of the internal analytic setting or structure. It is usually established during the analyst's training analysis, and in this way bears some affinity to the original construction of the infant's creation of the internal world and the origins of the individual's self-communication. In the same way that, as described by Winnicott (1969), that the infant experiencing omnipotence under the aegis of the facilitating environment creates and recreates the object, the creation and recreation of the analyst's 'internal frame' might also be usefully viewed as undergoing repeated recreation in a manner parallel. It seems that Bion, while possessed of his own fair share of pride and an investment in independent thinking, might have found Winnicott's entreaties more difficult to entertain during a time when his own internal analytic frame, the brick and mortar of his analytic attitude and sensibility, would be undergoing some major transformative change. Like Arthur Conan Doyle's famous story, 'The Adventure of Silver Blaze', the curious case of the analyst who seemed not to play with Winnicott may be most easily explained as a matter of Bion tending to the renovation of his own analytic playground in the midst of major shift and period of growth in his development as an analytic thinker.

References

Abram, J. (1996) *The Language of Winnicott: A Dictionary of Winnicott's Use of Words*. London: Karnac.

Abram, J. and Hinshelwood, R.D. (2023) *The Clinical Paradigms of Donald Winnicott and Wilfred Bion*. New York: Routledge.

Aguayo, J. (2023) *Introducing the Clinical Work of Wilfred Bion*. London: Routledge.

Bion, W.R. (1962) *Learning from Experience*. London: Karnac

Bion, W.R. (1963) *Elements of Psychoanalysis*. London: Karnac.

Bion, W.R. (1977) *A Memoir of the Future*. London: Karnac.

Caldwell, L. (2023) Reflections on the JAPA reviews of Winnicott's collected works. *Journal of the American Psychoanalytic Association*, 71, 519–532.

Civitarese, G. (2005) Fire at the theatre: (Un)reality of/in the transference and interpretation. *International Journal of Psychoanalysis*, 86, 1299–1316.

Civitarese, G. (2019) On Bion's concepts of negative capability and faith. *Psychoanalytic Quarterly*, 88, 751–783.

Di Ceglie, G.R. (2013) Orientation, containment, and the emergence of symbolic thinking. *International Journal of Psychoanalysis*, 94, 1077–1091.

Doyle, A.C. (1892) The adventure of silver blaze. In *Sherlock Holmes: The Complete Novels and Stories*, Volume I. New York: Bantom Dell, 1986, pp. 521–545.

Freud, S. (1925) Negation. *Standard Edition*, XIX, 233–240.

Hinshelwood, R.D. (2023) *W.R. Bion as Clinician: Steering Between Concept and Practice*. New York: Routledge.

Hinshelwood, R.D. and Torres, N. (2013) *Bion's Sources: The Shaping of His Paradigm*. New York: Routledge.

Keats, J. (1817) Letter to George and Thomas Keats, 21 December 1817. In H.G. Rollins (ed.), *The Letters of John Keats*, Vol. 1. Cambridge, MA: Harvard University Press, 1958.

Lacan, J. ([1964] 1981) *The Four Fundamental Concepts of Psychoanalysis*, ed. J.-A. Miller, trans. A Sheriden. New York: Norton.

Levine, H. (2024) On the question of the internal frame. *International Journal of Psychoanalysis*, 105, 234–241.

Mawson, C. (2018) Editor's Postscript. In C. Mawson (ed.), *Three Papers of W.R. Bion*. London: Routledge, pp. 24–33.

Ogden, T.H. (2019) Ontological psychoanalysis or "What do you want to be when you grow up?". *Psychoanalytic Quarterly*, 88, 661–684.

Parsons, M. (2007) Raiding the inarticulate: Internal setting, beyond countertrans-ference. In: *Living Psychoanalysis: From Theory to Experience*. New York, Routledge.

Rodman, F.R. (1987) *The Spontaneous Gesture: Selected Letters of D.W. Winnicott*. Cambridge, MA: Harvard University Press.

Rodman, F.R. (2003) *Winnicott: Life and Work*. Cambridge, MA: Perseus Press.

Roussillon, R. (2011) *Primitive Agony and Symbolization*. London: Karnac.

Vermote, R. (2011) On the value of 'late Bion' to analytic theory and practice. *International Journal of Psychoanalysis*, 92, 1089–1098.

Vermote, R. (2019) *Reading Bion*. London: Routledge.

Wilson, M. (2003) The analyst's desire and the problem of narcissistic resistances. *Journal of the American Psychoanalytic Association*, 51, 397–421.

Wilson, M. (2020) *The Analyst's Desire: The Ethical Foundation of Clinical Practice*. New York: Bloomsbury.

Winnicott, D.W. (1963) Communicating and not communicating leading to a study of certain opposites. In: *The Maturational Processes and the Facilitating Environment: Studies in the Theory of Emotional Development* (pp. 179–192). London: Hogarth, 1965.

Winnicott, D.W. (1969) The use of an object and relating through identifications. In: *Playing and Reality*. London: Routledge, pp. 115–127.

Winnicott, D.W. (1971a) *Therapeutic Consultations in Child Psychiatry*. New York: Basic Books.

Winnicott, D.W. (1971b) Transitional objects and transitional phenomena. In: *Playing and Reality*. London: Routledge, pp. 1–25.

Winnicott, D.W. (2017) Letter to W.R. Bion. In: *The Collected Works of D.W. Winnicott*, Vol. 3, Eds. L. Caldwell & H.T. Robinson. Oxford, UK: Oxford University Press, p. 433.

10 An Oracle (Perhaps a Miracle) at the British Psychoanalytical Society

Winnicott's Letter to Bion of October 5, 1967

Mauro Manica

Drawing on the coordinates set out in the above definitions of "oracle" and "miracle", I would first of all like to point out that the *place* where the extraordinary facts ("extraordinary" in the sense of "uncommon") that I am about to discuss happened was undoubtedly the British Psychoanalytical Society (BPS) and took the form of the series of events held on their premises in the 1960s.

Indeed, it was at one of these scientific meetings, held on June 16, 1965, that Wilfred Bion first presented his ideas on "memory" and "desire". The work was not published at the time; it was an oral presentation and the participants had not been provided with a written text ahead of the event. It was not until 2014 that the editor of Bion's works, Chris Mawson, was able to track down and transcribe the text of the 1965 paper in Vol VI of *The Complete Works of W.R. Bion* (Bion, 1965a).

In 1967, Bion published the essential part of that first work in the *Psychoanalytic Forum* under the title "Notes on memory and desire" (Bion, 1967a). This paper was later reprinted in *Melanie Klein Today, Mainly Practice* (vol. 2, 1988) edited by Elizabeth Bott Spillius.

In that same year, on 4 October, Bion presented another paper to the BPS, entitled "Negative Capability", which would later form the basis of some chapters of *Attention and Interpretation* (Bion, 1970), and which, as far as I can establish, has never actually been published, but could be considered complementary (Mawson, 2014) to "Memory and Desire", presented at the BPS in 1965.

In a letter dated October 5, 1967, Donald Winnicott wrote to Bion offering his observations regarding the unpublished presentation he had heard at the previous evening's event, where he had been one of the discussants. This role placed him at the very heart of a fundamental event in the development of Bion's ideas regarding not only *memory* and *desire* but above all relative to the possibility of revolutionizing the paradigm of psychoanalysis as known and practiced up to that moment.

In the space of three years (from 1965 to 1967) several fundamental moments occurred in Bion's thought: he published *Transformations* (1965b); he added a "Commentary" (1967b) to his more Kleinian influenced papers of

DOI: 10.4324/9781003502067-10

the 1950s; and by publishing this in *Second Thoughts* he was transforming himself into a truly Bionian Bion before becoming, starting from the 1970s, the beyond-Bionian Bion of *Memory of the Future*.

The *miracle*, the extraordinary event that was to transform psychoanalytic theory so significantly, seems to have occurred precisely during that three-year period. And if this is the "time" of the miracle, the space – the "place", as we have put it – in which the oracle, the revelation, takes place, seems to have been the BPS.

But what was the precise nature of this miraculous transformation? And what oracular role might Winnicott have played in participating in and contributing to the miracle? To put the question somewhat hyperbolically: how did he contribute to an event that aroused wonder, surprise, and amazement, but that also radically modified the substance[1] (*hypokeimenon*, in the Aristotelian sense) of psychoanalysis?

Winnicott's Letter

After attending the presentation of "Negative Capability" on the evening of October 4, 1967, the following day Winnicott wrote a short and impassioned letter to Bion.

The first thing to point out is that Winnicott makes no mention of either Bion's "Memory and Desire", which he had presented to the BPS in 1965, or to the publication in 1967 of "Notes on Memory and Desire".

Winnicott does not even make reference to the unusually emphatic and sententious tone that Bion had used in both works, a tone that partly accounts for the effective rejection by the psychoanalytic community of the ideas he had proposed regarding the occlusive effects on memory and desire of dependence in the analytic situation.

Even for a sensitive and open-minded psychoanalyst such as Luciana Nissim[2] (1987), reading "Notes on Memory and Desire" had initially aroused feelings of revulsion, bewilderment, and distrust, despite the fact that she had been fascinated both by the surprising content of the work and by the author's style, which she regarded as highly unusual for a scientific work.

Only after reading *Attention and Interpretation* (1970) did Luciana Nissim fully appreciate the exceptional nature of Bion's ideas and the bold description he gave of his own *modus operandi* vis-à-vis the patient – taking a stance that was stripped of memory and desire.

The point Bion (1970) was making in that revolutionary text could in fact not have been more explicit:

> To attain to the state essential for the practice of psycho-analysis I avoid any exercise of memory; I make no notes. When I am tempted to remember the events of any particular session I resist the temptation. [...] In this my practice is at variance with the view that notes should be kept or that psycho-analysts should find some method by

which they can record their sessions mechanically or should train themselves to have a good memory […] I resist any impulse to remember what happened or how I interpreted what happened on some previous occasion […]

A similar procedure is followed with regard to desires: I avoid entertaining desires and attempt to dismiss them from my mind. (It is not enough to try to do this in the session because that is too late: the habit of desiring must not be allowed to grow.) For example, I think it is a serious defect to allow oneself to desire the end of a session, or week, or term; it interferes with analytic work to permit desires for the patient's cure, or well-being, or future to enter the mind. Such desires erode the analyst's power to analyse and lead to progressive deterioration of his intuition […]. There are exceptions, all of a simple and obvious kind.

Some matters can be easily recorded and need not burden the mind, as, for example, the times of the sessions. It would be absurd if the analyst forgot to keep them and they are easily recorded on a timetable. The same may be true of age, members of the family, past illnesses, and other such facts as fancy might dictate. But these are to be recorded, together with addresses and telephone numbers, because they can be forgotten and because they lend themselves to record […].

Therefore, keep records for events whose background is sensible, such as the time at which a patient is to appear, but not for phenomena of central concern to the psycho-analyst, since their background is not sensible (pp. 267–269).

After reading this *lectio magistralis* on analytic attitude, Luciana Nissim declared herself "reassured" even though she went so far as to say that she was left with the impression that it was not always possible to attain the mental state Bion advocated. In her view, this still ought to be a goal or a direction to follow – I would say, a state of grace to be sought – and, above all, she thought it was fundamental that the analyst should try to live in the moment, with the patient, in the ongoing situation, so as to be mindful of any elements within it that may seem familiar but are in fact unknown both to analyst and the patient (Nissim, 1987, p. 266).

Moreover, in the paper he presented to the BPS on October 4, 1967, Bion himself had been less categorical than in the past and the guidelines he had laid down regarding memory and desire were only intended as suggestions for any expert analysts to experiment with, if they wished to do so. In a footnote (p. 67) to *Attention and Interpretation* he would make this point even more explicitly and precisely:

There are real dangers associated with the appearance; this is why the procedure adumbrated here is advocated only for the psycho-analyst whose own analysis has been carried out at least far enough for the recognition of paranoid-schizoid and depressive positions.

Winnicott seems implicitly aware of these risks and of the absolutely revolutionary potential contained in Bion's proposal. Accordingly, in the letter dated October 5, 1967 he drew Bion's attention to two fundamental issues: the first regards the use of words and language, while the second has to do with religion and its relationship with psychoanalysis.

On the question of language, Winnicott mentions how his wife Clare reminded him that the phrase "memory and desire" was a quotation from a poem by T.S. Eliot, the entire text of which she was able to provide.

The expression appears to have come from the opening lines of *The Waste Land*

> April is the cruellest month, breeding
> Lilacs out of the dead land, mixing
> Memory and desire, stirring
> Dull roots with spring rain.
> Winter kept us warm, covering
> Earth in forgetful snow, feeding
> A little life with dried tubers.
> Summer surprised us ...
>   (T.S. Eliot, 1922, The *Burial*
>   *of the Dead*[3])

Winnicott makes it clear that "for one reason or another", he has no difficulty in accepting the terms memory and desire as concepts that are "naturally interrelated in the poem"; however, he goes on to say that "in the application of the same idea to psycho-analytic work" the word that occurs spontaneously to him is *intention*, and that he believes the term *desire* to be incorrect. What he seems to be doing here is similar to Bion's explanation of the term memory. In answer to questions at the end of his presentation on June 16, 1965, Bion had distinguished between two types of memory: one that interferes with analytic receptivity and which relates to the already known, the already experienced (referring, in particular, to repetitive and obvious theories), and another which is more similar to a dream that suddenly resurfaces or "swims into view". When talking about this second type of memory, Bion said he preferred the term *evolution* (Mawson, 2014).

In suggesting that Bion should replace the term "desire" with *intention*, Winnicott is hinting at the possibility that there exist not only *wild thoughts* – "thoughts without a thinker" (Bion, 1977) – and preconceptions ([Bion, 1962, 1967b] Platonic and Kantian theories), but that there is also an inner principle or purpose – the entelechy (*en*, "inside" + *telos*, purpose) we know from Aristotle – which expresses itself in the drive of each human being to exist and become him- or herself.

The environment, then, must not impose its presence on the newborn (just as the analyst must avoid doing the same with the patient), but must create the conditions that allow the true Self spontaneous expression, even when contained in the need not to communicate (Winnicott, 1963). Although there remains a connection with Freud's thinking about dreams and desire, about the psychoanalytic method and the nature of the ego functions underlying memory and attention, the terms *intention* and *evolution* seem to give the analyst a glimpse of a new analytic attitude, a new technique and a new theory.

Moving on to the question of religion, Winnicott devotes the second and final part of his letter to "something quite separate":

> I'm very interested in the way you bring in the Bible story in your paper on catastrophic change and also quite frequently when you are talking. I, like you, grew up in the Christian tradition (Wesleyan) and I have no desire to throw away all that I listened to over and over again and tried to digest and sort out.
>
> (p. 247)

Similarly to Bion, Winnicott also seems to be referring to mystical thought not simply in terms of the influence of religious thinking on his conception of psychoanalysis, but rather in relation to something that affects his being and his ability to speak to the ontological dimensions of human experience.

Bion and Winnicott – as Luciana Nissim (1987) had pointed out – bring us face to face with further difficulties: the first is how to integrate into our usual way of thinking unusual concepts, such as the concept of F, the act of faith, by which Bion means faith in existence and in the possibility of intuiting the existence of a reality and an ultimate truth, namely the unknown, the unknowable, "the formless infinite", the "thing in itself" – designated as O. The second difficulty relates to being forced to reflect on the statement that

> The events of the psycho-analytic experience are transformed and formulated. The value of these formulations can be assessed according to the conditions under which the transformations are effected […] Their value therapeutically is greater if they are conducive to transformations in O [becoming][4]; less if conducive to transformations in K [knowledge].
>
> (Bion, 1970, pp. 39–40)

I find it extremely interesting that Michael Eigen (1981), in his study of "the area of faith" in Bion, Lacan, and Winnicott, should refer to Winnicott's concept of transitional phenomena (Winnicott, 1951) and to his subsequent paper on the use of the object (1969).

Eigen maintains that the area of faith in Winnicottian discourse is expressed particularly in these two papers – most notably in his "memorable" testimony of faith – namely when the subject says to the object:

> "I destroyed you", and the object is there to receive the communication. From now on the subject says: "Hullo object!" "I destroyed you." "I love you." "You have value for me because of your survival

of my destruction of you." "While I am loving you I am all the time destroying you in (unconscious) *fantasy.*" Here fantasy begins for the individual. The subject can now *use* the object that has survived.

(Winnicott, 1971, p. 151)

Here we find ourselves in an area which, to use Bionian terminology, could be regarded as standing under the sign of intuition or act of faith. The child needs to experience the object surviving its attempts at destruction in order to believe in the object's presence as something autonomous, separate and real. And the object must believe that in this act of destruction, the child wants to love it and feel loved by it.

Similarly, within the dimension of intermediality, the child and the mother must come to believe that the transitional object represents them concretely and simultaneously, even though neither is a participant in that relationship. The transitional object is at one and the same time the mother and the child. It is intuited in that sort of telepathic reciprocity whereby something *unknown* (Lacan, 1958–1959) or *formless* (Winnicott, 1971) begins to take on form: separateness in unison (at-one-ment), subjectivity in intersubjectivity.

Now that we have made the effort to convince ourselves that psychoanalysis is not only therapy but, above all, research and knowledge, we find ourselves having to take a further, even more arduous step.

The Question of Language and Theory

As we have seen, Winnicott and Bion tried to revolutionize the language of psychoanalysis, and by doing so they profoundly transformed analytic technique. By taking the unusual step of transforming technique, they also transformed the metapsychological framework of psychoanalysis, going so far as to encompass within its ontological soul (implicit in Freudian thought) a discourse that had inevitably aligned with the hard sciences of the era in which it was born.

With great determination Winnicott and Bion cut open the epistemological shell that had formed around psychoanalytic thought, thus freeing the more ontological, creative, and almost metaphysical, core within it.

Criticized vehemently by Ferenczi and Jung, the seeds of determinism had developed into ever more dogmatic propositions. And within these theoretical systems, Freud's truly revolutionary ideas, which unintentionally stood far removed from the idea that psychoanalysis should be about becoming and should deal with acausal connections, had died away, namely, ideas around the intersubjective essence of the mind – the "understanding" between mother and child (Freud, 1895, p. 423); the unconscious as a dreaming (group) function and not as an agency or place of the psyche (Freud, 1900); the idea that the principles of mental functioning concerned the here and now of the notation of psychic qualities by consciousness (Freud, 1911, 1921a); and the function of telepathy (Freud, 1890, 1900, 1901, 1921b, 1921c, 1925, 1933) as a premise for any theory of intuition (Manica, 2021).

Why does Winnicott, in his letter of October 5, 1967, question Bion on the subject of poetic and psychoanalytic language? *Intention* and *evolution*. Perhaps because he, like Bion, had become aware of the many limitations of a theory that focused exclusively on desire, namely that it was too intrinsically Hegelian[5] to include a theory of needs, a theory capable of understanding the earliest phases of the development of the mind. *Evolution* and *intention* shift the axis of psychoanalytic theory away from the epistemological dimension of memory and desire towards the ontological dimension of being and becoming.

What comes into play here is the present, the unknown, the session that will take place tomorrow. These are the words Bion wrote on the evening of June 16, 1965:

> The remarks I am making are addressed specifically to analysts who are seeing a patient tomorrow, or the day after. I think it would be helpful to focus not so much on what I am saying as on tomorrow's session; the one you are going to have tomorrow with the particular patient.
>
> (Bion, 1965a, p. 7)

And almost telepathically, Winnicott seems to attune himself to this idea two years later, again in the letter to Bion of October 5, 1967, when he writes:

> The memory includes memories of phenomena from external reality and certainly what is likely to turn up tomorrow in my analytic work cannot be covered by what I have in my own mind to want, precisely because I have to be able to bring the patient to be a separate person, just as the patient must come to be able to allow me to be outside his or her omnipotent control.
>
> (Winnicott, 1967, pp. 157–158)

In the period between these two dates, Bion laid down a challenge to the arrogance of a psychoanalytic discourse that claims to know what will happen before being able to actually dream it. And Winnicott makes his contribution to writing the future of this challenge. The patient is no longer simply the bearer of a desire that must always be stifled if thought is to be generated; the patient is also the bearer of a need that must be welcomed and supported even at the risk of possible exposure to the unbearable anguish of fragmentation.

In this way the theoretical construct of a psychoanalysis that focuses exclusively on desire, neutrality and frustration is subverted. The construct of a psychoanalysis of transference and countertransference that draws impermeable boundaries between patient and analyst is subverted.

In the "Commentaries" section of *Second Thoughts* Bion (1967b) writes:

> There is an emotional force field in which individuals appear to lose boundaries as individuals and become "areas", around and through which emotions play at will. The analyst and the patient cannot free themselves from the emotional field [...] It is a mental state that is more easily understandable if it is considered as the mental state of a group rather than of an individual, however going beyond the boundaries that we usually consider proper to the groups or individuals.
>
> (p. 157)

By analogy, if we take a Winnicottian perspective, we find ourselves in the area of the subjective object, the two-in-one, primary mirroring, the atonement which, to use the language of mystical thinkers, reestablishes union with the divine.

Bion and Winnicott write a version of psychoanalysis that speaks a new language and uses words capable of inventing an analytical attitude that "stir[s] dull roots with spring rain".

It is no coincidence that, in his letter of October 5, 1967, Winnicott posed the question of religion to Bion, as it had been Bion who had underlined and marked the passages of the Ascent of Mount Carmel by St. John of the Cross he felt were most significant:

> All these sensory means and exercises of the faculties [intellect, memory, will in their respective functions] must be left behind and in silence. [...] As a result one has to follow this method of disencumbering, emptying, and depriving the faculties of their natural rights and operations to make room for the inflow and illumination. [...] if a person does not turn his eyes from his natural capacity, he will not attain to so lofty a communication; rather, he will hinder it. If it is true that the soul must journey by knowing God through what He is not, rather than through what He is, it must journey, insofar as possible, by way of the denial and rejection of natural and supernatural apprehensions. This is our task now with the memory. We must draw it away from its natural props and capacities and raise it above itself (above all distinct knowledge and apprehensible possession) to supreme hope in the incomprehensible. [...]
>
> The annihilation of the memory in regard to all forms (including the five senses) is an absolute requirement. [...] the union cannot be wrought without a complete separation of the memory from all forms. [...] Once he has the habit [...] he no longer experiences these lapses of memory in matters concerning his moral and natural life.[6]

The Question of Religion and Technique

Why is it the case that in his letter of October 5, 1967 Winnicott emphasizes Bion's interest in the thought of the mystics and recommends he read *The Nazarene Gospel* by Robert Graves and Joshue Podro, which deals with an original reconstruction of the story of Jesus that met with the disapproval of all Christian churches? Are they both the victim of some sort of mystical delusion? Arguably, however, as Caper (1998) has suggested, Bion's expositions on memory and desire and his concept of O were misunderstood by some analysts and were mistaken as signals that he had turned to mysticism. In reality, though, the formulations that Bion borrows from mystical thinkers and applies to his concepts of container-contained (♀♂), dominion of O, and memory and desire constitute "a psychoanalytic model of mysticism and not a mystic model of psychoanalysis" (Caper, 1998, p. 420).

Bion is not going in search of God; he is looking for an absolute truth about the ultimate reality of the emotional experience that takes place during an analysis. He is looking for something that cannot be known but can only "become". And, along with Bion, Winnicott realizes that the scientific discourse of psychoanalysis is too limited to be able to deal with the ineffable nature of psychic experience.

In its essence, psychic reality has no sensorial basis. It cannot be apprehended through the senses, just as the reality of God can also not be apprehended. Anxiety has no smell, it has no shape or color, it cannot be touched or tasted. It cannot be known through the five common senses. At most it can be felt or "experienced" in the emotional field that is generated between patient and analyst. A "sixth sense" then becomes necessary, namely, the sense that mystics have attempted to reclaim and activate in an effort to develop faith in the existence of God, in the existence of the unknowable and the unknown.

The essence of psychic experience, as is also the case with God, requires an act of faith and can only be believed or intuited. In the same way as the good enough mother (Winnicott, 1952) senses and believes in the psychic states of her own child.

However, gaining access to intuition and faith requires an iron discipline, very similar to that advocated by the mystics. As Saint John of the Cross anticipated, we must strip ourselves of intellect (understanding), memory, will (desire) and sensory perception. Only in this condition can memory become *evolution* – not memory but the experience of "remembering"[7]. And only in this condition can desire be realized as *intention*.

It is not the past that is of interest in analysis, because insofar as it is the past it is unknowable. The tense/time of analysis is the present, the moment that takes place between us and the patient, the unknown, the not yet known. Because we can only undertake a (re-)construction of the past, a story, a narration, something able to create a past of which otherwise the only trace would be "debris" (Bion, 1978). Sometimes, it is only by starting from somatic traces that we can give life to something that has never been experienced on a mental level, and produce a previously impossible meaning.

If Bion's tone in the presentation he gave at the BPS of June 16, 1965 – and even more so in the 1967 work, *"Notes on Memory and Desire"* – had been categorical and dogmatic, in the paper on "Negative Capability"[8] it became (as Winnicott notes in his letter) more dialectical and cautious. He enjoins "expert analysts" to make the effort to acquire the discipline necessary to strip away memory and desire. Meltzer talks about willingness to run the risk of being devoured from within by madness as something similar to having a "shark" inside us (Meltzer, cited in Nissim [1987]).

Almost fifty years have passed since this proposal was made. Is it possible today to transcend the limits imposed by the fundamental rules of psychoanalysis? Can we today truly strip ourselves of memory, desire, understanding, and sensory perception? Can we set aside the occlusive theories we are so familiar with? Can we completely free ourselves from thoughts about when the current session will end, the prospect of fast approaching holidays, the need for the patient to heal, in order to actually face the unknown – the "shark" or the "lilac" bred out of the dead land – that lurks in every moment of the relationship?

I don't know. I really don't know if it is possible, but I think it is a goal we need to strive for. The only true goal of an analysis.

A Fiction by Way of a Conclusion

Let us imagine the situation of a female (or male) patient telling us that, on her way to the session, she broke her shoe. What possible ways are there to address this communication?

We could simply register it as an objective fact, but this would be of no relevance to the analysis. At most what would be required is the intervention of a shoemaker or a shoe salesman, someone with skills the analyst does not possess.

Or we could interpret the scene: either in the sense of a classic transference interpretation and, for example, refer it to the activation of a castration anxiety, prompted by the return of repressed infantile desires (obviously Oedipal, especially, if it was a lady's high heel that snapped!), set in motion by the relationship with the analyst; or in the sense of an interpretation that sees the scene as an act of monitoring the state of the patient's Self, registering the fear she feels at her lack of the resources needed to continue on the journey of analysis. The risk, however, would be that the interpretations provided would impede evolution by being saturated with memory and desire.

Alternatively, in unison (at-one-ment) with the emotions that have been generated in the analytic field, the attempt could be made to transform them in play or in dream. In this case one could dream the "broken shoe" as a pictogram that expresses the pain generated by the limping ♀♂ relationship or the PS↔D oscillation and which would call for an "I'm sorry" (Grotstein, 2000, 2007) from the analyst designed to heighten the dream-like qualities of the field. Or else the "broken shoe" could represent the possibility that the patient might finally be getting a pair of "new shoes", pointing to a development of functions which, for example, could be expressed in terms of the patient acquiring the ability to be alone or the capacity for concern or learning to put her true Self into action.

Or again, another possibility is that a reverie of the old partisan song *Fischia il vento* might appear in the analytic field:

> The wind whistles and the storm rages,
> broken shoes and we still have to go
> to conquer the red spring
> where the sun of the future rises…

In this case the lyrics of the song could give voice to the effort and hope of the analytic couple, who are engaged in a real battle to transform a group with a basic "fight/flight" assumption into a working group capable of generating spontaneity, creativity, and mental growth.

In reverie, the analyst finds himself "remembering" – in a kind of "swimming into view" – the torments and hopes of his adolescence: the struggles – in the family, at school, in life in general – to live more and more as oneself, in one's *meness*. Meanwhile, the patient talks about her adolescence, the pain of feeling anonymous, the girl "with the scratchy wool sweater and the tartan skirt" – the girl no one could see. L and H enter, emotions that color the field; a "red spring" enters which, as she goes through the pain, tinges the emotional field with new colors and helps it experience new emotions and new hopes. But if these emotions are to emerge, "negative capability" is required on the part of the analytic couple: "waiting", "patience" (PS), and the courage to live in a present of "hesitation".

Thus, starting from the moment of unison – "*I understand that it can be unpleasant and complicated to walk all the way here after your shoe has broken*" – the *dreaming ensemble* of the session begins to develop with its infinite possibilities of evolution.

In its simplicity, the analytic fiction helps us understand how the transition from psychoanalysis as a science of interpretations to psychoanalysis as a science of transformations can be represented: from K to O.

We must, however, also keep in mind that we cannot aspire to the numinous and terrifying quality of an absolute truth about an ultimate reality. We can intercept and become a personal and livable O, that which we are and that which each of our patients can be or become.

Stripping ourselves of any kind of memory or desire thus means stripping ourselves of the absolute in order to become infinite, so as to be able to interpret the infinite possibilities of being that each new patient and each new session challenges us to respect. An autistic O, a psychotic O, the neurotic O – all of which, in different proportions, live inside each of us. And without going through the experience of possibly going mad and being reborn in some remote corner of our existence, whatever traumatic experience we may have lived through, we will not make contact with the madness and the tenacious hope of being reborn that every patient confronts us with.

There is no effective analytic action that passes through K without having "stopped over" in L and H. If the analyst guards himself against the turbulence of his own emotional experience, even in -L or -H, he will not be able to dream in O and the analytic experience will be falsified because it will lose its ontological foundation, transforming into a form of pseudo-knowledge (-K) or pseudo-healing (-O).

Memory and desire refer to temporal dimensions that might concern the past and the future, while temporal terms such as "hesitation", "waiting", or "patience" undertake, as the philosopher Byung-Chul Han (2009) maintains, the task of establishing a positive relationship with what is removed from every available present. He states:

> [These figures] do not indicate a condition of deprivation. Rather, they are characterized by a *More of the Less*. The waiting does not expect anything concrete. Rather, it refers to what evades any kind of calculation. Likewise, hesitation does not mean indecisiveness, but is a relationship with what eludes any determined grasping. It is a positive drawing "toward what withdraws" [...] A thinker must patiently wait in this "draft, this current", instead of "seeking refuge from any draft too strong for them".
>
> (pp. 87–88)

So it is only in the present time of waiting, in the patience that establishes negative capability (Bion, 1970), in the here-and-now, in a present voided of memory and desire that the analyst can intuit the non-sensorial phenomena that constitute the fundamental facts of analysis.

Notes

1 In Aristotelian philosophy, *hypokeimenon* – literally "that which lies beneath" – refers to that which is hidden within the "sensible" thing and forms its *ontological* foundation.
2 Luciana Nissim was one of the most ground-breaking and brilliant Italian psychoanalysts, a proponent of a "kind" (*gentile*) psychoanalysis (Manica, 2019), understood as *a two-way affair* which develops between "two people talking in a room" (Nissim, 1984) in which the analyst must be prepared to replace the tradition of suspicious listening with *respectful listening*.
3 In T.S. Eliot, *The Waste Land* (2001). (M. North, Ed.) WW Norton.
4 The inserts between square brackets are mine.
5 The fact is that, starting from Freud and especially in the wake of its patrilineal developments (Lacan's contribution here is emblematic), psychoanalysis

had until that point suffered from the fundamental incompleteness of Hegel's theory of needs. In *The Phenomenology of Spirit*, and in particular in the chapter on self-consciousness, Hegel (1807) seems not to have grasped the essentially intersubjective structure of need. He understood it as a unilateral relationship of negation of the other: "I am thirsty. I drink", "I drink, I deny the object, I annihilate it". But how can one deny the object on which one depends for survival? "I drink" is already imbued with intersubjectivity. We owe an eternal debt to Winnicott for having provided psychoanalysis with an adequate theory of needs.

6 Kavanaugh, K. and Rodriguez, O. trans. (1964) St. John of the Cross, *The Ascent of Mt Carmel*, Book 3, Chap. 2, § 2, Washington, D. C., I C S Publications.

7 In *Attention and Interpretation*, Bion (1970) wrote: "There is something that has often been called 'remembering' and that is essential to psycho-analytic work; this must be sharply distinguished from what I have been calling memory" (p. 312).

8 *Negative capability* is an apophatic concept Bion took from a letter the poet John Keats wrote to his brothers.

References

Bion, W. R. (1962) *Learning from Experience*, CWWRB, IV.

Bion, W. R. (1965a) *Memory and Desire*, CWWRB, VI.

Bion, W. R. (1965b) *Transformations: Change from Learning to Growth*, CWWRB, V.

Bion, W. R. (1967a) Notes on Memory and Desire, *The Psychoanalytic Forum*, **2**: 272–273, 279–280.

Bion, W. R. (1967b) *Second Thoughts*, CWWRB, VI.

Bion, W. R. (1970) *Attention and Interpretation*, CWWRB, VI.

Bion, W. R. (1977) *Taming Wild Thoughts*, CWWRB, X.

Bion, W. R. (1978) A *Paris Seminar*, CWWRB, IX.

Bott Spillius, E. edited by (1988) W.R. Bion *Notes on Memory and Desire*, in *Melanie Klein Today. Mainly Practice*, vol. 2, Routledge, London and New York.

Byung-Chul, H. (2009) *The Scent of Time. A Philosophical Essay on the Art of Lingering*, Polity Press, Cambridge.

Caper, R. (1998) Review of: The clinical thinking of Wilfred Bion, Symington, J., Symington, N. (1996), *The International Journal of Psychoanalysis*, **79**: 417–420.

Eigen, M. (1981) The area of faith in Winnicott, Lacan and Bion, *The International Journal of Psychoanalysis*, **62**: 413–433.

Freud, S. (1890) *Psychical (or mental) Treatment.*, S.E., 7.

Freud, S. (1895) *Project for a Scientific Psychology*, S.E., 1.

Freud, S. (1900) *The Interpretation of Dreams*, S.E. 4 & 5.

Freud, S. (1901) *The Psychopathology of Everyday Life.*, S.E., 6.

Freud, S. (1911) *Formulations on the Two Principles of Mental Functioning*, S.E.

Freud, S. (1921a) *Group Psychology and the Analysis of the Ego.*, S.E., 18

Freud, S. (1921b) *Dreams and Telepathy.*, S.E., 18.

Freud, S. (1921c) *Psychoanalysis and Telepathy*, S.E., 18.

Freud, S. (1925) *Some Additional Notes on Dream-interpretation as a whole.*, S.E., 19.

Freud, S. (1933) *New Introductory Lectures on Psycho-analysis.*, S.E., 22.

Grotstein, J. S. (2000) *Who Is the Dreamer, Who Dreams the Dream? A Study of Psychic Presences*, The Analytic Press, Inc., Hillsdale, New Jersey.

Grotstein, J. S. (2007) *A Beam of Intense Darkness. Wilfred Bion's Legacy to Psychoanalysis*, Karnac, London.

Hegel, G. W. F. (1807) *Phenomenology of the Spirit*, Cambridge University Press, Cambridge 2018.

Lacan, J. (1958–1959) *Desire and Its Interpretation, Book VI*, Polity Press, Cambridge 2021.

Manica, M. (2019) *Dalla psichiatria alla psicoanalisi. Per una pratica terapeutica gentile*, FrancoAngeli, Milano.

Manica, M., (2021) *Coscienza e intuizione*, Alpes, Roma.

Mawson, C. (2014) *Editor's Introduction*, in CWWRB, VI.

Nissim, L. (1984) "...Due persone che parlano in una stanza..." (Una ricerca sul dialogo analitico), in *Rivista di psicoanalisi*, XXX, 1: 1–17.

Nissim, L. (1987) La memoria e il desiderio, in C. Neri, A. Correale, P. Fadda (a cura di) *Letture bioniane*, Borla, Roma 1987.

Winnicott, D. W. (1951) *Transitional Objects and Transitional Phenomena*, CWDWW, 3.

Winnicott, D. W. (1952) *Letter to Roger Money-Kyrle*, 27 November 1952, CWDWW, 4.

Winnicott, D. W. (1963) *Communicating and Not Communicating Leading to a Study of Certain Opposites*, CWDWW, 6.

Winnicott, D. W. (1967) *Letter to Wilfred R. Bion*, 5 October 1967, CWDWW, 8.

Winnicott, D. W. (1969) The Use of an Object and Relating through Identifications, in *Playing and Reality*, Routledge, London and New York.

Winnicott, D. W. (1971) *Playing and Reality*, Routledge, London and New York.

11 Reading What Is Not in a Book
Dreaming and Playing with Words

Elena Molinari

Periodically, I try to find out who I have become and am becoming as a psychoanalyst by writing about that process as best I can.

(Ogden, 2016, p. 21)

"Destroy the Object" to Learn to Dream

I have always felt grateful to Bion for his teaching about keeping "memory and desire" at bay in therapy, until the day Winnicott entered a session and brought with him the *intention* of remembering what had happened. Above all, he brought the idea of allowing both the therapist and the child patient the freedom to talk about it openly and to engage in a different kind of play.

During a session, just before the summer break, when the experience of separation once again became a real experience between my patient and me and posed a potential re-enactment of trauma, Clara asked to sit in the adults' room, requesting that I read her a story. I suggested that she choose a book from the children's room, but after a brief search, she returned and said she wanted a grown-up book instead.

As if by chance, Winnicott's book "Children" slipped from the shelf – at least that is the way it seemed to me as she had not stopped to read the titles.[1] *"I want this one,"* she said, lying down on the couch. "Read it to me, please."

I only vaguely remembered the contents of the book, but as I skimmed through the index, I was surprised at how many of the collected essays touched on Clara's difficulties: adoption, the true self, and psychosomatic disorders. I began pretending to read, all the while grappling with how to reconcile what Clara had unconsciously revealed, what Winnicott seemed to be suggesting, and how to communicate it to a nine-year-old.

I remembered Clara's tragedy and the many adventures she had led me through during our play, where we had often found ourselves at risk of being

DOI: 10.4324/9781003502067-11

attacked by wild animals. This brought to mind the film "The Life of P,"[2] which I used as inspiration to begin.

Analyst: *Once upon a time, there was a boy who lived in a circus with many animals. But one day, while crossing a stormy sea, their ship capsized, and everyone died: his family and all the animals except for the tiger. The two of them survived and found themselves alone together on a small lifeboat.*

Clare: *It's a good thing that Jordan didn't come to the trip, or he would have died too.*

Jordan is Clara's family cat, who had obviously stayed at home on the day of the accident and still lives with her and one of the families that host her. I was struck by how Clara introduced the topic of death and separation so directly.

Analyst: *Both the boy and the tiger were very hungry, and the tiger was also furious because she had lost everything: her forest, her friends, and even the ability to run since the boat was so small compared to the jungle where she used to live.*

Clara tossed and turned on the couch, a sign of her emotional struggle, as if testing her ability to move within the limited space of the couch.

After a few minutes of silence, I added:

The boy was angry too, but he didn't want to upset the tiger. He wanted to stay with her, especially at night, because he felt lonely.

Clara: *He wanted to stay with the tiger because he was afraid of having nightmares.*

Analyst: *Yes, and he was also afraid that if he said something wrong, the tiger would leave or eat him. He was in a really tough spot.*

Clara remained silent, thoughtful, perhaps searching for a way to resolve the dilemma.

Analyst: *The boy wanted to be close to the tiger because she was soft and warm, but when he saw her teeth, he felt like running away.*

Clara: *I have an idea. He could stay close to the tiger during the day, and if he notices that she wants to eat him, he could jump into the sea. But at night, since he can't control things then – because when you close your eyes, you don't know what's going to happen – he should stay a bit further away.*

After a brief silence, Clara noticed how the problem that had left through the door seemed to return through the window and added:

But at night is when he would want to be closest to the tiger.

After another pause, during which Clara seemed to be trying to get out of the dilemma, she said:

Do you know that Jordan sometimes sleeps on my bed even though Mum doesn't want him to be there?[3]

I think Clara found the solution by associating the surviving cat with her ability to oppose her mother.

Analyst: *Having Jordan around and disobeying a little is an excellent idea! Before, when you got scared, you had to hide under the covers and stay completely still.*

    I wanted to communicate to Clara how she sometimes took refuge in herself or in the passivity of acquiescing to others as an antidote to fear.

Clara: *So how does the story end?*

Analyst: *It ends with them arriving on an island, where the tiger is happy to run among the trees. Even though they live a little apart, the boy and the tiger still care for each other.*

    Clara seemed thoughtful, and a little skeptical of my hasty, happy ending.

Clara: *Apart like in heaven?*

Analyst: *Not that far apart. Apart and together, like in a house.*

Clara: *I don't think they'd be very happy living far apart. But if they aren't as far apart as in heaven, they could meet up sometimes and have parties together.*

    It seemed to me that Clara had done a better job than I of reconciling the elements of unerasable pain with the desire to find compensatory experiences in reality.

    The session was over, and together we walked to the door, where her father had come to pick her up. In the waiting room, Clara asked me, *"Do you think the boy told the tiger that he was angry too?"*

Analyst: *I think he did.*

The Psychoanalytical Theory

In the letter Winnicott wrote to Bion on October 5, 1967 (Winnicott 1968), there is both a manifest content and an underlying emotional thread, with several key passages that merit attention.

The intent is not to analyze Winnicott's emotions, which would be an unwarranted analytical intrusion, but rather to explore within his style of thought a preliminary reflection on my own emotional response, which the letter has unexpectedly helped me to understand more clearly.

As I reread the letter, my mind shifts between the different theoretical assumptions of the two correspondents, imaginatively recreating a situation similar to a debate after a conference. What happens to me in these circumstances is that I find myself in tune with different, sometimes quite opposing, hypotheses as they are presented. At times, I am in complete agreement with Bion when I reflect on his description of the mental state "without memory and desire," which he proposes as the optimal condition for connecting with the emotional truth of the session. At other times, I feel in tune with Winnicott as he, in contrast to Bion, seeks to clarify how the two subjects of analysis can establish a creative bond between them by reconciling their subjectivities.

For a long time, I viewed what was happening to me with some embarrassment, considering it a sign of poor conceptual coherence. Only later was I able to emerge from the oscillation that had captured me like a wave, to find a more stable cognitive grounding.

Unexpected help in overcoming this experience came from Winnicott's letter, parts of which I briefly revisit.

In the first lines of the letter, after expressing his admiration for Bion's conference, Winnicott recounts that, once back at home and in a state of deeper self-reflection, he used conversation with his wife Clare to explore his doubts and uncertainties about what he had heard, particularly regarding the combination of the words: *memory and desire*.

The letter does not reveal Clare's position, but we do learn that she is aware of the origin of the expression and provides her husband with the entire poem. Clare thus does not seem to take sides, but by opening the field, acts as a conduit for Winnicott's subsequent thoughts. Indeed, immediately after recounting the conversation with Clare, Winnicott presents his reflections on the relationship between patient and analyst and how it can be infected, used, or influenced positively or negatively.[4] Winnicott appears to be working on clarifying his own ideas and experiences regarding play, and initially finds Bion's proposition to be quite distant from his own ideas.[5]

In this experience of contrast, he illustrates how elements of his memory, his desire, and, naturally, those of his patient may be necessary for the evolution of the process and declares that he prefers the word intention rather than desire.

Winnicott lays the groundwork here for how this intentionality is a prerequisite for the destruction of the object on which the true self is based. This creative destruction is necessary in analysis for individuals who have not been able to enjoy a facilitating environment, but it is also necessary for the analyst, who must be able to detach from the known in order to grasp the emotionally vivid and creative aspects.

To this first part of the discussion on a distinctly analytical topic, mainly concerning how the analyst can advance the process, Winnicott adds a second part that he declares to be completely separate from the first. Indeed, the tone changes, but the thread of the elaboration seems to continue on a more emotional and personal level. The object of admiration is no longer the content of Bion's lecture and the discussion of his hypotheses, but rather Bion's use of metaphors informed by biblical stories. According to Winnicott, this narrative style would affirm their common cultural background in Catholicism.

While in the first part Winnicott explored the distance from Bion, in this second part he seems to reflect on their closeness, not only on an intellectual level but also on a personal one.

Considering the etymology of the word religious,[6] which is the subject of the recommended book, one might wonder how much the idea of connection continues to pervade in various forms and how much rivalry and ambivalence are contained in the fact that the recommended book is out of print. Bion will be able to get closer to Winnicott only by making the effort to obtain it from the library.

Therefore, through the few lines of the letter, the reader participates not only in a comparison of ideas but also in an experience set against the backdrop of the desire to maintain a connection. At the same time, for this connection to be authentic, it must undergo a process of critical distancing.

Although Winnicott points out that in primary development, the process of "destruction of the object" is not a reactionary anger toward frustration, in this letter, he seems to grant the reader access to how emotional ambivalence supports freedom of thought (Winnicott, 1969).

The letter can therefore be seen a conduit to the process through which a new idea develops, and, what I wish to emphasize, is that it hinges on the possibility of maintaining a connection with someone or something conceived by others while also allowing the possibility of distancing oneself from it.

Focusing on this oscillatory movement, has enabled me to feel less uncomfortable when I find myself in tune with different hypotheses during a debate. Through this perspective, I have surmised that my identification with various interlocutors stems from a predominant drive to maintain connection – perhaps influenced by my being a woman. It is only in a situation of greater security, when I am at ease within myself, that I can confront the divergence involving the elimination of a part from which, at times, a creative spark may emerge.

In particular, in a clinical experience which I now describe, a declared adherence to post-Bionian field theory mingled with a more intimate need to revisit something of the process of destroying the "beloved theoretical object" in order to play with my young patient.

In other words, freeing oneself from a cherished idea is an intellectual aspect of that necessary destruction of the object that ensures freedom not only for the patient but also for the analyst.

From this arose a question: How is it possible to preserve the ontological intersubjectivity of the field while retaining an element of intentionality?

The possibility of oscillating between different ideas, viewpoints, or more dreamlike modes to more playful ones may perhaps be an aspect of mental functioning that involves an intimate need not to adhere to a single theory.

In the two clinical fragments of the analysis of a young girl, I try to show how adhering to Bion's suggestion to proceed without memory and desire in search of emotional attunement was necessary and beneficial until the introduction of a creative "Winnicottian" story, full of memory and intentionality, facilitated the evolution of the analytic process.

Playing Without Memory and Desire

Clara is a nine-year-old girl who became an orphan at the age of five after losing her parents and her younger sister in an accident. Clara had strongly insisted on taking that trip, and this fact had intensified her pain with an unbearable sense of guilt for, from her perspective, causing the incident. She was the only survivor, and regaining the ability to move and walk again had required numerous surgeries and an extended period of rehabilitation. In addition to the physical and psychological trauma, from the very first days after the accident, two sets of relatives, who were potential adoptive parents, had started a fierce legal battle over custody and possible adoption.

The level of conflict has been and remains very high and it seems to completely disregard Clara's vulnerability and the potential consequences of pressuring her to conform to the rules and desires of the two sets of relatives, who are distant in their life choices, educational models, and relational styles.

Clara's greatest difficulty compared to a child with separated parents is having an excessive number of adults relating to her in a parental capacity. Moreover, both families involve Clara in an excessive number of extracurricular activities for a young child, perhaps giving them the satisfaction of offering her plenty of opportunities while also creating a relational distance that enables the adults to avoid engaging with her too directly.

Ultimately, for each family, she embodies a loss that is hard to overcome.

The dead are present not only and not so much in memory but in a climate of war where the other, who becomes the enemy, allows one to distance oneself from one's own flaws and evade the anguish of death.

Whoever accuses the other first in any minor daily issue adheres to the same logic dictated by war: shoot first to avoid being killed.

Gradually, this environment has intensified the conflict of loyalty that Clara feels toward each relative, making it difficult for her to process the multitude of inputs she receives, both cognitively and emotionally. Clara tries to cope by employing hyper-adaptation (Winnicott, 1964, 1965). In therapy, she struggles intensely to process her trauma and to find her true self. This struggle is also manifesting in signs such as a mild eating disorder, academic difficulties, and the development of tics.

Following my report to the juvenile court, requesting that the judge take into account the child's increasing distress, there have been some minor adjustments to Clara's daily schedule, allowing her to have small moments of life less intruded upon by adults and their demands.

Shortly afterward, it is no coincidence that the early stages of play oriented toward processing the trauma appear.

The need to avoid being driven by a desire to prematurely address the tragic feelings associated with the accident, while also keeping the complicated family dynamics at least partly outside the therapeutic relationship, in order to focus on the here and now of our interaction and to be able to speak to her step by step following the dream we could create together, was a principle I had to remind myself of many times (Ogden, 2007, 2016). I wanted our meetings to be a new experience for both of us, an experience where the trauma could surface when we were both ready to face it. Although Clara appeared capable of engaging in a relationship, she protected herself from it by using very strong defenses.

In the first three years of therapy, she never played anything besides board games or drawing. Clara engaged with me in sequences of repetitive actions or shared some school activities, placing me in the role of the child who could not carry out the task. For a long time, engaging in play and developing unpredictable interactions was impossible for her. The need to control the object pervaded the relational field, making the traumatic aspects almost entirely inaccessible. This strategy of self-containment and compartmentalizing unbearable memories allows the child to avoid being psychically overwhelmed by the trauma (Bromberg, 2006; Fabozzi, 2018) but it also inhibits the child's ability to engage in a lively and spontaneous relationship.

During the fourth year of therapy, Clara began to play spontaneously at a slightly more childish level than her age, almost as if picking up the thread it had been interrupted.

The game began by staging "journeys" that went from the children's room to the adults' room; these journeys involved crossing turbulent seas and jungles filled with ferocious animals, during which Clara shared with me the need to take care of injured baby animals.

The level of danger gradually intensified, and we faced terrifying tsunamis, escaping in various ways, sometimes by migrating to other planets by spaceship.

In these situations, for a certain period, there also were violent, bloody scenes, and at times, I had the impression that Clara was experiencing brief hallucinosis of images she had captured during her rescue, when hospital reports indicate she was conscious.

Clara enacted the arrival of ambulances and rescue teams in many different ways, openly questioning why some could be saved while others could not.

Then this type of play came to an end, and Clara began asking me to draw. First, she assigned me the role of the pupil, keeping the position of control for herself; then, she began doing her own drawings.

One day, while we were quietly drawing on our own sheets of paper, occasionally glancing at each other's work, Clara sketched a natural landscape with trees, a meadow, a caravan, and a swimming pool. I noticed how the theme of travel had found a less dramatic form of expression in her imagination.

I commented that traveling by caravan allowed you to bring along some home comforts, which could be quite nice. Perhaps encouraged by my remark, Clara added that a caravan could also carry an inflatable swimming pool, which could be stored under the floor.

At this point, she took another sheet of paper and drew the car they had the accident in, but told me she could not quite remember its name. I said it for her and added that sometimes this kind of car can be dangerous.

There was a long silence, and then Clara told me not to be afraid because the car was equipped with a sponge that, in case of a crash, would make it bounce without breaking.

I was deeply moved as I witnessed her ability to use imagination to mend the destruction she had experienced, and I felt how genuine this was, especially because she had found a place where, for a long time, both "memory and desire" had been kept at bay (Levine 2012).

Concluding Considerations

If in Bionian theory, being without memory and desire is the mental state necessary for dreaming together with the patient about the unconscious emotions that arise in the session as the relationship develops, then the destruction of the object is the condition that Winnicott considers essential for accessing the possibility of being oneself and playing creatively.

In the dialogue between Winnicott and Bion, as derived from the letter at the center of this book, there is not only a theoretical or personal contrast but also an attempt to explore areas that are partly overlapping and partly distinct within the analytic relationship: dreaming and playing.

Winnicott explores both his intellectual and experiential closeness to and distance from Bion. He plays with words with his wife Clare and then directly with Bion, proposing a sort of "hide and seek" inasmuch as the book that seals their connection exists, but it is not readily available.

I like to think that being able to read the entire poem through Clare's mediation opened a gateway for Winnicott to dream without memory and desire, and the need to be himself instead came through playful confrontation. Both Bion and Winnicott, each in their own way, addressed the challenge of harmoniously integrating aspects that seem opposing or complementary. They introduced into psychoanalysis the continuum that Derrida (1978, 1981) suggested as a possible development of the dichotomous philosophy of Western thought (Bitan, 2012; Civitarese, 2018).[7]

The concept of oscillation, rooted in Bionian thought, describes something close to what Winnicott suggested regarding the necessity of not applying divergent logic when encountering paradox (Winnicott, 1969).

A dreamlike mental state or one capable of using words or objects to create a play situation are two distinct aspects, yet they are continuous, like the two faces of a Möbius strip. Not having to choose one over the other to remain faithful to a singular theoretical framework allows us to oscillate and explore with the patient the proximity to the emotions encountered by both the patient and analyst at a given moment in their interaction. This oscillation facilitates approaching the emotional resonance that promotes transformation more effectively. The intersubjectivity of creating together is fully preserved by adhering to what the child proposes to the analyst, and this adherence in play can only be achieved at the intersection of the analyst's mind being free from memory and desire while also being aware of the development of the play itself.

With Clara, it was necessary to spend a lot of time dreaming without memory and desire for the more difficult emotions to be somewhat tamed. Then, by creating a story, I wrote her my personal letter in which I was able to express my admiration for her ability to survive catastrophe, and by dismantling the theoretical object of love within myself, I allowed her to rediscover her mother's eyes watching her as she becomes herself (Ogden, 2024).

Notes

1 A collection of essays published by Cortina in 1997 and intended for dissemination. The essays focus on various topics, such as psychosomatic pathologies of childhood and problems relating to adoption and foster care, as well as more specialized topics, such as autism and schizophrenia.
2 "The Life of P" is a film directed by Ang Lee in 2012.
3 Clara refers to the parents of one of the families, who first took her in, as Mum and Dad. This family also has other biological children.
4 In this letter, we can see a fragment of how Winnicott's theory and his tension in being himself also arise from his experience (Ehrlich, 2021).
5 However, the cross-section of experience that we become aware of functions as an anticipation of the effectiveness of a narrative interpretation or of the possibility of poetically dreaming together something that expands our ability to think. (Bezoari et al., 1989; Ferro, 2002; Ogden, 2007).
6 From Latin *religio -onis*, it is similar to *religare*, «to bind».
7 Bollas (2013) argues that the East found a way to develop the collective mind while preserving the individual idiom. In Western culture, the personal self and the social self mix, as in poetry, the central expression of the self, which unites the particular and the universal.

References

Bezoari, M., & Ferro, A. (1989). Listening, interpretations and transformative functions in the analytical dialogue. Journal of Psychoanalysis, 35, 1014–1050.

Bitan, S. (2012). Winnicott and Derrida: Development of logic-of-play. International Journal of Psychoanalysis, 93, 29–51.

Bollas, C. (2013). China on the mind. London: Routledge.

Bromberg, P. M. (2006). Standing in the spaces: Essays on clinical process, trauma, and dissociation (Rev. ed.). New York, NY: Routledge.

Civitarese, G. (2018). Hymenality in psychoanalysis: A reading of boundaries and bridges: Perspectives on time and space in psychoanalysis. International Journal of Psychoanalysis, 99, 275–286.

Derrida, J. (1978). Writing and difference (A. Bass, Trans.). Chicago, IL: University of Chicago Press.

Derrida, J. (1981). Positions (A. Bass, Trans.). Chicago, IL: University of Chicago Press.

Ehrlich, R. (2021). Winnicott's idea of the false self: Theory as autobiography. Journal of the American Psychoanalytic Association, 69(1), 75–108.

Fabozzi, P. (2018). Winnicott's subjective object: Merging experiences as preconditions of being. Psychoanalytic Quarterly, 87, 73–99.

Ferro, A. (2002). Some implications of Bion's thought: The waking dream and narrative derivatives. International Journal of Psychoanalysis, 83, 597–607.

Levine, L. (2012). Into thin air: The co-construction of shame, recognition, and creativity in an analytic process. Psychoanalytic Dialogues, 22(4), 456–471.

Ogden, T. H. (2007). On talking-as-dreaming. International Journal of Psychoanalysis, 88, 575–589.

Ogden, T. H. (2016). Some thoughts on practicing psychoanalysis. Fort Da, 22, 21–36.

Ogden, T. H. (2024). Giving back what the patient brings: On Winnicott's "Mirror-role of mother and family in child development". The Psychoanalytic Quarterly, 93, 413–430.

Ogden, P., Minton, K., & Pain, C. (2006). Trauma and the body: A sensorimotor approach to psychotherapy. New York, NY: Norton.

Winnicott, D. W. (1964). The concept of the false self. In Home is where we start from: Essays by a psychoanalyst (pp. 65–70), ed. C. Winnicott, R. Shepherd, & M. Davis. New York, NY: Norton, 1986.

Winnicott, D. W. (1965). The concept of trauma is about the development of the individual within the family. In The collected works of D. W. Winnicott, ed. L. Caldwell & H. T. Robinson. Oxford University Press, pp. 169–188.

Winnicott, D. W. (1968). Letter to W. Bion. In The collected works of D. W. Winnicott, ed. L. Caldwell & H. T. Robinson, Vol. 8. Oxford University Press.

Winnicott, D. W. (1969). The use of an object. International Journal of Psychoanalysis, 50, 711–716.

12 'What Life Itself Is About'

Michael Parsons

The letter Donald Winnicott wrote to Wilfred Bion on October 5, 1967 (Winnicott, 1987: 169–170) is as interesting for its form, and the context of its writing, as for its content.

It will be useful to have the following timeline in mind:

April 7, 1896: birth of Winnicott.
November 17, 1952: Winnicott writes a letter to Melanie Klein.
May 4, 1966: Bion presents 'Catastrophic Change', which Winnicott refers to in the letter he will write on October 5, 1967.
December 7, 1966: Winnicott presents 'The Location of Cultural Experience'.
April 25, 1967: death of James Strachey, Winnicott's first analyst.
October 4, 1967: Bion presents 'Negative Capability'.
October 5, 1967: prompted by the previous evening's meeting, Winnicott writes the letter to Bion which is the subject of this book.
November 12, 1968: Winnicott presents 'The Use of an Object and Relating Through Identifications' to the New York Psychoanalytic Society.
January 22, 1971: death of Winnicott.

The first part of Winnicott's letter to Bion is all about memory and desire. Then he writes: 'The rest of this letter has to do with something quite separate'. A letter of two halves, evidently. The 'something quite separate' is the way Bion referred to the Bible in his paper on catastrophic change. Winnicott writes: 'I, like you, was brought up in the Christian tradition (Wesleyan) and I have no desire to throw away all that I listened to over and over again and tried to digest and sort out'. So having finished with memory and desire, Winnicott moves on to something else which turns out to be about desire ('I have no desire to throw away') and memory ('all that I listened to over and over again'). Not such a letter of two halves after all.

Winnicott's pre-emptive negation of any link between what he has just said and what he is about to say recalls Freud's patient who said: 'You ask who this person in the dream can be. It's *not* my mother' (Freud, 1925: 235). This made Freud think 'So it *is* his mother', and sure enough, the second

DOI: 10.4324/9781003502067-12

half of Winnicott's letter is anything but separate from the first. What is going on here?

The two parts of Winnicott's letter are responses to two different papers by Bion. The 'very interesting evening' that prompted the first part was Bion's presentation the day before on the subject of 'Negative Capability'. The paper on 'Catastrophic Change' that Winnicott mentions in the second part had been presented by Bion the previous year on May 4, 1966.

Despite the link between the not-so-separate parts of the letter, there is a noticeable shift between them. In the first part, Winnicott is 'not quite settled' in his mind about what Bion said regarding memory and desire. His response is not a commentary, thought out and articulated, on Bion's paper. It is more an attempt by Winnicott to sort out his own ideas. This gives it a spontaneity, extending sometimes to an apparent confusion. Winnicott tells Bion that what may turn up in a session

> cannot be covered by what I have in my own mind to want, precisely because I have to be able to allow the patient to exist as a separate person ... So you see why it is that I find myself unhappy with your word desire in this context. Instead, he finds himself 'using the word intention and not feeling desire to be correct'. This reads as though Winnicott thinks Bion is endorsing the idea of desire. Winnicott disagrees and explains why he thinks intention is a better description of the analyst's attitude. Bion had not been as dogmatic about memory and desire, the evening before, as he was in an earlier paper (Bion, 1967) but his view was still clear. Did Winnicott not understand that, far from advocating desire, Bion was opposed to it?

Winnicott also seems to be adrift in not picking up that the phrase 'memory and desire' is a quotation. He needed his wife Clare to 'remind me again' that it comes from the opening lines of T. S. Eliot's *The Waste Land* (Eliot, 1923). Evidently Winnicott knew the poem, and he mentions Bion using the phrase before. Even so, he appears to have missed the reference. This is surprising. Poetry mattered to Winnicott, as we shall see, and he is making a point here about its nature.

The second part of Winnicott's letter is very different. He has something definite that he wants to say to Bion. He explains clearly why he is interested in Bion's 'Catastrophic Change' paper, and links this to a book that has impressed him. He thinks the book might interest Bion too, and gives a lucid description of it. If his thinking seemed somewhat adrift before, now it is straightforward and direct.

Both the papers by Bion that Winnicott responds to here were presented at Scientific Meetings of the British Psychoanalytical Society. The Society's archives contain audio recordings of both events. On each occasion, Winnicott himself was in the chair and opened the discussion. The recording for May 4, 1966 (Archive, S-P-1-19A, S-P-1-19B) comprises Bion's presentation of his paper on 'Catastrophic Change', Winnicott's response, and the discussion that followed, while the recording for October 4, 1967 (Archive, S-P-1-A-40) only has Bion giving his paper on 'Negative Capability', without Winnicott's response from the chair or the subsequent discussion.[1]

The 'Catastrophic Change' paper was circulated in advance, in the British Society's in-house Bulletin (Bion, 1966), and at the meeting Bion commented and elaborated on it rather than reading the prepublished text. On the recording we hear Winnicott, as chairman, discouraging speakers in the discussion from presenting comments they had prepared beforehand. It was more important, he said, to respond in the moment to what Bion was saying. Winnicott valued spontaneity, as his letter following Bion's 'Negative Capability' paper shows. On that occasion the paper had not been published in advance, so when Winnicott opened the discussion there was no choice but to respond in the moment. It is unfortunate that the recording does not include what Winnicott said, but his letter to Bion the next day reads like a continuation of his spontaneous response; he is still trying to work out what he thinks. The change in how his mind works, half-way through the letter, is not a break between its two parts. It is a movement from one to the other. Having been adrift to begin with, Winnicott needed to find a way to anchor himself.

It is certainly true that Bion's way of presenting his ideas could make his listeners feel at sea. He could disrupt their habitual thought processes in a way that was both exciting and disturbing, and he was aware of this. In the recording of his presentation on Negative Capability he begins with a preamble:

> Now one point I would like to make clear is that although it may seem strange, as I understand that what I write does seem strange, I don't think that I am saying anything that isn't already known.

Then he says:

> Well now, there's another point. People often feel that I don't really give clinical examples. Now this evening, I want to take as my clinical example the session that you are going to have with your patient tomorrow, that is to say the session that has not taken place.

This seems crazy but, in another way, absolutely right. Of course it is my own work that Bion's paper aims to help me with, and of course what matters are the sessions I am going to have, not ones that are over and done with. Listening, I feel both disorientated and excited.

The same thing happened to Donald Meltzer after Bion's 'Catastrophic Change' paper sixteen months earlier, where we do have a recording of the discussion. Following the paper Meltzer said: 'Now when I listen to Dr. Bion, I get drunk with a kind of delight because everything he says is so new and so exciting'. Despite the delight, this turns out to be a complaint.

Meltzer continues: 'I want to really express my resentment at this sort of drunkenness that he induces in me, and complain about how he does it and why I think he should not'. An interesting point of difference then appears between Meltzer and Winnicott. When he opened the discussion after the paper, Winnicott took Bion to task for reducing his large ideas to the parochialism, as he put it, of Melanie Klein's paranoid-schizoid and depressive positions. Meltzer, on the other hand, says:

> It is when Dr. Bion does not really condescend to inform us how it is linked with the things we have ordinarily been thinking, that he promotes in us a kind of excitement that takes us off into new channels without providing us with an anchorage.

Meltzer then picks up Winnicott's reference to Klein and says he thinks Bion's ideas in fact link very clearly to the paranoid-schizoid and depressive positions. He goes on:

> Now as soon as I can recognise that he is taking us the next logical step from the advances posed by 'Envy and Gratitude' [Klein, 1957], I stop being drunk and begin being really puzzled and worried about the quality of my work, and wonder what is wrong with it that needs to be improved by what Dr. Bion is talking about … It seems to me that Dr. Bion is talking about the kind of things that I have found myself worrying about …

Interestingly, Meltzer arrives here at what Bion said the following year before reading the 'Negative Capability' paper: that his ideas are to do with what is already known. But Meltzer does not like the way Bion makes what is familiar feel new and disorientating. He wants his anchorage, as I think Winnicott was looking for one in the second part of his letter to Bion. Klein's ideas are not the anchorage for Winnicott that they were for Meltzer. It is the use Bion made of the Bible that drew Winnicott back to the 'Catastrophic Change' paper. That is what connects with his need of an anchorage.

We should notice that the 'Catastrophic Change' meeting might have been in Winnicott's mind anyway. He had chaired Bion's presentation then, and he knew that the present meeting on October 4, 1967 was probably the last time he would do so. Bion was on the verge of emigrating to Los Angeles, and something of what this meant to Winnicott shows in what he said after Bion finished speaking. There was a coffee break before the discussion, and the coffee was evidently a bit delayed. We hear Winnicott apologise for this, and then he says:

> I will not speak immediately about the paper, but just to waste a little time, in a good way, Dr. Bion will, I hope, remember when he goes abroad that he is still a member of this Society and that we count on him to come back and continue to give these papers of this kind, which

is one of a series. And it is a tremendous loss to us to have Dr. Bion going, and he has just got to remember that we shan't forget him.

Bion and Winnicott were perhaps the most original and creative minds in the
British Society at this time, and they were important interlocutors for each
other. Winnicott's sense of loss, personal as well as for the Society, is clear.
    What about the connection, though, between Bion's use of the Bible
and the question of an anchorage? In the discussion after the 'Catastrophic
Change' paper, Bion responded to Meltzer's complaint about being deprived of an anchorage by agreeing that what he is recommending does
have this effect. Nevertheless, he said, one has to accept it:

> There is something peculiar about the operations of what is [sic] or-
> dinarily understood as memory and desire which makes one particu-
> larly unfitted to intuit what was actually happening in the session.
> And I think it is related to this question of the anchorage. If you try
> to do this [to give up memory and desire], then I think you have an
> unpleasant and anxious experience in which you feel you lose your
> anchorage. And one is constantly trying to find it. One is constantly
> trying to fall back on something or other like a cure ... something with
> which one is familiar, as a protection against what is really an unpleas-
> ant situation, a situation in which anything may happen ... Therefore
> it is important to be seeing the patient tomorrow as if that patient had
> never been seen: a very difficult thing—it is much easier to talk about
> than to do. And the difficulty is made worse by this fact that one loses
> one's anchorage and it is a nasty feeling, as you will soon find out if
> you try that and if you have any sort of success in trying it.

Winnicott would certainly have recognised what Bion was talking about.
On December 7 1966, just over six months later, he gave his paper 'The Location of Cultural Experience' to the British Society. Again there is a recording
(Archive, S-P-1-A-29A) which shows that what he said at the meeting was
virtually identical to the paper as it was later published (Winnicott, 1971:
95–103). While reading the paper, however, Winnicott made some interesting spontaneous interpolations. In one of these he talks about times when

> gradually much of the excitement and the activity of the analysis dies
> down; eventually there may be reached periods in the analysis when
> there tends to be quiet (see above pp. 127–128). The analyst wonders
> whether he is earning his guineas and he tends to fish around to
> find some material for interpretations that are certainly true, though
> they may not be apposite or well-timed. I am talking of course about
> myself and the early stages of my analytic career, in which I could
> never leave a long gap, and I simply thought I was failing and I would
> fish around for something to say, and I remember it only too well,

and with shame. I am asking for a watch to be kept for the significant silence or quiet period. Dr. Bion has recently referred to this, of
course in quite different language.

Winnicott makes a link between his own emphasis on waiting, and the
temptation to interpret for the sake of it, and Bion's stress on giving up
memory and desire, and the temptation to look for another anchorage
instead.

This question of anchorage is at the heart of Winnicott's letter to Bion.
His father was a leading figure of the local Wesleyan (Methodist) church,
and Winnicott had a strongly religious upbringing of a conventional sort
(Rodman, 2003: 383 n. 27). He did not want to throw away what this had
given him, nor his efforts to 'digest and sort out' what it meant. He needed,
though, to free himself from its literal-minded conformism which required,
for example, belief in miracles. It was an anchorage for him, but one that he
needed to let go of, in the way Bion described to Meltzer. The problem for
Winnicott was how to let go of it but, at the same time, keep hold of what
he valued about it.

The Nazarene Gospel Restored (Graves and Podro, 1953) offered a solution.
Winnicott's excitement about it is evident. He calls it 'an amazing book',
and says 'a tremendous amount of erudition and research' makes it 'absolutely fascinating and very important for the understanding of the Bible
story'. It is a daunting volume, over a thousand pages long and heavy in
the hand. There is no narrative thread, and reading it is hard work. It consists entirely of biblical quotations set against one another. Inconsistencies
are pointed out, and learned commentaries on the texts, including those of
the church fathers and the Talmud, suggest what the original events lying
behind them must have been. User-friendly the book is not, and might easily seem the opposite of exciting. It offered Winnicott, however, a way of
abandoning his religious anchorage that was also, at the same time and in
the same process, a way of preserving it. For Winnicott to be as excited as
he was by the book shows what relief he felt at being able to do this.

For Winnicott, Bion was an interlocutor about more than clinical technique. He writes to Bion as someone who shares a Christian background
and will recognise the struggle Winnicott has had with his religious upbringing. One can see why the 'Catastrophic Change' paper evoked this
response. Its primary theme is the concept of the container and contained.
Bion discusses how the prevailing institutional establishment, in any given
field, may be confronted with a genius, or 'mystic' in Bion's terms, who
introduces a 'messianic' idea into that field. What happens then? Can the
mystic be contained in such a way that the messianic idea can be made use
of constructively by the rest of the group? Does the messianic idea shatter
the establishment by its explosive force? Or does the establishment contain
it so ruthlessly as to squeeze the life out of it, and it goes to waste? Bion
illustrates this with extensive reference to Jesus and the Jewish religious

establishment, and to later developments in Christianity as well. He quotes several passages from the Gospels, refers to Saint Augustine and Meister Eckhart, and even the Jewish mysticism of Isaac Luria. Not surprisingly, Winnicott saw Bion as someone thoroughly grounded in Christianity, who had made use of it for himself in an unexpected and creative way, just as Winnicott was trying to do on his own account.

The question of tradition and originality was important to Winnicott:

> In using the word culture I am thinking of the inherited tradition … something that is in the common pool of humanity, into which individuals and groups of people may contribute, and from which we may all draw *if we have somewhere to put what we find* … In any cultural field *it is not possible to be original except on a basis of tradition*.
> (Winnicott, 1971: 99)

This echoes T. S. Eliot, the poet whose work Winnicott knew and forgot when Bion quoted it. In his essay *Tradition and the Individual Talent*, Eliot insisted that original writing in the present day can only be significant by virtue of its relation to the literary tradition of which it forms part (Eliot, 1920).

A dramatic statement of this link between tradition and present-day creativity comes from a contemporary Japanese potter whose family have been pottery masters for eleven generations:

> Tradition is to receive past knowledge, break it down and use it in a creative way, and to hand down that knowledge again as a true history.
> (Ohi, 1997)

A potter makes things with his hands, and there are videos of Toshiro Ohi, whose statement this is, which show the intense physicality of his work. For such a maker to talk of 'breaking down' his tradition has a quality of violence about it. The same violence is there in the way Winnicott needed to break down the religious tradition his parents enjoined on him.

On November 12,1968, Winnicott presented his paper 'The Use of an Object and Relating Through Identifications' to the New York Psychoanalytic Society (Winnicott, 1971: 86–94; see Rodman, 2003: 323–348). It is not an easy paper and Winnicott's meaning is not always clear. There are valuable discussions of it by Thomas Ogden (2016) and Jan Abram (2013; 2022: 33–58). Its central theme is that in order to use an object, as against simply relating to it, a subject must first destroy the object, and find that it survives being destroyed. Only then can the object be made use of. This is just what Winnicott did with Christianity. It was presented to him in a particular form by his parents, especially his devout father. According to Clare, he was taught by his father 'to read the Bible and find in it whatever he could as a personal guide' (Rodman, 2003: 12). This form of religion was one Winnicott could not make use of. In a lecture in 1962 he said:

> Religion (or is it theology) has stolen the good from the developing individual child, and has then set up an artificial scheme for injecting this that has been stolen back into the child, and has called it 'moral education' … Theology, by denying to the developing individual the creating of whatever is bound up in the concept of God and of good-ness and of moral values, depletes the individual of an important as-pect of creativeness.
>
> (Winnicott, 1965: 94–95)

However, he did not want 'to throw away religion just because the peo-ple who organise the religions of the world insist on belief in miracles'. Although he rejected belief in dogmas that belonged to the conventional religion of his parents, he still wanted to make space for what he valued in that tradition. This meant finding a way in which the object he needed to destroy could survive that destruction, in a new form that did let him make use of it. This is what *The Nazarene Gospel Restored* provided. What interested him so much about Bion's 'Catastrophic Change' paper was that it seemed to show Bion going through the same experience, and Winnicott wanted to compare notes about it.

This link between Winnicott's letter and the 'Use of an Object' paper is not by chance. The paper was presented in New York just a year after he wrote to Bion, and he must have been working on it at the time of his letter. He had in fact been developing ideas of destruction and survival for some years. In 1963, while writing a review of Jung's *Memories, Dreams and Reflections* (Win-nicott, 1964), he had a powerful dream about which he wrote to a colleague:

> It refers to a deep layer of destructiveness, yet to a somewhat sophis-ticated (ego-wise) coping with destructiveness. In health the infant is given (by ordinary devoted Mum) areas of experience of omnipotence while experimenting with excursions over the line into the wasteland of destroyed reality. The wasteland turns out to have features in its own right, or survival value, etc., and surprisingly the individual child finds total destruction does not mean total destruction.
>
> (Winnicott, 1989: 229–230)

It is interesting that Winnicott should write about survival in the 'waste-land'. In 1963, Bion had not yet written about memory and desire, but was Eliot's poem already an unconscious reference point in Winnicott's mind?

In 'Notes made on a train' in 1965, Winnicott wrote:

> What can a human being do with an object? At the beginning the re-lation is to a subjective object. Gradually subject and object become

separated out, and then there is the relation to the objectively perceived object. Subject destroys object. This splits up into (1) subject
preserves object; (2) subject *uses* object; (3) subject *destroys* object.
(Winnicott, 1989: 231)

This already describes the shift, which is crucial in the 'Use of an Object'
paper, from a subjective object to one that is an objective part of external
reality. But (2) and (3) are the wrong way round. In 1965, Winnicott had
not yet seen that destroying the object is what makes it possible to use
it. It took until 1968 to understand and articulate this in the 'Use of an
Object' paper. In 1967 when he wrote to Bion, he was in the middle of
working it out.

Winnicott was excited about *The Nazarene Gospel Restored*, and the use
Bion made of his own religious upbringing, because they resonated with
something he was not only working out theoretically, but which mattered
to him at a deep level personally. In delivering his paper on Negative
Capability, the evening before Winnicott wrote to him, Bion twice made
a point of mentioning the analyst's growth. Once, as he was imagining
progressively more serious clinical situations and how to deal with them
(see below, p. 142), he said:

> I want to suggest that this kind of game is a sophisticated version of
> the child's game, which we can exploit for purposes of exercising our
> minds, or doing whatever it is that a child does. I suggest that it is
> related to the process of the psychoanalyst's growth.

Another time he said:

> I would like to make a sort of parallel to movement from paranoid-
> schizoid to depressive, using terms like 'patient' for the paranoid-
> schizoid position and 'secure' for the depressive position. That is to
> say that if one was an ideal analyst, then one would pass through
> the phase of being patient—I use that term particularly because
> I want to retain the idea of suffering in it—to this other position
> of being secure, retaining also the meaning of it as being without
> anxiety, without care. In that way, then, I would suggest that the
> analysis becomes a dynamic experience for the analyst himself, and
> his growth.

Winnicott does not refer to these comments in his letter, but hearing Bion
highlight how the analytic process contributes to the analyst's own personal growth would have carried particular meaning for him.

Fifteen years earlier, on November 17, 1952, Winnicott wrote a letter to
Melanie Klein (1987: 33–38). It seems that Klein had reacted negatively to a
paper of Winnicott's on 'Anxiety Associated with Insecurity'. This disagreed

with Klein's insistence that early infant development was a matter only of intrapsychic, instinct-driven experience. Winnicott said in the paper:

> Analysts ... often speak as if the infant's life starts with oral instinc-tual experience and the emerging object relationship of instinctual ex-perience. Yet we all know that an infant has the capacity to feel awful as a result of something that is quite in another field, that is to say, that of infant care ... Before object relationships the state of affairs is this: that the unit is not the individual, the unit is an environment-individual set-up ... often we think we see an infant when we learn through analysis at a later date that what we ought to have seen was an environment developing falsely into a human being, hiding within itself a potential individual.
>
> (Winnicott, 1975: 98–100)

In his letter, Winnicott tells Klein he had hoped for a creative discussion of what he thought were new ideas, expressed, as they were bound to be, in his own way and his own language. What he got instead, he says, was a reductive attempt to restate what he had said in standard Kleinian terms. 'If you make the stipulation that in future only your language shall be used for the statement of other people's discoveries then the language becomes a dead language, as it has already become in the Society'. In the rest of the letter, which is long, thoughtful and clearly heart-felt, he en-larges this criticism. He tells Klein how damaging to her extremely signifi-cant work he thinks it is, that her ideas are being turned into a dogmatic creed—'Kleinism'—which inhibits their creative development and harms relationships in the Society. A *festschrift* for Klein's 70th birthday was being prepared at the time, and at the end of his letter Winnicott says: 'I am writ-ing all this down to show why it is that I have a real difficulty in writing a chapter for your book although I want to do so very badly'.

This letter is a milestone in Winnicott's development both personal and psychoanalytic. With it he frees himself from adherence, not just to Melanie Klein's ideas, but to any system that would constrain his freedom to think and express himself in whatever way he needs to. His key statement in this regard comes at the beginning of the letter: 'The first thing I want to say is that when something develops in me out of my own growth and out of my analytic experience I want to put it in my own language' (Winnicott, 1987: 37). The phrase to notice here is 'out of my own growth'. Winnicott links his personal growth and his analytic experience together, as being conjointly the source of his creativity. When Bion, in his Negative Capabil-ity paper, highlighted the same link between the 'dynamic experience' of doing analysis and the analyst's growth, it was another reason for Winni-cott to recognise him as a kindred spirit.

In this letter to Melanie Klein, Winnicott was refusing to have a doctrinaire systematisation of Kleinian theory imposed on him. He believed Klein's ideas were valuable, but he thought the refusal by her and her followers to allow space for anyone else's creative development of them rendered them lifeless. Faced with this dogmatism, Winnicott needed to do the same with it as he did with his parents' religious dogmatism. He needed to break it down and destroy it, in order to make creative use of what survived the destruction.

If Winnicott had submitted to the creed either of his parents' religion or of Melanie Klein and her followers, he would have been living by compliance. This concept comes from another paper of his entitled 'Creativity and its Origins' (Winnicott, 1971: 65–85). He says there that a relationship to the world based on compliance carries a sense of futility and is 'a sick basis for life', for the reason that such a way of living is essentially uncreative. His disappointment with Klein was because his paper had been, in his words, 'a creative gesture', and all she seemed interested in was for him to comply with her way of thinking. His complaint about religion too was that it 'depletes the individual of an important aspect of creativeness' (see above, p. 130). Creativity is what mattered to him, and he wanted a kind of religion that he could make use of creatively, as he wanted to use Klein's ideas creatively in his own way.

A religion that stays open to fresh creativity, and a psychoanalysis of which the same is true, are expressions of a certain cultural attitude. Winnicott is tentative about trying to define culture: 'Perhaps I have said enough to show both what I know and what I do not know about the meaning of the word culture' (1971: 99). The importance culture had for him personally, and his uncertainty in approaching it, are clear in the obituary he wrote of James Strachey, his first analyst.

> I longed to get to know him but always I had the awful feeling that he was nothing if not erudite and sophisticated, which I was not. He was at home in an area which I had discovered too late, since I had not met the cultural life (except in the form of an evangelical religion) until I was at public school. Strachey had grown up in it, in this third area of living, the area of cultural experience. Strachey's familiarity with literature, music and ballet filled me with envy and made me feel somewhat boorish when in his company … He was so infinitely enriched by what he had gathered in from the cultural experience that he did not depend on distractions for feeling glad to be alive.
> (Winnicott, 1969: 130–131)

Strachey died in April 1967. Six months later Winnicott repressed his knowledge of where the words 'memory and desire' came from. It may be worth noting that the opening section of The Waste Land, where the phrase appears in the third line, is called 'The Burial of the Dead'.

Winnicott's mention of 'this third area of living, the area of cultural experience' is a reference to his paper 'The Location of Cultural Experience' (1971: 95–103), which he had presented a year earlier in 1966. Its central idea is that cultural experience takes place, not in the area of internal psychic reality, nor that of external reality, but in a third area intermediate between those two, 'the *potential space* between the individual and the environment' (Winnicott, 1971: 100). This potential space is continuous with the transitional space of infancy and the play space of childhood. Following on from them, 'this third area, that of play, expands into creative living and into the whole cultural life of man' (Winnicott, 1971: 102).

As well as the literature, music and ballet that Strachey knew, Winnicott offers other examples of cultural life when he asks: 'What are we doing when we are listening to a Beethoven symphony or making a pilgrimage to a picture gallery or reading *Troilus and Cressida*?' (Winnicott, 1971: 105). Winnicott does not use language casually. His question *'What are we doing when we ...?'*, and his comment that Strachey was enriched by *'what he had gathered in* from the cultural experience' [my italics], show that cultural experience, for him, is not something that simply happens; it is an activity to be engaged in (Parsons, 2024: 358–359). This shows very clearly in the interpolation mentioned earlier that Winnicott made while presenting 'The Location of Cultural Experience'. After recollecting his difficulty in waiting, and the temptation to 'fish around for something to say' because it is so hard to give up using interpretation as an anchorage, Winnicott went on:

> Certain patients have taught me that it is in between the patient and the analyst that, when there is mutual trust, something tends to start up that has immense significance. This something does not need interpreting, and it cannot be produced by interpretation. It amounts to a filling up of the potential space between the patient and the analyst with imaginative material that comes as a creative act from the patient.

Again, his emphasis is on the creativity of what occurs in the potential space.

Winnicott had to find his way to this understanding, just as he did with regard to the use of an object. In that instance, he knew in 1965 about destroying and using the object, but the sequence 'subject destroys object, object survives destruction, subject can use object', was not arrived at until 1968. Again with cultural experience, he had the elements in place before he worked out the relationships between them. In 'Communicating and not Communicating Leading to a Study of Certain Opposites', which he presented at the British Society in 1963, he writes:

> One should be able to make a positive statement of the healthy use of non-communication in the establishment of the feeling of real. It may be necessary in so doing to speak in terms of man's cultural life, which is the adult equivalent of the transitional phenomena of infancy and early childhood, and in which area communication is made without reference to the object's state of being either subjective or objectively perceived.
>
> (Winnicott, 1965: 184)

Winnicott sees that cultural life belongs to an area that is intermediate between subjective and objective, being a continuation of the transitional space of infancy. However, in his summary at the end of the paper he writes:

> The two extremes, explicit communication that is indirect, and silent or personal communication that feels real, each of these has its place, and in the intermediate cultural area there exists for many, but not for all, a mode of communication which is a most valuable compromise.
>
> (p. 192)

The word 'compromise' has a somewhat negative, *faute de mieux* connotation. A compromise may be valuable, as being the best solution available, but it is still a substitute: something to be accepted because what was really wanted is not possible. Winnicott did not yet see that the fact of this area being intermediate, between subjective psychic reality and objective reality with its explicit communication, was the very thing that gives it the creative potential to generate cultural experience. That had to wait another three years to be stated in 'The Location of Cultural Experience'.

Here is another of the informal asides Winnicott made while presenting 'The Location of Cultural Experience'. Towards the end of the paper, in its published form, comes the following passage (1971: 101).

> Yet *for the baby* (if the mother can supply the right conditions) every detail of the baby's life is an example of creative living. Every object is a found object. Given the chance, the baby begins to live creatively, and to use actual objects to be creative into and with.

What we hear on the recording of the meeting goes like this:

> Yet *for the baby* (if the mother can supply the right conditions) every detail of the baby's life is an example of creative living. Every object is a found object.
>
> There is a vast amount of poetry that is about these things that I am prosaically describing. Poetry is, in a sophisticated way, the very stuff that fills the potential space in that particular medium. [He pauses] I don't know why I have chosen to say four lines:
>
> > Go and catch a falling star,
> > Get with child a mandrake root.
> > Tell me where all past years are
> > Or who cleft the devil's foot.
>
> I was led to this by the word 'mandrake' which I was looking for.

> Given the chance, the baby begins to live creatively, and to use actual objects to be creative into and with.

Reading a paper to his colleagues, Winnicott stops and recites some lines of poetry, says he doesn't know why he is doing so but the poem has a strange word in it that he was looking for, doesn't explain why that word interests him, and carries on reading his paper. As well as showing how important poetry was to Winnicott, it is an astonishing example of his spontaneity. One sees why colleagues seem to have found him, just like Bion, both delightful and frustrating.

There is more to say about this interpolation. Seven months earlier, Winnicott chaired Bion's 'Catastrophic Change' paper about mystics and messianic ideas; now he is writing about the transitional space of infancy extending into adult life; and in less than a year's time he will write to Bion about *The Nazarene Gospel Restored*. Infancy and childhood, and questions of unorthodox religion, are occupying his mind. Winnicott does not know why he speaks these four lines, but listen to the phrases in them: 'get with child', 'where all past years are', 'the devil's foot'. Mandrakes have myths about sexuality and procreation attached to them; and the author of the lines is John Donne, whose poems about his religious strivings are famous. Winnicott's connection to his unconscious, and his freedom in speaking from it, are remarkable.

Winnicott's letter to Bion and the one to Melanie Klein show how his work as an analyst and issues that occupy him personally are bound up together. This interpolation is another example, and it is even clearer in a paper he gave, also in 1966, about split-off male and female elements in both sexes (Winnicott, D.W., 1989: 168–192). He recognised that a male patient was talking about penis envy, and said to him:

I am listening to a girl. I know perfectly well that you are a man but I am listening to a girl, and I am talking to a girl. I am telling this girl: 'You are talking about penis envy'.

In the subsequent exchange with the patient, Winnicott said:

It was not that *you* told this to anyone; it is *I* who see the girl and hear her talking, when actually there is a man on my couch. The mad person is *myself*.

The patient responded:

I myself could never say (knowing myself to be a man) 'I am a girl'. I am not mad that way. But you said it and you have spoken to both parts of me.

Winnicott comments:

This madness which was mine enabled him to see himself as a girl *from my position*. He knows himself to be a man and never doubts that he is a man.

Is it obvious what was happening here? For my part, I have needed to live through a deep personal experience in order to arrive at the understanding I feel I have now reached.

When I gave myself time to think over what had happened I was puzzled. Here was no new theoretical concept, here was no new principle of technique. In fact I and my patient had been over this ground before. Yet here we had something new, new in my own attitude and new in his capacity to make use of my interpretative work. I decided to surrender myself to whatever this might mean in myself, and the result is to be found in this paper that I am presenting.

(Winnicott, 1989: 170–173)

Winnicott's biographer, Robert Rodman, underlines the connection I am pointing to between Winnicott's analytic work and his inner life.

Winnicott's continuing attempt to understand himself in the context of advancing age reached a number of climactic expressions in the early 1960s … He wrote with newfound confidence, having found it possible to bring together his personal striving and his professional observations and speculations.

(Rodman, 2003: 264)

Rodman mentions Winnicott's 'advancing age'. He was born in 1896, so at the beginning of the 1960s he was 64, and 71 when he wrote to Bion—by no means old in today's terms. From the late 1940s onwards, however, he had a succession of heart attacks and chest problems, and his health was always precarious. He died only three and a quarter years after his letter to Bion.

After Winnicott's death, Clare found some notes he was making for an autobiography (Winnicott, C., 1989: 3–4). First there was a prayer, with his initials to show it was his own: 'D.W.W. Oh God! May I be alive when I die'. Then he went on:

I died.

It was not very nice and took quite a long time as it seemed (but it was only a moment in eternity).

There had been rehearsals (that's a difficult word to spell. I found I had left out the "a". The hearse was cold and unfriendly).

Let me see. What was happening when I died? My prayer had been answered. I was alive when I died. That was all I had asked and I had got it.

Winnicott may have wondered, in the 1960s, how much longer he had to live. The 'rehearsals' were presumably his heart attacks and pulmonary illnesses, and his analyst's ear heard the word 'hearse' in the background. His reference to 'a moment in eternity' is interesting, given his attempts to make creative use of the religion he was brought up in. What comes through most powerfully is Winnicott's conviction that being alive, in the full sense of the word, means more than just existing. His work has been called 'a kind of biography of the sense of aliveness as it unfolds in infancy and throughout a lifetime' (Eigen, 1996: xxi; see also Parsons, 2014). It is a biography of his own personal sense of aliveness as well.

When Winnicott described his envy of Strachey's immersion in culture, he said that Strachey was so enriched by his cultural experience that 'he did not depend on distractions for feeling glad to be alive'. Almost in passing, Winnicott shows why cultural experience matters: it contributes to the sense of being fully alive. The obituary for Strachey was written soon after 'The Location of Cultural Experience', and in that paper Winnicott stresses the point twice.

> We tend to think of health in terms of the state of ego defences. We say it is healthy when these defences are not rigid, etc. But we seldom reach the point at which we can start to describe what life is like apart from illness or absence of illness. That is to say, we have yet to tackle the question of *what life itself is about*.
>
> (1971: 98)

> What I say does affect our view of the question: what is life about? You may cure your patient and not know what it is that makes him or her go on living. It is of first importance for us to acknowledge openly that absence of psychoneurotic illness may be health, but it is not life. Psychotic patients who are all the time hovering between living and not living force us to look at this problem, one that really belongs *not to psychoneurotics but to all human beings*.
>
> (1971: 99–100)

Winnicott is saying that *all human beings*—neurotic or not, analytic patients or not—are necessarily confronted with the problem of *what life itself is about*. The word 'problem', and the italics, show the personal urgency this carried for him.

What is at stake in cultural experience also comes across in a talk on 'Playing and Culture' that Winnicott gave in March 1968:

> Play is always exciting. It is exciting *not* because of the background of instinct, but because of the precariousness that is inherent in it, since it always deals with the knife-edge between the subjective and that which is objectively perceived. What holds for playing and culture

also holds for the St. Matthew Passion at which I am almost certain to find colleagues when I go to the Festival Hall in a few weeks' time.

(1989: 205–206)

To listen to the St. Matthew Passion is exciting, Winnicott says, because it means balancing precariously on the knife-edge where cultural experience is located.

One can fall off a knife-edge in either direction. In a seminar in 1964, Winnicott described the ordinary forward movement of maturation like this:

An important aspect of growth is the change from relating to sub-jective objects to a recognition of objects that are outside the area of omnipotence, that is to say that are objectively perceived but not ex-plained on the basis of projection.

(1989: 101)

Cultural experience requires a kind of growth that involves not just this forward direction of movement, but a back-and-forth fluidity, a capacity to entertain both the subjectivity of the infant's sense of omnipotence, and the perception of objective reality, without anchoring oneself in either of them.

In the seminar, Winnicott's next sentence was:

In this area of change there is the maximum opportunity for the indi-vidual to make sense of the aggressive components.

Winnicott would not write the 'Use of an Object' until 1968, four years later. The importance of aggression in that paper has been highlighted by Abram (2013), but its positive function was already in view in this 1964 seminar. To progress from relating to subjective objects to a recognition of what is perceived objectively puts an end to the sense of omnipotence. There is aggression in this, as when Winnicott put an end in his mind to the miracles he had been brought up on. To hold open the potential space of cultural experience is a further progression involving rejection in both directions. It refuses to accept either subjective omnipotence or objective perception as the guarantee of reality. This balancing on a knife-edge requires the kind of growth that Bion called for in analysts when he asked them to do, in their own minds, what children do in their play space (see above p. 131).

My use just now of the phrase 'without anchoring oneself' is another reference back to earlier discussions. Donald Meltzer, listening to Bion talk about catastrophic change, felt deprived of his familiar anchorage in Melanie Klein's ideas and did not like it. Bion's answer was yes, Meltzer was being deprived of his anchorage and yes, the feeling is an uncomfort-able one, but it is necessary nevertheless. To accept what Bion was saying,

Meltzer would have needed to destroy his anchorage. Not, that is, to destroy Klein's ideas but to destroy them *as an anchorage*. This would let him discover that the ideas survived, and he could then begin to make use of them in a new way.

Winnicott did recognise that he had to destroy his anchorages. His fragment of autobiography shows him feeling that he had succeeded in being alive. His title indicates, however, that there was a cost to this. The autobiography was to be called 'Not Less than Everything', and inside the cover of the notebook was a fuller version of the quotation: 'T.S. Eliot "Costing not less than everything"'. Given how intertwined his professional life was with his inner psychic life, it is no surprise that the cost of aliveness was there in both of them.

In his clinical work, the anchorage that needed destroying was his recourse to interpretations. As well as confessing how in difficult silences he would 'fish around for something to say', he wrote:

> It appals me to think how much deep change I have prevented or delayed in patients *in a certain classification category* by my personal need to interpret.
>
> (Winnicott, 1971: 86)

In challenging situations, making interpretations could be a way for Winnicott to reassure himself. But retreating from a problem to a routine kind of solution is not a way of being fully alive, and using an interpretation—even if it happens to be true—to defuse one's anxiety and uncertainty is not a way of being alive clinically. Knowing he could always fall back on interpreting something was an anchorage for Winnicott, and becoming more alive in the consulting-room meant destroying it. This cost him an automatic kind of confidence; instead, he had to trust something in himself without knowing what form it would take or where it would lead. Analysing the man who was a girl with penis envy meant entering an area of madness in himself. There was a cost, in this analysis, to Winnicott's sanity. He said elsewhere, though, that 'we are poor indeed if we are only sane' (Winnicott, 1975: 150), and his willingness to pay that cost allowed the analysis to progress and enriched him personally as well.

The cost of being alive is there in all psychic life. Winnicott emphasises that the problem of *'what life itself is about'* belongs *'not to psychoneurotics but to all human beings'*. 'To feel that life is real, to find life worth living' depends, he says, on 'a well-established capacity in the individual for total experience, and for experience in the area of transitional phenomena': in the intermediate, potential space, that is to say, where cultural experience is located (1971: 98–100). To have a 'capacity' for something means it is not automatic. It may be located in a certain kind of space, but one has to go to meet it. Winnicott's comment about Strachey "gathering in" his cultural experience, and his question 'What are we doing?' when we listen to a Beethoven symphony, show that cultural experience is not passive. The cost of feeling that life is real, and worth living, is the risk of balancing oneself precariously on 'the knife-edge between the subjective and that which is objectively "perceived" (1989: 206)

There is no obligation to do this. One can listen to the St. Matthew Passion without being poised between what is given from outside and what one creates from inside. This will feel safe, the music will still be enjoyable, but it will be a less creative experience. For Winnicott and his colleagues to leave the Festival Hall feeling more alive than when they went in, they would need to have put themselves at risk in their listening.

Listening to Bion could be a risky experience. He had a subversive way of making his listeners question what they took for granted. André Green said he 'makes us witnesses to the process of the unfolding of his thought' (Green, 1992: 585). A witness, though, can be detached, and this is what Bion makes difficult. In David Bell's words:

> Bion is a writer who has an effect on his reader, and one that is most peculiar. It is as if the very thing that he discusses takes place in the act of reading him.
>
> (Bell, 2011: 81)

Hearing Bion in person could produce the same effect. When he spoke on 'Catastrophic Change', Donald Meltzer found that what Bion was talking about—giving up one's usual reference points—started happening in his own mind, and it made him feel drunk. I mentioned how disorientated I too felt while listening to the recording of Bion's paper on Negative Capability. I heard Bion say that his clinical example would be a session of mine (*What? Did I hear that right?*) which has not happened yet (*Hold on! This is mad!*). I had a moment of not being sure who was who, between Bion and myself, until I could recover my balance and think about what he meant. In his letter to Bion the next day, Winnicott seemed adrift in certain ways, as I noted to begin with. He was responding both to the content of the paper and to his own experience of listening to it.

The paper itself was never published. The recording in the British Society's archives shows that it contained elements from other papers, especially 'Memory and Desire' (Bion, 2014: 7–17) and 'Notes on Memory and Desire' (Bion, 2014: 203–210), dating from 1965 and 1967. Aspects of it also appear in 'Opacity of memory and desire', Chapter 4 of *Attention and Interpretation* (Bion, 1970: 41–54). As regards what Winnicott heard Bion say on October 4, however, the recording is all we have.

Certain passages of the recording have been mentioned already, but it is worth quoting at some length, partly as a record of its content, but also to convey the flavour of what listening to it might have been like.

The early part of the paper seems to pull the rug out from under its own feet. Bion's reason for wanting listeners to take their own session as a clinical example, and not one of his, is that 'we have to use a very inadequate method of communication with each other'. Patient and analyst have a chance of understanding each other, because they are talking about what is happening in the moment. However:

> When it comes to lateral communication, as this evening here, it is a different matter because I have to ... talk about experiences which you haven't had ... and as I think everybody knows, you get a peculiar effect as a result of this. You get a situation in which you have no doubt, say about an interpretation that you have given, and that it was apposite at the time. And it is extraordinary to find that what you say really causes no echoes, because what one says in the lateral communication is so different, and is so inadequate to describe what took place in the consulting-room.

In similar vein:

> There are certain points ... where we float off the edge, as it were, of our vocabulary, that we are trying to talk about experiences which we may all know but which we experience differently. And I think this is a serious matter, because I think very often we have arguments and controversies in the Society ... but they are a waste of time because the apparent controversy is really stirred up through inadequate means of publication; that is to say inadequate means for this lateral communication that I talk about, communicating what one analyst has experienced to somebody else who obviously has not had that experience, even if he thinks it is a similar experience ... The point that I would like to make, although the conditions don't exist for it, is that one should consider these kinds of extra-sessional meetings as being much more in the nature of games, and in doing this, to exploit what we know of children's games.

Listening to this, Winnicott might have thought he was now on home ground. But Bion's games are not Winnicott's games. Bion is obliged to fall back on games because, he says, the reality he wants to communicate cannot be communicated. Instead, he asks the audience to play a game of imagining versions of a wrist-scratching situation, starting from a patient scratching their wrist apparently trivially, leading up to one who threatens to slash their wrists, is admitted to hospital, does slash their wrists and is found by nurses in a bath full of blood. Bion offers possible ways of thinking about these situations: do they have a direction, from inward to outward or outward to inward? What quality of violence do they exhibit? How do they work as communications? He is at pains to say that 'in all this, I am not suggesting any answers. I am merely suggesting a method of playing a game producing questions'. He does not suggest answers because they would be irrelevant:

> I said that this was about tomorrow's session. The point about it is that we haven't the slightest idea what will happen in tomorrow's session, and we therefore do not know anything at all about it. And one thing quite certain is that we are unlikely to be presented by a recognisable event which bears a recognisable relationship to what I have been saying this evening.

If communication is so limited, and what Bion is describing has no relationship to what will happen in their session tomorrow, the audience might wonder what they were there for. But there is even stranger stuff to come. Bion quotes something that Freud wrote to Lou Andreas-Salomé:

> I know that in writing I have to blind myself artificially in order to focus all the light on one dark spot, renouncing cohesion, harmony, edifying effects and everything which you call the symbolic element.
>
> (Freud, 1972: 45)

He applies this to clinical work:

> When it comes to the actual session, what we suffer from is not lack of knowledge, lack of theory, lack of training, so much as too much knowledge, too much theory, and too much light. Now for this particular search in which we are engaged, I don't think that a bright light, if I can use this model, is required so much as to get the situation so obscure that the dimmest object, the faintest scrap of light will show up. Therefore, the important thing is to be able to exclude as much as you can, in order to bring a sort of penetrating shaft of darkness to bear on the obscure spot.

This is where Bion brings in John Keats' description of negative capability: 'when a man is capable of being in uncertainties, mysteries, doubts, without any irritable reaching after fact and reason'. For Bion, a capacity for tolerating half-truths and incomplete knowledge is essential. Without it, 'one finds sooner or later, usually sooner, one starts reaching out for psychoanalytic interpretations. That I think is wrong'.

Winnicott might have felt that this again was familiar territory. He knew about not fishing around for interpretations, and had made the link between himself and Bion the year before when presenting 'The Location of Cultural Experience'. As with games, though, what looks familiar may not be quite what it seems. Bion goes on:

> This brings me to the point which I have discussed before, of the importance of memory and desire. What I want to suggest about this is a really very simple exercise. Instead of telling you what I mean by

> memory and desire, I think it would be a good thing just to try out …
> trying to do without the intrusion too much of whether it is the end
> of the session or not.

He is not just offering ideas; he sets his listeners an exercise. He wants them
to experience what he is talking about, because this 'simple exercise' leads
on to seeing how truly disturbing it is to be an analyst.

> I think that one should gradually, in this kind of way, come to one's
> own definition of what is meant by memory and desire. And then …
> one can consider extending this to things that are not simply of a triv-
> ial nature. But the curve, as it were, rises very steeply. It's pretty easy
> to get to the point I am talking about—well enough, anyway, to get
> clear on one's own definition of memory and desire. It is not so easy to
> know where the process should stop.
>   The effect is to intensify the analytic experience very much; so
> much indeed that the psychoanalysis of patients moves into the cen-
> tre of the analyst's life, and you get an effect that is rather similar to
> being analysed. In the same way that one's analyst is always a very
> important person, and this is reflected in dreams and suchlike, in the
> same way the practice begins to be reflected in the analyst's dreams
> and so on, and it becomes possible to focus more the origins of these
> various anxieties … by recognising that they derive from the intense
> experience not of being analysed but of psychoanalysing.

Bion says that if you really do this, and face your patient tomorrow as
nearly as possible free of memory and desire,

> then you get a situation in which what is going on in the analysis is a
> whole lot of discrete and meaningless episodes in which the pattern
> is not discernible. Now that is difficult to tolerate. It requires nega-
> tive capability, otherwise one will rush in with an interpretation to
> get out of the dilemma of tolerating mysteries, half-truths and so on.

> This procedure ought to be used with caution … without being in too
> much of a hurry, and expecting to find repercussions in one's own at-
> titude and outlook of a disagreeable kind.

> One ought to proceed cautiously, setting one's sights pretty low, espe-
> cially on this question of memory and desire, of suppressing them or
> getting rid of them, because I think in a very extreme form this comes
> awfully near to what the psychotic does, that his attempt to defend
> himself against overstimulation by the world of reality rather takes
> the form of destroying his ability to have any contact with stimuli
> from the real world and it plunges him into a contact which is far too
> intense to stand with what we ordinarily call the unconscious.

At the end of his paper, Bion has arrived somewhere disturbing. He is telling his colleagues that practising psychoanalysis as he thinks it should be practised brings one 'awfully near' to risking one's sanity. One can imagine Winnicott remembering the man who was a girl with penis envy.

I started by saying that the way Winnicott wrote to Bion the day after hearing this paper suggested he had made a strange mistake; that he thought Bion was endorsing memory and desire, not arguing against them. The passages I have quoted, however, are unequivocal; it would be hard to misunderstand them as being in favour of memory and desire. Bion had given his paper 'Memory and Desire' at the British Society on June 16, 1965 and his ideas were much debated. Winnicott must have known very well that Bion thought memory and desire were a hindrance. But the confusion I observed in his phrasing in the letter is still there, as well as his repressing where the words 'memory and desire' came from. Something else is going on. What is it about memory, desire and intention that this letter is trying to clarify?

Here is an interpretation. I emphasise that I do not suggest this is what Winnicott himself was thinking. It is my interpretation of what his letter represents; which may, nevertheless, help us understand the conflict underlying Winnicott's perplexity.

When he wrote the letter, Winnicott was working on his 'Use of an Object' paper. In October 1968, just a year after writing to Bion, he showed the paper to Anna Freud and the following month he presented it in New York (Rodman, 2003: 323; Abram, 2013: 305–311). As I said earlier, the theme of the paper, in a nutshell, is: subject destroys object, object survives destruction, subject can use object. What is the most important object for a psychoanalyst to be able to use? Surely, psychoanalysis itself.

Winnicott thought analysts should not resort to interpretation to reassure themselves they understood the patient; Bion thought interpretations should not be driven by memory and desire. There is an overlap, but it is only partial. They are not talking about the same thing. While presenting 'The Location of Cultural Experience', Winnicott referred to 'periods in the analysis when there tends to be quiet'. Rather than fishing around for something to say, he was 'asking for a watch to be kept for the significant silence or quiet period'. However, when he added: 'Dr. Bion has recently referred to this, of course in quite different language', he was not being quite accurate. Winnicott is referring to particular episodes in the course of an analysis. For Bion, on the other hand, seeing a patient as though you have never seen them before, with no desire for anything to come of seeing them, should be the analyst's state of mind all the time. Analysts have to strive to maintain that attitude, not just at certain times, but constantly.

Striving is needed because this is an unpleasant state of mind, as Bion emphasised to Donald Meltzer in the discussion after his 'Catastrophic Change' paper. When he said, in the paper on 'Negative Capability', that rejecting memory and desire produced disagreeable repercussions in the analyst, he added:

> I did hear that when I spoke about this before, that many people thought this was an easy procedure, that all that you did was to forget your work and not bother about it. Well it isn't. It is not that. It's a tougher discipline than that and it is a nasty one, anyhow for quite a long time, perhaps forever, for all I know.

All analysts try not to let their free-floating attention be distracted, but Bion often insisted fiercely that he was talking about much more than that. Here are some examples. He writes of

> a watchful avoidance of memory … The psychoanalyst should aim at achieving a state of mind so that at every session he feels he has not seen the patient before. If he feels he has, he is treating the wrong patient.
>
> (2014: 206–207)

> You should spend your time banishing any memory of the patient whatsoever, in preparation for the session, and any aim or ambition as regard to his cure … I think it is a matter which you will find is extremely difficult, and you have only got to think of it for a moment to see how inherently improbable it is.
>
> (2014: 12)

> Every session attended by the psychoanalyst must have no history and no future. What is 'known' about the patient is of no further consequence: it is either false or irrelevant.
>
> (2014: 205)

> Do not remember past sessions. The greater the impulse to remember what has been said or done, the greater the need to resist it … Desires for results, 'cure' or even understanding must not be allowed to proliferate … These rules must be obeyed *all* the time and not simply during the sessions.
>
> (2014: 206)

What is the analyst left with, as a result of all this insistence on what not to do?

> The consequences … are peculiar … It really is a sort of positive lack of anything in one's mind, if one can put it like that; that the darker the spot that you wish to illuminate, the darker you have to be—you have to shut out all light in order to be able to see it.
>
> (2014: 13)

Bion could have been more careful of his language here. A 'wish' to illuminate a spot, even a dark one, might seem suspiciously like a desire. Nonetheless, he realises that this 'tough', 'nasty', and 'inherently improbable' discipline is something different from psychoanalysis as most analysts understand it.

> I would like to stress once more that it is very different from the view that we are all used to — the view that we fall back into very easily: the more critical the situation, the more we try to remember something or other, even if it is only an appropriate theory.
>
> (2014: 13)

The state of mind Bion asks for is the opposite of what is usually thought of as analytic. It is not free-associative listening. On the contrary, it requires the active expulsion of thoughts from the mind. The 'positive lack' in one's mind which this produces is not a void; it is what Bion elsewhere calls a 'no-thing', something that exists as an absence. Even a positive absence, however, does not offer anything for associations to join up with. And if the 'rules' are to be obeyed all the time, and not just in sessions, there is no room for theory. Are we talking about psychoanalysis at all any longer?

I mean the question seriously. Of course Bion was a psychoanalyst, and an important one, and of course he says a lot more about what memory is and is not, about what he means by 'evolution' as opposed to memory, about forgetting being as bad as remembering and so on. He works hard not to be misunderstood. Even so, I want to suggest that what he is doing in the papers and passages I have quoted is to destroy psychoanalysis in the mind of his readers and listeners.

This is an outrageous statement. Nevertheless, when Winnicott wrote to Bion as he did about memory and desire, I think he was writing to him as the subject who destroys the object which is to be made use of. Too shocking a thought, maybe, to find its way into words, and Winnicott was still on the way to clarifying that for the object to be made use of, it does have to be destroyed first; hence the ambiguity and apparent confusion in his phrasing. Evidently, though, he saw a need to counter what Bion said about memory and desire, and his choice of the word 'intention' for doing so is significant. As I remarked, the rejection of memory and desire called for by Bion is a permanent condition for the analyst, while Winnicott's advice against premature interpretations was in order not to interrupt 'the significant silence or quiet period'. With the concept of the analyst's intention, however, Winnicott introduces a state of mind that is not intermittent. It does not come into play only in certain episodes or at certain times in the analysis; it is at work all the time. In this way, it is the counterpart of Bion's rejection of memory and desire. However, it describes the analyst's attitude from a positive rather than a negative point of view. While Bion's exclusion of memory and desire represents 'subject destroys object',

Winnicott answering it with the analyst's intention represents 'object survives destruction'.

It is important to understand that this is not a criticism of Bion. Subject destroying object and object surviving destruction are part of a process. Both are necessary in order to make it possible to use the object. This process is never completed, in the sense of arriving at an end-point that means it can stop happening (Abram, 2022: 43). The 'Use of an Object' paper shows this in regard to the way a patient makes use of the analyst: for a patient to go on using the analyst, the patient has to go on destroying the analyst and the analyst has to go on surviving. Winnicott has the subject saying to the object:

> I love you. You have value for me because of your survival of my destruction of you. While I am loving you I am all the time destroying you in (unconscious) *fantasy*.
>
> (1971: 90)

He says the same, in distinguishing this kind of destruction from the destructiveness of anger:

> *There is no anger* in the destruction of the object to which I am referring, though there could be said to be joy at the object's survival. From this moment, or arising out of this phase, the object is *in fantasy* always being destroyed.
>
> (1971: 93)

It is the survival of the object that keeps the destruction at the level of fantasy. This is what Winnicott's italics emphasise. The object may fail to survive. An analyst might be unable to tolerate a patient's attacks, and retaliate; with a cruel interpretation, perhaps, or by forgetting to be there for a session. Then the analyst has failed to survive as an analytic object, and the destruction has succeeded. It is no longer at the level of fantasy, and this will have to be addressed in the analysis. Provided the object survives, though, it can go on being destroyed 'in (unconscious) *fantasy*'. In that case, Winnicott says,

> This quality of 'always being destroyed' makes the reality of the surviving object felt as such, strengthens the feeling-tone, and contributes to object-constancy. The object can now be used.
>
> (1971: 93)

When Winnicott, in his letter to Bion, introduces the idea of the analyst's intention, he leaves open what the nature of the analyst's intention might be. The 'Use of an Object' paper, that he was working on at the time, makes it clear that the analyst's intention is to survive; and to survive as an analytic object that can be used by the patient.

To be an analyst for his patients was, of course, Bion's intention too. The problem with memory and desire for him was that they got in the way of what he meant by psychoanalysis. Here is an example from the recording of his Negative Capability paper that illustrates this clearly.

> I think that this was brought home to me, really, by a very severely disturbed patient who I recognised was constantly stimulating me to try to think what he had said, or I had said, on some previous occasion, and to stimulate me to want to cure him, or do something or other for him, other than psychoanalysis. And this is where one gets into difficulties because it is so difficult to avoid feeling that really one wants to do something for one's patients and so on.

It would be easy to say that my comments on Bion 'destroying psychoanalysis', and on Winnicott's 'intention' as a counter to Bion's rejection of memory and desire, are misplaced and fail to recognise Bion's commitment to psychoanalysis. That would miss the point I am trying to make. In this brief vignette Bion shows that holding on to what he considered an analytic position involved exactly the process Winnicott describes in 'The Use of an Object'. *Subject destroys object*: the patient destroys Bion as an analytic object by getting him to try to remember things or to cure him. *Object survives destruction*: the patient's destruction of the object remains at the level of (unconscious) fantasy, because Bion refuses to look for memories or feel a desire to do something for the patient. *Subject can use object*: this makes it possible for the patient to go on using Bion in the way he wanted to be used as an analyst.

The important question then becomes whether the patient has, or will be able to find, the capacity to use Bion in this way. For Winnicott the idea of 'capacity' was crucial. To find life real and worth living, he said, depends on a capacity for experience (see above pp. 140–141). In the 'Use of an Object' he writes: 'To use an object the subject must have developed a *capacity* to use objects' (1971: 89). I asked earlier what is the most important object for analysts to be able to use. The 'being able' is what matters. To rephrase the question: what object above all must analysts have the capacity to use? Again, the answer has to be psychoanalysis itself. How are they to develop this capacity? On a small scale, there is a lesson in this vignette of Bion's. On a larger scale, Winnicott's letter to Bion has sent me on an extended, free-associative field trip. It started with needing to let go of anchorages; it arrives back not far from there, with the understanding that psychoanalysis has to be continually destroyed, and continually survive, in order to be continually made use of.

Because Winnicott invested himself so personally in his analytic thinking, he resonated strongly with other analysts who did the same. Marion Milner, with whom he had a close connection, is an outstanding example (Parsons, 2000: 23–34). Bion was another whose own psychic life was closely bound up with his psychoanalytic ideas (Brown, 2012; Roper, 2012). It is a further reason for Winnicott to have recognised him as a kindred spirit. Playing occupied different places in their respective psychoanalytic imaginations. This unpacking of Winnicott's letter, though, has shown how they played together—perhaps not always consciously—to open up the orthodoxies they had inherited and rethink psychoanalysis for the next generation.

Note

1 'Catastrophic Change' as it was prepublished in the British Society's *Bulletin* appears in Bion's *Complete Works* vol. 6 (Bion, 2014: 27–43). 'Container and contained transformed', Chapter 12 of *Attention and Interpretation* (Bion, 1970: 106–124), is an amended version of the paper. Bion's paper on 'Negative Capability' has never been published (see p. 141).

References

Abram, J., ed. (2013). DWW's notes for the Vienna Congress 1971. In *Donald Winnicott Today*, ed. Abram, J. London: Routledge, pp. 302–330.

Abram, J. (2022). *The Surviving Object: Psychoanalytic Clinical Essays on Psychic Survival-of-the-Object*. Routledge: London and New York.

Archive. The British Psychoanalytical Society Archive, GB, BPASA.

Bell, D. L. (2011). Bion: The phenomenologist of loss. In *Bion Today*, ed. Mawson, C. London: Routledge, pp. 81–101.

Bion, W. R. (1966). Catastrophic change. *Bulletin of the British Psychoanalytical Society*, no. 5: 13–25.

Bion, W. R. (1967). Notes on memory and desire. *Psychoanalytic Forum*, 2: 272–273, 279–280. Reprinted in *Cogitations*, London: Karnac, 1992, pp. 380–385.

Bion, W. R. (1970) *Attention and Interpretation: A Scientific Approach to Insight in Psycho-Analysis and Groups*. Reprinted in *Seven Servants*. New York: Aronson, 1977.

Bion, W. R. (2014). *The Complete Works of W.R. Bion*, ed. Mawson C., vol. 6. London: Karnac.

Brown, L. J. (2012). Bion's discovery of alpha function: thinking under fire on the battlefield and in the consulting room. *International Journal of Psychoanalysis*, 93: 1191–1214.

Eigen, M. (1996). *Psychic Deadness*. Northvale, New Jersey: Aronson.

Eliot, T. S. (1920). Tradition and the individual talent. In *The Sacred Wood*, pp. 42–53. London: Methuen, 1920.

Eliot, T. S. (1923). *The Waste Land*. London: Hogarth.

Freud, S. (1925). Negation. *Standard Edition* 19:235–239.

Freud, S. (1972). *Sigmund Freud and Lou Andreas Salome: Letters*, ed. Pfeiffer, E. London: Chatto & Windus/International Psychoanalytic Library.

Graves, R. & Podro, J. (1953). *The Nazarene Gospel Restored*. London: Cassell.

Green, A. (1992) *Cogitations*, by W. R. Bion. *International Journal of Psychoanalysis*, 73: 585–589.

Klein, M. (1957). *Envy and Gratitude: A Study of Unconscious Sources*. London: Hogarth.

Ogden, T. (2016). Destruction reconceived: On Winnicott's 'The use of an object and relating through identifications'. *The International Journal of Psychoanalysis*, 97: 1243–1262.

Ohi, T. (1997). *History of Ohi Ware*. Kanazawa: Ohi Museum.

Parsons, M. (2000). *The Dove that Returns, The Dove that Vanishes: Paradox and Creativity in Psychoanalysis*. London: Routledge.

Parsons, M. (2014). *Living Psychoanalysis: From Theory to Experience*. London: Routledge.

Parsons, M. (2024). Freud and the two Michelangelos. *Psychoanalytic Inquiry*, 44: 358–368.

Rodman, F. R. (2003). *Winnicott: Life and Work*. Cambridge: Perseus.

Roper, M. (2012). Beyond containing: World War I and the psychoanalytic theories of Wilfred Bion. In *History and Psyche: Culture, Psychoanalysis and the Past*, ed. Alexander, S. and Taylor, B. London: Palgrave Macmillan, 129–147.

Winnicott, D. W. (1964). Memories, Dreams, Reflections: by C.G. Jung. *International Journal of Psychoanalysis*, 45: 450–455. Reprinted in *Psychoanalytic Explorations*, London: Karnac, 1989: 482–492.

Winnicott, D. W. (1965) *The Maturational Processes and the Facilitating Environment: Studies in the Theory of Emotional Development*. London: Hogarth.

Winnicott, D. W. (1969). James Strachey – 1887–1967. *The International Journal of Psychoanalysis*, 50: 129–131. Reprinted in *Psychoanalytic Explorations*, pp. 506–510.

Winnicott, D. W. (1971). *Playing and Reality*. London: Tavistock.

Winnicott, D. W. (1975) *Through Paediatrics to Psychoanalysis*. London: Hogarth.

Winnicott, D. W. (1987). *The Spontaneous Gesture: Selected letters of D.W. Winnicott*, ed. Rodman, F. R. Cambridge MA and London: Harvard University Press.

Winnicott, C. (1989). D.W.W.: A reflection. In *Psychoanalytic Explorations*, ed. Winnicott, D. W., 1989, pp. 1–18. London: Karnac.

Winnicott, D. W. (1989). *Psychoanalytic Explorations*. London: Karnac.

13 Winnicott and Bion

Communicating and Not Communicating[1]

Bruce Reis

Introduction

My thesis for this chapter will be speculative. I assert that in the complicated context of the British Psychoanalytic Society at the time, D.W. Winnicott and W.R. Bion, shared a fractured and indirect dialogue around psychoanalytic topics. This unusual dialogue occurred during a time of the growing ascendency of the Kleinian school within the Society that complicated what might have otherwise been a straightforward conversation between these key figures. Winnicott's (1963) paper "Communicating and Not Communicating Leading to a Study of Certain Opposites" (C&NC) I suggest, was in part, his indirect communication with Bion.

Context

Winnicott presented his paper "Anxiety Related to Insecurity" to the British Society on November 5, 1952. Already the Society was deeply influenced by the work of Melanie Klein; and she, as well as many of her supporters were in the audience for the presentation. Winnicott had been much influenced by Klein but began to bridle against the predominance of the Kleinian approach within the Institute. Joona Taipale (2021, pp. 35–36) well describes the scene:

> Kleinian thinking had established a strong position at the Society: Klein had released many of her most influential publications, her ideas were frequently discussed at the meetings, she had numerous devoted followers, and her conceptualizations and theorizations were increasingly becoming the language that the presenters at the Society were expected to be using when conveying their thoughts to the audience.

Winnicott, of course, did not state his own ideas in a Kleinian language; and on November 17, 1952 he wrote to Klein expressing the importance for him of remaining true to his own expression of psychoanalytic

DOI: 10.4324/9781003502067-13

thought. In a self-deprecating fashion that characterizes many of his letters he wrote:

> I can see how annoying it is that when something develops in me out of my own growth and out of my analytic experience I want to put it in my own language. This is annoying because I suppose everyone wants to do the same thing, and in a scientific society one of our aims is to find a common language. This language must, however, be kept alive as there is nothing worse than a dead language… What I was wanting…was that there should be some move from your direction towards the gesture that I make in this paper. It is a creative gesture and I cannot make any relationship through this gesture except if someone come to meet it…I feel that corresponding to my wish to say things my way there is something from your end, namely a need to have everything that is new restated in your own terms.
>
> (Rodman, 1987, p. 34)

After referring to his own theorizing as a "creative gesture" he critiques the popularity of "Kleinism" within the Society and particularly among Mrs. Klein's supporters. He does so in a manner that is not always respectful to the way in which her ideas were being used (though he manages the tact of mostly holding himself back from critiquing her directly) and calls upon Mrs. Klein to "destroy this language called the Kleinian doctrine…" (p. 35). Not surprisingly, Winnicott's plea to Mrs. Klein was not taken up, though Klein was careful to not publicly criticize Winnicott and privately, Taipale (2021) reports, based on his own research, that there is no record of her having responded to this letter. Taipale (2021, p. 36) describes

> Winnicott made a statement in his own way, hoping that the scholarly environment would play along, as it were, but instead he was advised to curb, moderate and modify his creative impulses and to comply to what was there already.

At the very end of the letter, we see what its most prescient passage may be. Winnicott writes of his own "difficulty" and his own "illness," which I take to mean his need to re-write others thought in his own language, a subject of this letter, and of his larger work around issues of compliance and creativity. He writes:

> This matter which I am discussing touches the very root of my own personal difficulty so that what you see can always be dismissed as Winnicott's illness, but if you dismiss it in this way you may miss something which is in the end a positive contribution. My illness is

something which I can deal with in my own way and it is not far away from being the inherent difficulty in regard to human contact with external reality.

(p. 37)

Indeed there may be something to Winnicott's diagnosis of this problem in himself as evidenced by his redefinition of many Kleinian conceptualizations, for example, omnipotence as understood within the Kleinian scheme, compared to a diametrically opposed conceptualization of omnipotence in his own thought.

Winnicott was preoccupied by his opposition to the Kleinian movement in the British Society and his concerns about the long-term implications of Kleinism, as reflected in his letters to Segal, Money-Kyrle, Rosenfeld, and others in the years following this letter to Mrs. Klein.

Bion and Winnicott: Similarities and Dissimilarities

The personal histories of Bion and Winnicott, as many have noted, share some interesting intersections. While Winnicott was raised with eight women taking care of him and a depressed mother and a neglectful and rigid father (Rodman, 2003); Bion grew up largely without his parents, having been sent at the age of eight to school in England while his parents stayed in India. As Vermote (2019) observes both men were the products of the Edwardian school system, with Bion attending boarding school near Oxford and Winnicott in Cambridge. Both subsequently attended medical school, Bion in London and Winnicott at Cambridge. Both were enthusiastically involved in sports and both volunteered to serve in World War I, Winnicott in the British Royal Navy, and Bion in the Tank Corps. And both men remarried in 1951, Bion after the death of his first wife. Winnicott after divorce from his first wife of 20 years. Vermote (2019, p. 21) writes:

Both were typically British upper-middle-class gentlemen and shared the same British humour and irony. Winnicott had a lively style and was experienced by some as a bit effeminate partly due to his high-pitched voice, while Bion was tall and had an athletic, austere, even somewhat military outlook. Winnicott was a playful man wearing nice suits...and driving an oldtimer two-seat Rolls Royce, while Bion was remote. In studying their work I have the feeling that Winnicott can be seen as an intuitive poet at heart full of paradoxes in his clinical work and research, while Bion was an art and poetry lover but with a more scientific state of mind in clinical work and writings.

The thesis of my chapter involves the theoretical relationship that Bion and Winnicott shared. Both were prominent members of the British Society and were present for each other's paper presentations there. But while

Winnicott wrote letters to Bion, ostensibly without a response, and while they seldom directly took up each other's work in their own published papers, I speculate that Bion and Winnicott were in conversation with each other through their published work; that each influenced the other and reacted to the other, while developing their own idiomatic theoretical systems. I find Winnicott's (1963) paper "Communicating and Not Communicating Leading to a Study of Certain Opposites" to be a particularly representative paper as regards the communication between Bion and Winnicott I propose to have occurred.

Winnicott himself may have been only partially aware that his writing of this paper was a part of his dialogue with Bion and the Kleinian school. At the very beginning of the paper, he contrasts his understanding of his discovery within himself of his "right to not communicate" with what he supposes a Kleinian would make of such a claim ("in another language") suggesting that, immediately, his thoughts regarding his own contribution are compared to Kleinian thought. Perhaps more tellingly as will be described below with reference to Bion, Winnicott writes within the paper

> …it is more difficult for an analyst to be original than for anyone else, because everything that we say truly has been taught us yesterday, <u>apart from the fact that we listen to each other's papers</u> and discuss matters privately" (emphasis added).

It is of particular interest that Winnicott writes "listens to" rather than "reads."

Winnicott the Gatherer and Bion the Colonialist

While Winnicott and Bion shared similarities in their backgrounds one important difference between them concerns how each of them "used" others. Winnicott, it could be said was sensitive to the role of the other in helping to develop or release one's own idiom; whereas Bion, it could be said concentrated on making usable his own productions once they have been given meaning by another. Both men made use of the conceptions of others, but the ways in which they did so reflect a great deal about their personalities. Winnicott creatively elaborated existing ideas based on intuitions that arose in clinical interactions without any claim as to whether or not his elaborations were true to the original source. Bion appropriated ideas, altered their meanings while presenting them as true to their source.

As I illustrate below, Winnicott "gathered" and even "stole" ideas to make them his own while Bion co-opted other's ideas, colonizing them so as to purpose these ideas for his ends.

In Winnicott's *Primitive Emotional Development* (1945, p. 145) Winnicott writes of how his ideas are shaped by those of others "I gather this and that, here and there, settle down to clinical experience, form my own theories and then, last of all, interest myself in looking to see where I stole what." Goldman (2025) notes that Winnicott's idea about language as "indirect" may have been his creative elaboration, following his reading of Ella Freeman Sharpe's (1940) "Psycho-Physical Problems Revealed in Language: an examination of metaphor" although that paper is not cited as an influence. Winnicott clearly drew upon various sources such as the Romantic poets, British empiricists, Lewis Carroll, Darwin, the fourteenth-century Lollards, and John Wesley (Goldman 1993; 2012). The difference is that while Winnicott uses other's ideas to shape his own, Bion adopts other's ideas and changes them to suit his aims. Indeed, I would call the approach "colonial," consistent with Bion's upbringing, to take the idea, and make it his own (e.g., his conceptions of intuition, or faith, the unconscious, dreaming). This is one way to regard his colonization of Winnicott's ideas regarding mother-infant nonverbal communication in infancy and casting them in his Kleinian frame; repackaging Winnicott's primary maternal preoccupation as maternal reverie (Bion, 1962).

In addition to the analytic theories Bion drew upon and innovated upon (e.g., Freudian, Kleinian) he also adopted ideas from mathematicians, scientists, philosophers, Christian mystics, poets, and writers. Hinshelwood and Torres (2013) provide a partial list in their recent volume Bion's sources; including but not limited to Henri Bergson and Alfred North Whitehead's work on metaphysics and process philosophy; Kurt Lewin's work on a "social field of forces" within groups; philosopher R.B. Braithwaite's work on the philosophy of science; Jung's conception of container-contained; Henri Poincare's notion of the selected fact; Milton's concept of the void and the formless infinite; the Christian mystical tradition of Meister Eckhart and St. John of the Cross; the work of writers such as Joyce and Pound; Keats's "negative capability"; and Kant's philosophy of the "thing-in-itself."[2]

We tend to ignore the question of whether Bion's use of these ideas remains faithful to their original intent. Yet in an important chapter from the book Bion's sources (Hinshelwood & Torres, 2013) philosopher Kelly Noel-Smith (2013) takes up problematic aspects of Bion's adoption of Kant's work, and the widespread assumption "that Bion understood Kant and used Kant's terms correctly" (p. 135). To the contrary, she suggests, Bion "misappropriates certain key Kantian terms, even when claiming a direct analogy between his use of the term psychoanalytically and Kant's use of the same term philosophically" (p. 135). Noel-Smith's reading conflicts with such assumptions, and perhaps reveals Bion's (mis)understanding of these issues, as reflected in a quotation she employs from Bion:

> The use I make of an existing theory may seem to distort the author's meaning; if I think so I have acknowledged it, but otherwise it is to be assumed that I believe I am interpreting the author's theory correctly.

It would represent serious difficulties in psychoanalytic theory construction were Bion's understandings of some of the key terms he employs from other disciplines applied incorrectly by him. For instance, if Bion's explicit use of Kantian terms such as "things-in-themselves" or "empty thoughts" are not what Kant meant by using these terms; and if Bion's concept of O may not correspond to Kant's conception of the "thing-in-itself" as Bion suggested it did; and in addition, if this were the case for terms taken from other disciplines too, then it would be very difficult to know what Bion was actually talking about.

Attempts to Directly Communicate

In 1954, Winnicott developed the conception of holding, its importance in normal development, and in clinical work with "patients whose analyses must deal with the early stages of emotional development before and up to the establishment of the personality as an entity" (Winnicott, 1955, p. 17). The emphasis was on patients who needed to establish a sense of a self instead of resolve internal conflict. This paper, later published (1955) as Metapsychological and clinical aspects of regression within the psychoanalytical set-up, Hinshelwood (2018, p. 203) notes was "read in March 1954, just 18 months prior to Bion's paper on this same differentiation [of the psychotic from the non-psychotic personalities], read in October 1955 (although published in 1957)." Given the modifications Bion made to what arguably started as Winnicott's ideas we can easily agree with Hinshelwood conclusion that "…certain aspects of Winnicott's core theories, as he developed these independently of Klein from 1945, were being taken by the Kleinians and put back into their concepts" (pp. 203–204).

In October of 1955 Winnicott wrote to Bion, praising him as "the big man of the future in the British Psycho-Analytical Society" (p. 89) and urging him to leave the confines of the Kleinian group in order to "emerge as President of the whole Society" (p. 90). This letter follows Bion's presentation of a paper to the British Society that would later be published as Differentiation of the Psychotic from the Non-Psychotic Personalities (Bion, 1957). At the beginning of his paper Bion makes clear that he will focus his discussion on "mechanisms" in the personalities of individuals who develop schizophrenia and will not discuss any role the environment could play. He describes a patient who, after arriving 15 minutes late for his appointment, turned from side to side on the couch. Eventually the patient said "I don't suppose I shall do anything today. I ought to have rung up my mother." The patient paused and then said "No; I thought it would be like this." A longer pause ensued and then "Nothing but filthy things and smells, I think I've lost my sight" (Bion, 1957, p. 270). Bion associated the patient's movements to a motor discharge of stimuli and acknowledged that his statements regarding his mother left him "in the dark" (p. 271) though he does go on to associate to what little he feels he knows about the patient's mother to suppose her "bringing up of her children was ignorant and painstaking in the extreme" (p. 271). Aguayo (2018) notes that Winnicott called out Bion on his implicitly talking about "environment" even though he said we would not do so. More importantly for my purposes, the disagreement between these men centered on the issue of communication, and Winnicott's suggestion that the patient's movement on the couch followed by his feeling he ought to have called his mother represented an opportunity for an interpretation on the subject of the difficulties the patient experiences in making a communication. In his letter he then offers Bion what he would have said to such a patient:

> A mother properly oriented to her baby would know from your movements what you need. There would be a communication from your movements what you need. There would be a communication because of this knowledge which belongs to her devotion and she would do something which would show that the communication had taken place. I am not sensitive enough or oriented in that way to be able to act well enough and therefore I in this present analytic situation fall into the category of the mother who failed to make communication possible. In the present relationship therefore there is given a sample of the original failure from the environment which contributed to your difficulty in communication. Of course you could always cry and so draw attention to need. In the same way you could telephone your mother and get a reply but this represents a failure of the more subtle communication which is the only basis for communication that does not violate the fact of the essential isolation of each individual.
>
> (Rodman, p. 91)

Winnicott drives home his point about communication by repeating the word seven times in this short paragraph. We might indeed say that his efforts against Kleinism was something of an "illness" or a "personal difficulty" for him as it seems he could not put down this cause, but repeated it again and again, so that when it shows up in his letter(s) to Bion, it is by this time his well-established position/complaint. Again, we witness what appears to be Winnicott's naivete in writing to Bion, the analysand of Mrs. Klein and a loyal ally to her at the time[3]; and again we see Winnicott building up Bion with praise as he is simultaneously critical of him for his association to the Kleinian group, in a manner similar to his earlier letter to Mrs. Klein herself.

Winnicott's letter to Bion of October 1955 suggests to him that his patient was attempting to communicate with the analyst in a manner both verbal and nonverbal; and that Winnicott may have responded with a recognition of the patient's movements that spoke to the need being expressed to a mother who would receive the communication and respond to it out her state of "ordinary devotion."[4] Mancia (2023, p. 277) notes …"in the writings that followed the paper read on October fifth—beginning with

"On Arrogance" (1957) – Bion deepens his interest in the patient's communicative intentions, the analyst's receptive capacity, and the mother's original failure to receive the child's modes of communication."

According to Hinshelwood (2023, p. 67) in 1955 Bion was among a group of analysts beginning to consider whether projective identification may also take a communicative form; and he became "very interested in the method of communication between baby and mother, which is clearly not language" (Hinshelwood, p. 74). In 1959, Bion developed his model of container-contained, which would become integral to his clinical technique. Bion considered this to be "a direct, non-symbolic form of communication typical of early infancy" (Hinshelwood, 2023, p. 68). Bion writes:

> From the infant's point of view she should have taken into her, and thus experienced, the fear that the child was dying. It was this fear that the child could not contain. He strove to split it off together with the part of the personality in which it lay and project it into the mother. An understanding mother is able to experience the feeling of dread that this baby was striving to deal with by projective identification and yet retain a balanced outlook.
>
> (Bion, 1959, pp. 312–313)

Applying this model to adult treatment Bion writes:

> When the patient strove to rid himself of fears of death, which were felt to be too powerful for his personality to contain he split off his fears and put them into me, the idea apparently being that if they were allowed to repose there long enough they would undergo modification by my psyche and could then be safely reintrojected.
>
> (Bion, 1959, p. 312)

I hear an echo in the first quote from Bion of Winnicott's having written to him of "a mother properly oriented to her baby" and in the second quote of a mother who would do something in response to the infant's distress.

In October 1964 the philosopher John Wisdom, who was involved with psychoanalytic ideas, presented a paper at the British Society on innovations contained in the work of Bion. Winnicott attended this paper presentation, and while he remained silent during the question and answer period, he wrote to Wisdom shortly thereafter. In that letter Winnicott again built up Bion, while complaining that the parallels to his own contributions had been "scotomized" in Wisdom's presentation; and Winnicott comes as close as he ever had to openly asserting the value of his own work vis a vis Bion's. It is not Bion he takes to task however, but it is the "terrific opposition" of Melanie Klein and failure of Wisdom in his role as reporter. He writes to Wisdom, "You related Bion's work to Freud and Klein which is the important thing. But *in your role of commentator* you do need to relate his work to contemporaries, including me" (p. 144, original italics). In his letter he lays claim to conceptions Wisdom praises Bion for employing – of tantalizing objects, reverie, as introduced into the lexicon by Marion Milner and utilized by Winnicott as a conception of creating something (i.e., symbolic realization) in the mother-infant dyad (via primary maternal preoccupation) and in adult therapy; and for the notion of "what happens depends...." Of the latter Winnicott writes that "Melanie Klein absolutely would not allow this, and my relation to her was (though always warm and good) impaired by her adamant objection to "what happens depends..." (p. 145)".

According to Caldwell (2018, p. 222) a search of the Collected Works of both Bion and Winnicott "...does indeed confirm that Bion ignores Winnicott except for some dismissive references, while [Winnicott's work] contains frequent references to Bion that directly attempt to engage with his work...." Aguayo (personal communication) observes that in the handful of citations to Winnicott's work, Bion sounds rather sarcastic and contemptuous, making clear that the former's ideas are not for him. Indeed, his derision of Winnicott's ideas appears to me intentional as when in the Tavistock Seminars (June 28, 1976) he states

> To get back to the psychoanalytic view: it is quite useful to talk about 'transference' and 'countertransference'. Or, as Winnicott puts it, the transitory object; it is in transition, from goodness knows where to goodness knows what, from oblivion to amnesia....
>
> (Bion, CW, 9:10)

Communicating and Not Communicating

In the paper <u>Communicating and Not Communicating Leading to a Study of Certain Opposites</u>, Winnicott (1963) once again takes up the issue of infant-caretaker nonverbal communication, making it central to the theme of the paper. He presents an earlier version the paper in 1962 in San Francisco, prior to its publication. Goldberg (2021 p. 453) conjectures

> Perhaps the prospect of an audience still relatively unfamiliar with his work was itself appealing: presenting groundbreaking ideas to an American audience might have seemed less constraining and intimidating than trying to find a receptive ear among London analysts already deeply invested as stakeholders in their intracommunal struggles over psychoanalytic truth.

While discussing the development of an infant's capacity to use symbols, Winnicott describes language as a form of "indirect communication." Thus symbolic communication is subtly placed in contrast with and perhaps secondary to what he calls direct communication or communication not involving the use of symbols that is "<u>for ever silent</u>" (original emphasis, p. 188). For Winnicott direct communication paradoxically involves silence, and simple going on being as <u>healthy</u> forms of communication. Parenthetically it is of note that approximately during the same period Khan presented a paper entitled "Silence as Communication" at the Menninger Clinic, published later that same year in the Bulletin of the Menninger Clinic and subsequently in the book Privacy of the Self (1963), suggesting that Khan and Winnicott were discussing these matters.

Winnicott's development of the idea of healthy direct communication and non-communication may be read as a response to Bion's having taken Winnicott's insights regarding mother-infant communication and recasting them within a Kleinian understanding as a form of projective identification. Hinshelwood's observation that Bion around the mid to late 1950s became "very interested in the method of communication between baby and mother, which is clearly not language" (Hinshelwood, 2023 p. 74) and his development of the technical model of container-contained around the idea of "a direct, non-symbolic form of communication typical of early infancy" (Hinshelwood, 2023, p. 68) would seem to support at least in part his use of such notions from Winnicott's work, especially given that Bion, in a broader sense, was not particularly interested in basing his analytic scheme in a paradigm of mother-infant relatedness.

In C&NC Winnicott also emphasizes the importance of the analyst's holding open the possibility for "the patient's non-communicating as a positive contribution" (p. 188) and differentiates a healthy non-communicating from a refusal to communicate. I read these formulations as pertaining to the lack of response he received from both Klein and Bion to the letters he sent them. Perhaps this is Winnicott's "doing something with" the refusal of Klein and Bion to communicate. Indeed, much of the section of the paper under the sub-heading "Opposites" (of communication) may be read as critique of Kleinian understanding and practice – for example, in writing of the dangers of interpreting with patients "instead of waiting for the patient to creatively discover"[5] (p. 189).

Furthermore, if Communicating and not Communicating is read as a dialogue with Klein and Bion then we can understand Winnicott's emphasis in this paper on subjective objects to be a statement in contrast to Klein's idea of the infant having distinct objects from birth; and his emphasis on the "feeling of real" as a very personal creation to be in contrast to her conception of "reality" as external and objective.

At the same time, Winnicott's emphasis on direct communication may be taken to have to do with an experience of the individual around issues of being (and becoming). In a rather remarkable sentence toward the end of this paper Winnicott writes: "In the development of the individual infant living arises and established itself out of not-living, and being becomes a fact that replaces not-being as communication arises out of silence." The sentence is situated in a paragraph that recasts Klein's (and Freud's) ideas regarding life and death instincts. Here Winnicott replaces these terms with "being" and "non-being," which he also uses to open up the terms "deadness" and "absence of liveliness" to a more phenomenological use. We should keep in mind that the sentence above is particularly relevant to what Winnicott calls in this paper "cull-de-sac" communication or communication with subjective objects, that is, not necessarily communication with actual others; which highlights the point that for Winnicott the importance of the presence of the object was not for "relationship" but to facilitate a developmental process of growth for the individual (Winnicott, 1958).

The remarkable sentence is followed by another just a few paragraphs later: "In healthy development the infant (theoretically) starts off (psychologically) without life and becomes lively simply because of being, in fact, alive." This appears to be a very early idea of the birth of the human pre-subject – born without psychological life and gradually becoming alive (psychologically). It also appears highly related to Winnicott's way of working analytically. Here Winnicott links silence, and silent communication with the development of the individual. The function of this communication is not evacuative as it may be for a Kleinian, or even transformative (of mental content) as it may be for a Bionian, but as the ground for becoming that is associated with the experience of real, and liveliness: "To be alive is all" writes Winnicott.

There is one more point that bears considering before moving on. If, as I've suggested, C&NC is a paper in which Winnicott is in dialogue with Klein and Bion, then what are we to make of his introduction of the issue of subjective objects that must have no contact with externality; objects that carry all the sense of real? Winnicott built his theoretical challenge to the dominance of Kleinism by insisting on the real external object. So how are we to understand that in this paper he would seem to afford what one might think of as an internal object so much importance? We might read this as another, less appreciated innovation of Winnicott's, in the sense that by rejecting the Kleinian distinction between an inner and outer world at birth he is not putting the subjective object experience "inside" the infant as a facet of its inner world. Rather the experience of the world is continuously created beyond the dichotomous frame of internal or external. Furthermore, he considers this condition something the individual does not leave behind in development. Winnicott considers it operational throughout life and accords it significant importance as a sort of "balance" to the demands of false or compliant object-relating. He writes:

> I am postulating that in the healthy (mature, that is, in respect of the development of object-relating) person there is a need for something that corresponds to the state of the split person in whom one part of the split communicates silently with subjective objects.

> (p. 184)

Winnicott therefore not only rejects the internal/external dichotomy at the beginning of life, he also suggests there to be a certain danger to that dichotomy in the experience of the mature individual.

Influence, Collaboration, Collegial Love, and Rivalry

The 1950s and 1960s had the flavor of a gold rush within the British Society as analysts vied to theorize early infantile life in their own terms. Within this setting there existed rivalry, but also collaboration and…love. While Winnicott felt unrecognized by Klein and Bion for his contributions his relationship with other colleagues was quite different. For instance, Margaret Spelman (2023) called the relationship between Winnicott and Marion Milner one of "collegial friendship and love" (p. 19), noting there existed a "thinking environment of the pair's friendship" (p. 21) in which was found "reciprocity" (p. 21). James Anderson (1981), a psychoanalyst and psycho-biographer reports that Marion Milner described their "last communication" to him thus:

I'll tell you something. The last communication I had with him. I had a student in training who was in supervision with him. And – he shouldn't have done it, of course – he sent a message to me via the student: Tell her, 'it doesn't matter which of us thinks of it.' Because I can't tell you. Do you see what I mean?…there was a lot of interchange when we talked. You couldn't say which of us had a thought of something (sic).

On July 10, 1967 Winnicott again wrote to Bion upon learning of his intention to move to California:

I have been told, of course, about your proposal to leave England in the new year and to spend a few years in Los Angeles. This will be very good for Los Angeles and I think you may do a really good job there. The trouble is, however, that we shall miss you a very great deal in this country. Your position here and your personality in what you stand for in the work is of the very greatest importance to us and we can ill afford to lose you.

In this case, there is record of Bion having replied:

Dear Winnicott, many thanks for your kind letter and generous remarks. Francesca and I both look forward, with some trepidation… Naturally we hope good will come of it; what it costs to uproot from all our friends and associates here is painfully obvious but we shall have to wait to see what the compensating…may be—and hope. With all good wishes to Clare and yourself from Francesca and me.

(quoted in Rodman, 2003, pp. 313–314)

Not long after, Winnicott again wrote Bion, on October 5, 1967, on the occasion of Bion's having presented his paper on "Negative Capability" at the Institute. Winnicott no longer offers him obsequious complements. He writes that his wife Clare reminds Winnicott that in invoking the terms "memory" and "desire" Bion is quoting T.S. Eliot, suggesting that Bion did not make the attribution himself in his talk or previously when Winnicott had heard Bion use these terms; and that she supplies him with "the whole poem" (p. 169). Reeves (2010) notes Winnicott's well-attested predilection for Eliot's Four Quartets, writing of the

> ...immense emotional significance the poem came to hold for him. It seemed to enshrine certain key insights he had independently arrived at...affording them imaginative expression in a way that seems in turn to have released his own creative and aesthetic sensibilities.
>
> (p. 383)

Reeves suggests Eliot's work is explicitly and unconsciously used by Winnicott throughout his writing, including in the paper C&NC.

By the mid to late 1960s both men had continued their conversation into new areas, such as what it means to search for or discover the unknown. Most notable is how far they had ventured from the Kleinian influence of their earlier years. Vermote (2019, p. 24) writes:

> Bion advocated an attitude of no memory, no desire, no understanding, no coherence in order to get in contact with the unknown O of a psychic experience and to facilitate a transformation in O. In his much-discussed paper 'The use of an Object and Relating though Identifications', Winnicott (1969) suggested silence and not giving clever interpretations to allow the patient to discover the yet unknown real object once he had been able to destroy his transference illusions.

Perhaps it was in part due to reading C&NC that led Bion into the mystic, drawing on St. John of the Cross and Meister Eckhart, and developing Milner's notion of reverie as a method of finding emotional truths. Winnicott comments in C&NC, in what seems almost an aside, that is apropos of nothing,

> In thinking of the psychology of mysticism, it is unusual to concentrate on the understanding of the mystic's withdrawal into a personal inner world of sophisticated introjects. Perhaps not enough attention has been paid to the mystic's retreat to a position in which he can communicate secretly with subjective objects and phenomena, the loss of contact with the world of shared reality being counterbalanced by a gain in terms of feeling real.
>
> (pp. 185–186)

What was Bion's reaction to having read this in Winnicott's 1965 paper?

Perhaps the conversation I am speculating took place between Winnicott and Bion also extends to their clinical approaches to the issue of Being. Winnicott was fascinated by the issue, which comprises a large and important part of C&NC, but which also extends throughout his work (Abram, 1996). Where Winnicott was writing of the experience of formlessness at the core of the incommunicado self, an experience that was deeply personal and beyond knowing, Bion, adopting the clinical position of reverie and of not (already) knowing would write of entering states of mind without memory or desire to clear his consciousness so that he may gain knowledge of something formless, thinking of this as an ultimately uncommunicable "truth" in a fashion not dissimilar to the way Winnicott would think of communication with subjective objects as "carrying all the sense of real." These issues around what's real and true were linked for Winnicott to a fundamental mystery at the heart of communication. As Ogden (2018) observed, Winnicott explored in C&NC "what we cannot conceive of, much less put into words, the experience at the core of our being." One needn't be a mystic, nor is an elaborate metapsychology needed to encounter this mystery; all that is required for Winnicott is being alive. He writes:

> We have to recognize this aspect of health: the non-communicating central self, for ever immune from the reality principle, and for ever silent. Here communication is not nonverbal; it is, like the music of the spheres, absolutely personal. It belongs to being alive. And in health, it is out of this that communication naturally arises.

Notes

1 I would like to thank Dodi Goldman for his helpful comments on successive versions of this chapter.
2 It is one thing to borrow a term from another discipline, import it into psychoanalysis and change its meaning in doing so (as Bion [1961] did with the term "valency", which he took from physics and made a feature of his approach to groups). However, the effect of doing this not with one term, but with scores of terms, drawn from disparate fields, including some terms that are central conceptions in the theory and practice of psychoanalysis (e.g., unconscious, or dream) has the large-scale effect of transforming psychoanalysis into Bion's psychoanalysis – taking it over by taking over its common language and concepts, refusing dialogue and replacing that with a private language.
3 It is of note that Rodman (2003, p. 314) reports an undated personal communication with Bion, in which Bion tells him "I told Melanie that did not want to be a Kleinian".
4 A state that later is referred to by Winnicott as Primary Maternal Preoccupation.
5 Yet we know for other published material that Winnicott also did not wait to interpret, nor for the patient to creatively discover (e.g., Winnicott, 1970).

References

Abram, J. (1996). The Language of Winnicott: A Dictionary of Winnicott's Use of Words. London: Karnac.

Abram, J. & Hinshelwood, R.D. (2023). The Clinical Paradigms of Donald Winnicott and Wilfred Bion: Comparisons and Dialogues. New York: Routledge.

Aguayo, J. (2018). D.W. Winnicott, Melanie Klein, and W.R. Bion: The Controversy Over the nature of the External Object – Holding and Container/Contained (1941–1967). Psychoanalytic Quarterly, 87, pp. 767–807.

Anderson, W.J. (1981). Unpublished transcript of Anderson's interviews with Marion Milner. Cited in: Spelman, M.B. "Winnicott and Milner – recognizing the legacy of collegial love" Chapter 4 in M.B. Spelman & J. Raphael-Leff (Eds.) The Marion Milner Tradition. New York: Routledge.

Bion, W.R. (1957). Differentiation of the psychotic from the non-psychotic personalities. International Journal of Psychoanalysis, 38: 266–275.

Bion, W.R. (1959). Attacks on Linking. International Journal of Psychoanalysis 40: 308–315. Reprinted in Second Thoughts. London: Heinemann, 1967; Bott Spillius, E. (Ed.) Melanie Klein Today, vol. 1. London: Routledge, 1988. In: the Complete Works of W.R. Bion, vol. 6, pp. 138–152. London: Karnac.

Bion, W.R. (1961). Experiences in Groups. London: Tavistock.

Bion, W.R. (1962) Learning from experience. London: Tavistock.

Caldwell, L. (2018). A Psychoanalysis of Being: An Approach to Donald Winnicott. British Journal of Psychotherapy, 34, 2, pp. 221–239.

Goldberg, P. (2021). "Not Final, Not Complete": Winnicott's Remarkable Presentation on Communication, San Francisco, October 8, 1962. JAPA, 69, 3, pp. 451–468.

Goldman, D. (1993). In Search of the Real: The Origins and Originality of D.W. Winnicott. New Jersey: Jason Aronson.

Goldman, D. (2012) Weaving With the World: Winnicott's Re-Imagining of Reality. Psychoanalytic Quarterly 81, pp. 1–23.

Goldman, D. (2025). A Shimmering Landscape. New York: Routledge..

Hinshelwood, R.D. (2018). Intuition From Beginning to End? Bion's Clinical Approaches. British Journal of Psychotherapy 34, 2, pp. 198–213.

Hinshelwood, R.D. & Torres, N. (2013). Bion's Sources. New York: Routledge.

Hinshelwood, R., Abram, J. (2023). The Clinical Paradigms of Donald Winnicott and Wilfred Bion. New York: Routledge.

Khan, M. (1963). Silence as Communication. In The Privacy of the Self. New York: International University Press, pp. 168–180.

Mancia, M. (2023). A Letter From Winnicott to Bion: An Imaginative Conjecture to Illustrate a Paradigm Transformation. Psychoanalytic Quarterly 92, 2, pp. 263–288.

Noel-Smith, K. (2013). Thoughts, thinking, and the thinker: Bion's philosophical encounter with Kant. In: R.D. Hinshelwood & N. Torres (Eds.) Bion's Sources. New York: Routledge.

Ogden, T.H. (2018). The Feeling of Real: Winnicott's "Communicating and Not Communicating Leading to a Study of Certain Opposites." International Journal of Psychoanalysis, 99, 1288–1304.

Reeves, C. (2010). Redeeming Time: Winnicott, Eliot, and the Four Quartets. American Imago, 67, 3, pp. 375–397.

Rodman, F.R. (1987). The Spontaneous Gesture: Selected Letters of D.W. Winnicott. Cambridge, MA: Harvard University Press.

Rodman, F. R. (2003). Winnicott: Life and Work. Cambridge, MA: Perseus Publishing.

Sharpe, E. F. (1940) Psycho-Physical Problems Revealed in Language: An Examination of Metaphor. International Journal of Psychoanalysis, 21, pp. 201–213.

Spelman, M.B. (2023). Winnicott and Milner – recognizing the legacy of collegial love. In: M.B. Spelman & J. Rapheael-Leff (eds). The Marion Milner Tradition, pp. 19–26.

Taipale, J. (2021). The Illusion of Contact: Insights From Winnicott's 1952 Letter to Klein. International Journal of Psychoanalysis, 102, 1, pp. 31–50.

Vermote, R. (2019). Reading Bion. New York: Routledge.

Winnicott, D.W. (1945). *Primitive Emotional Development*. Reprinted in: *Through Pediatrics to Psychoanalysis*, pp. 145–156. London: Hogarth, 1958, republished 1987.

Winnicott, D.W. (1955). Metapsychological and Clinical Aspects of Regression Within the Psycho-analytical Set-up. International Journal of Psychoanalysis, 36, pp. 16–26. In: The *Collected Works of D.W. Winnicott,* vol. 4, pp. 201–217. Oxford: Oxford University Press.

Winnicott, D. W. (1958). The capacity to be alone. The Maturational Processes and the Facilitating Environment: Studies in the Theory of Emotional Development. Madison, CT: International Universities Press.

Winnicott, D. W. (1963). Communicating and not communicating leading to a study of certain opposites. In: The Maturational Processes and the Facilitating Environment. London: Hogarth Press, 1965, pp. 179–192.

Winnicott, D.W. (1965). Communicating and Not Communicating Leading to a Study of Certain Opposites. International Journal of Psychoanalysis, 64, pp. 179–192.

Winnicott, D.W. (1970). Two further clinical examples. In: T*he Collected Works of D.W. Winnicott*, vol. 9, part 2, article 13, Oxford: Oxford University Press.

14 Holding and Containing

Winnicott, Bion, and Klein on Infancy and the Infantile[1]

Stephen Seligman

Winnicott's letter to Bion of 5 October 1967 (Winnicott, 1964) reflects the subtle differences between his metatheory and Bion's, with the latter's greater loyalty to Kleinian theory. Here, he emphasizes two interrelated points: the salience of external reality and the imperative for an experience of separateness as an essential aspect of psychoanalysis. It follows that analysts should not, and cannot abolish their own experience, including their memories—and by implication, their desires.

> ....The memory includes memories of phenomena from external reality and certainly what is likely to turn up tomorrow in my analytic work cannot be covered by *what I have in my own mind to want* (italics mine), precisely because I have to be able to allow the patient to be a separate person, as the patient has to come to allow me to be outside his or her omnipotent control.
>
> (Winnicott, 1967)

Winnicott's argument about therapeutic action parallels his developmental theory. Indeed, this letter precedes the presentation of "the use of the object" paper by a year, and its outlines are suggested here: the object emerges from the child's omnipotence through its paradoxical destruction/survival (Winnicott, 1969).[2]

More generally, analytic theories' views of development and analytic therapeutic action are usually correlated. This is particularly true for images of infancy and "the infantile." Infancy is taken to reflect what is most basic in human nature before culture has interceded. In most of the established analytic theories, "the infantile," "the primitive," and infancy are closely associated, with all these terms linking to a conception of a kind of original asociality, rooted in the dual instincts, which are cast as emerging from the body, outside of and prior to mental life. Bion follows this, although with greater subtlety than his predecessors Freud and Klein, as he describes a pathway for a kind of progressive transformation in the infant-mother relationship. Winnicott, however, makes a more distinctive break

DOI: 10.4324/9781003502067-14

with those same predecessors, as he begins with the constructive movements of natural growth, activity and imagination.

The term primary usually signifies "that which is most basic," and analytic theories have traditionally associated the temporal priority of infancy (i.e., it comes first) with ontological primacy: infancy is the not only the first stage, but where we find what is most essential. This follows along with the idea that infancy is prior to the integration with, or interposition of, language. The primary is taken as presented in its purest form in infancy, as in "primary process," "primary narcissism," "primary identification," "primary maternal preoccupation," and the like. Further, that which is primary is linked to the primitive, such that regression to infancy is linked to psychosis.

Freud, of course, originated this set of linkages, as he elaborated and buttressed his ideas about the irrationality and boundarilessness at the core of human nature through his images of infantile primary narcissism, "the oceanic feeling," and the baby as living mostly in primary process. Klein moved the field toward infancy as the central metaphor for psychic life as she originated the theory of the originary internal objects. Still, "the Kleinian baby" remained located in the mostly solipsistic world of primitive phantasies and the Death and Life instincts, leading to the initial paranoid-schizoid organization, marking the infantile, the primitive and something like the psychotic. Klein authorized object relations theory, but the nature of those objects was defined by the instincts, especially the Death Instinct.

In the more recent decades, this core orientation has been dislocated to varying degrees, by developments in psychoanalytic theory as well as infant development research. I mostly put the latter aside here and note that both Winnicott and Bion shifted attention to the mother–infant *relationship*, extending Klein's placing infancy at the center. But this convergence should not obscure their substantial differences. As I elaborate, Bion maintained a kind of compromise with the original one-person dual instinct theory, while Winnicott went further in placing the baby **in primary relation to** the actual caregiver: when Bion emphasizes the baby presenting something problematic that has to be re-processed by the mother, he is retaining the Kleinian idea that the whole developmental process starts with the infant's proto-experience of unmanageability. This engenders the necessity for projective identification, whether normal or pathological. The mother's task is to be receptive to these, so as to render them manageable; she must begin with a kind of passive receptivity—the "negative capability" to which Bion refers in the paper to which responds.

Winnicott's baby has no need for projective identification as long as good-enough care is provided, which is what happens more often than not; projective identification in the first developmental stage is a breakdown product of inadequate care. For him, the infant's omnipotence is creative and reassuring, rather than destructive; it does not have to be restrained. For him, omnipotence is creative and not destructive. Some may find that this interest in the positive is not "psychoanalytic," but Winnicott's descriptions of babies and mothers are not direct accounts of what can be observed on the surface but depend on his interest in the radical effects of personal imagination from the beginning of life. Winnicott's commitment to observing infants directly while also capturing their distinctive psychic reality is one of his most exquisite (if less inconspicuous) paradoxes. As he is watching actual parent-infant dyads, he sees activity on both partners and in both the observable and highly subjective domains.

Although Bion's later work went far beyond the conventional Freud-Klein tradition, the image of the infant that remains most definitive and influential is that of his extraordinary paper on "… thinking" (Bion, 1962). There, Bion deploys a particular image of the infant—and the infantile— to re-conceive the psychoanalytic process and the origin and development of the psyche, including containment, alpha- and beta-process, and normal projective identification. His reading of the infantile features the emotional-somatic proto-experience of a painful increase in tension and frustration which must be relieved by projections and the intercession of a caregiver who absorbs them. Bion's (1962) nuanced formulation of a preconception of a breast that can "mate" with the awareness of the breast itself, or alternatively that will be left with a "no-breast" that is "not there" "and by not being there gives… painful feelings underpins his conception of psychic development organized around the dynamics of mental formations emerging through the vicissitudes of frustration, representation, transformation, and more. Bion builds his baby around absence; gratification is incidental in the "thinking paper," noted in the first sections and hardly mentioned thereafter. Rather, his interest is in how psychic growth emerges from the mother's processing of the baby's distress, communicated through projective identification, when his "preconceptions" are not met by the outside world.[3]

This parallels, and in some sense, originates, the contemporary Kleinian dedication to the analyst's containing and interpreting projective identification as the central mode of therapeutic action. This "Klein-Bion analyst" listens "without memory and desire" so as to be prepared to accept and process those projections, while the "Winnicottian analyst" is proposing a facilitating environment which depends on allowing her presence to felt, if only in the background. Winnicott, in a typically paradoxical formulation, emphasizes the *activity of the analyst's receptivity and patience*, much like the mother's. Commonalities between both Bion's and Winnicott's clinical innovations and their images of infancy are conspicuous here.

But, while these orientations may be complementary much of the time, the differences in emphasis are important, as Winnicott says in the 1967 letter to Bion. Although Winnicott did appreciate that Bion made room for the environment in a way that Klein did not. he continued to feel that Bion hewed closer to Klein's downplaying of that outside world. In a letter to John Wisdom, the discussant of one of Bion's papers, he (1964) explicitly distances himself from Klein, with particular reference to the salience of the outside world:

> It is important to me that Bion states (obscurely of course) what I have been trying to state for 2½ decades but against the terrific opposition of Melanie. Bion uses the word reverie to cover the idea… that the infant is ready to create something, and in good-enough mothering the mother lets the baby know what is being created. Winnicott then explicitly likens this to 'therapy,'" and goes on: "Bion says 'What happens will depend….' Melanie Klein absolutely would not allow this, and my relation to her was (though always warm and good) impaired by her adamant objection to 'what happens depends …' Bion goes deeper than Melanie here, or finds a way of stating what Melanie would not allow.
>
> (Letter to John O. Wisdom, 26 October 1964)[4]

Winnicott indeed notes that Bion goes further than Mrs. Klein in including the environment, but, as we shall see, not far enough. This is already suggested in his use of the word, "cover," with its double sense of explication *and* concealment. This becomes more explicit when he suggests that Bion stayed closer to the original Kleinian formulations in a way that left him stuck with some torturous theorizing. He goes on to claim his own originality.

> ….Bion, however, finds himself in a muddle and postulates the infant's need for a breast—a "bad breast" which has to be exchanged for a good one……I think my way of using mother's good-enough adaptation to ego needs has something more straightforward than this, without violation of the facts and findings in direct observations and in the work of those of us who treat the occasional "borderline" case….I like Bion's treatment of this subject, and I can learn something from it. But if you (not he) are talking about it you ought to say: this is what D.W.W. has been trying to get us to see for two or three decades. In a way, all that Bion has done is to divert our attention from the main issue to alpha and beta functions.[5]
>
> (Letter to John O. Wisdom, 26 October 1964)

I take Winnicott to imply that Bion is hewing closer to the original Kleinian view, that the natural state of the newborn infant is one of vulnerability, impulsivity, haunted by destructiveness and on the edge of catastrophic anxiety. This conception starts with an image of an infant whose psychic life starts out separate from his environment, to which he turns for relief. (With some qualms, I'll call the baby, "he.") But Winnicott's baby starts out in a relationship, beginning with his sexual conception,[6] through intrauterine life, and then in the first caregiving relationship. Winnicott's babies are generally well-enough cared for, and so they are generally not having to manage much anxiety. Rather, they are most often more or less "relaxed"— a term that he uses artfully.

Winnicott is thus fully committed to an *object relations* theory. For him, drives don't appear until later in development. He thus offers an even more radical departure from the Freud/Klein instinct theory than is sometimes apparent. In those, mental life originates with instincts which are prior to *the lived experience of the body* and have to be mediated by phantasies in order to constitute mental life. But Winnicott's baby emerges through rather ordinary sensorimotor activity in relation to the mother's body and his own needs; embodied, rather than organized and driven by phantasies which are necessary to give a form to those instincts. The psychic and the somatic are part of a single space, where human vitality begins, at risk if the baby is deprived of adequate care, since his mind and his body are already present for him in a more or less integrated way. Further, this "psychesoma" is psychically continuous with and ensconced in the presence of the mother. Paradoxically, infantile psychic life, then, is inseparable from the body and the caregiving environment, with mind/body and subject/object undifferentiated, rather than with a mother who is psychically taken as a phantasmatic internal object (i.e., "the breast"), rather than an actual physical presence. If things *are* going well, then, Winnicott's baby does not need to have any phantasies and projective identification is not necessary, since there are no endogenous destructive motives to be overcome, nor an outside that is experienced as such.

For Winnicott, then, the entire bodies and psyches of infant and mother form up the infant's world, in dynamic transaction, in a sensorimotor matrix that normally and naturally accommodates the baby's needs and developmental potentials. Progressive development is a natural motive force, potentiated and supported by maternal care and bodily growth. This formulation of the infantile flows from Winnicott's daily pediatric practice and into his analytic-technical proposals about the analytic setting and presence. Like his Middle Group colleagues, he pursues a frankly developmental theory of therapeutic action: analytic provision of the right kind, painstaking as that may be, can mobilize potentials which had been derailed by environmental deprivation, deficits and trauma. At the basic level, this is a matter of relationship and environmental provision, not "containment."

This has core clinical implications. For Winnicott, relationships are primary factors in growth and development in psychoanalysis, as in childhood. The analyst's presentation of a holding environment facilitates the resumption of previously arrested developmental potentials; this is not a passive stance, since it requires a kind of active patience and attention, with precise, analytic understanding of the emerging psychic situation. The emotional strains on both analytic partners can be quite profound, with tolerance and endurance usually required. All of this follows

Winnicott's image of what mothers do with their babies to help them grow psychologically.

Along these same lines, this approach also involves more spontaneity and dyadic intermixing that we find in the Kleinian emphasis on containment and interpretation. Winnicott is an intersubjectivist and developmentalist, as he maintains his commitment to the radical imagination of the primary process. The stress is not on listening "without memory or desire," but rather on an absorptive and engaged approach, one that may well highlight an understanding of the patient's traumatic and/or deprived history. This may well stay in the background for long periods of time, or be expressed in direct, emotional displays or activity, but is hardly ever far from view.

This is a radical departure from the Kleinian-Freudian emphasis on the transformation of "primitive" psychic phenomena into less primitive experience as the salutary process in both early childhood development and analytic progress. This further clarifies Winnicott's letter to Wisdom and his general position: Winnicott is critical of a constraint (if not a mistake) in the Bionian framework's stress on the transformation of beta to alpha, which we see further articulated in Bion's Grid. Again in keeping with his core, radical Object Relations orientation, Winnicott is most attuned to relationships, featuring them at the internal psychic core without neglecting the outside world; his notion of "illusion" is central here (Winnicott, 1953; Seligman, 2018b). Winnicott is oriented through the Freudian project of seeing the role of imagination and the radically subjective in all phases of psychic life, but he doesn't feature "primitivity" or instincts in general, especially in his view of infancy in particular. Rather he emphasizes adaptation and the transaction between actual environments and the creativity of the child's psychosomatic experiencing; that is, a particular form of relating. This may be even more apparent in his theory of the transitional phase than in his theory of the earliest parent-infant relationship, generally reflected in his clinical approach to "subneurotic" psychopathology, depending as it does on how the analytic space remobilizes previously arrested growth potentials.

In other words, Bion's formulation of the infantile posits a baby who finds himself in an incomplete originary state that must be transformed by external intervention from something less organized to something more organized. As I understand it, this remains central in some respects throughout his evolution, as the technical emphasis is on transformation of the more primitive into something more organized, rather than on a more continuous path of progressive development as a natural phenomenon. Winnicott's baby does not await the transformation of his experience through the intercession of someone else's less primitive mode of experiencing, rather is prepared to be (and become) himself if given the right environment. Normal social caregiving relations entail an active transition to mature object relations that evolve through bodily and imaginative activity, which is intrinsic to being human and part of what he considers the inherited potential of our species. This is also one of the many radical implications of the theory of the transitional object and playing as crucial to therapeutic process: playing is not something one does without memory or desire.

In short, then, all of this parallels his clinical approach, as it stresses the analyst's provision of a facilitating environment in which the patient's own developmental potentials can emerge. The analyst's contribution is more a matter of presence than of any specific activity. This apparently subtle difference from the Klein-Bion idea of "containment," which is not always recognized by some of my colleagues who blur the differences between that term and Winnicott's "holding." (This may be particular to the United States.)

Winnicott's entire project, then, rests on and is permeated by his radical departure from the usual analytic view of the infantile. His three-phase developmental model features the movement from the environmental object (or subjective object), through the transitional object, to the "objective object" which can be "used." This shapes his account of psychopathogenesis and psychoanalytic mutative action, including the emergence of two-body relations, the capacity for concern, "the use of the object," illusion, "the capacity to be alone," and more.

Winnicott's breakthrough account of infancy, then, is at the core of his bold and capacious re-working of analytic theory. He deconstructs and rebalances several apparent dichotomies that define the psychoanalytic field: internal/external; subject/object; mind/body; between monadic and dyadic positions in psychic life, and between what can be observed and what can be inferred through analytic engagement: these constitute the paradoxically matrices within which life goes forward. In addition to taking issue with Klein's view of the normal infant's relating to a distinct (if phantasized) object ("the breast"), he is also revising Freud's theory of primary narcissism as a state of non-relating: For him, the relation to the environmental object is indeed a relationship, continually supported under good-enough conditions, in a dynamic transaction with the outside world. Here we see a different kind of primariness, as the first phase *is* an object relationship: in an exquisitely Winnicottian paradox, the "environmental mother" is felt as a "subjective object" that the baby does not experience as other than himself, and this object relationship requires the mother's—again—"*primary* maternal preoccupation" (Winnicott, 1956/1975). He differentiates himself here even more from Klein than from Freud, since this primary object relationship is more like Freud's undifferentiated primary narcissism than Klein's more differentiated internal object world. Still, as I have said (Seligman, 2021), he departs from Freud in that he nonetheless regards the primary state as one of relation, or as he calls it, "relating" (Winnicott, 1969).

Winnicott, then, is insisting that the actual, observable activity of infant care is accessible to the baby (even as the baby does not know that), and in parallel, that environmental provision is quite salient for both analytic theorizing and practice. But—and this is a rather important matter--Winnicott remains committed to the fundamental role in the infant's subjective experience of that which can be observed; here he is very much in the Freudian mode. The actuality of the mother matters directly to the baby, but it does not register for him in the same way that it does for any observer. This commitment to the internal version of the outside world, then, reflects a paradoxical affinity with Freud which is not always so obvious.[7]

As is typical, then, Winnicott's novel theory of this first stage of development depends on a particular paradox, around the complex duality of psychic and "objective" realities. He is of course very interested in the maternal environment and the actual mother, but his most exceptional contribution to the understanding of perinatal psychology involves the mother's and baby's psychosomatic states: the infant is radically absorbed in the relationship with his mother, whom he lives with as an environment—not a separate person (or even a separate thing). In tandem, her primary maternal preoccupation is a special psychic-physiologic set-up that allows her to surrender to infant's needs so as to "become an environment": (Two of the three major sections of the "Theory of the Parent-Infant Relationship" are devoted to "the role of maternal care" and "changes in the mother.") The infant's core existence is "absolutely" dependent on the quality of maternal care—both physiologically and psychically. Although the infant is not aware that he is living in an environment with another person, he must be protected from awareness of that very dependency, and from the otherness of the mother and the environment generally.

The dense and paradoxical primary situation here is that the infant is thoroughly intertwined with what is around him as he doesn't realize that there *is* a world other than himself; this is the wholesome omnipotence which Winnicott regards as so fundamental to healthy development throughout the life cycle. This is the normal condition most of the time: the "harmonious interpenetrating mix" to which Balint (1968/1975) refers is what usually happens, such that Winnicott's baby is mostly relaxed, "going-on-being," rather than managing the recurring threat of catastrophe through phantasmatic maneuvers such as splitting and projective identification. Klein's and Bion's images of infancy analogize infancy to psychosis and other severe pathology. In positing the projective identification/containment pathway to "thinking," and other new psychic structure, Bion does open the door halfway to another view. But frustration and absence the Klein-Bion tradition overgeneralizes from the difficulties seen in the consulting room.

It is, then, not surprising that consulting remain the first, primary psychic situation. The Winnicott would have qualms about the notion of listening "without memory or desire," as this is a move in the direction of absence. Bion's model parallels Freud's view that the analyst's abstinent, free-floating attention facilitates the emergence of infantile phantasies. But the Winnicottian infantile does not entail fantasy,[8] unless there are environmental failures for which fantasies must compensate. For both Freud and Klein, fantasy emerged from the inevitable movement of the Life and

Death instincts into the body and the image-generator of the psyche. But Winnicott conceives of instinct in the first place as emerging through senso-rimotor activity and need, in relation to the environment; his baby doesn't have to contend with innate destructiveness. In an appreciative statement of his "Personal View of the Kleinian Contribution," he (1962/65) de-clared, "I simply cannot find value in his [Freud's] idea of a Death Instinct" and rejected both "paranoid-schizoid" and "depressive position" as "bad name(s)" (pp. 176–177). This is all a reflection of his fundamental commit-ment to the primary place of relationships—both internal and external, which takes Object Relations Theory to a new dimension. Like most of his Middle Group colleagues, he is a "full throated" Object Relations theorist (Seligman, 2018a), while Bion and Klein are in some sense suspended between object relations and instincts.

This further clarifies how Winnicott's use of the term, "omnipotence" differs from most other analysts'. For him, normal infancy does indeed rest on an omnipotent platform, but that omnipotence consists in not having to pay attention to one's needs, nor having to notice whatever effort needs to be made; in other words, not having to think about anything, including not having to fantasize. Omnipotence is *not* an all-powerful, controlling relationship to an object with a kind of otherness. Rather, it is a paradoxical relation to a subjective object, to an entire environment which is felt to be so unobtrusively responsive that its presence need not be noticed, but is, rather, an underlying background for security and vitality. And in reverse, if that environment does need to be noticed (even as it makes itself *felt*), then the developmental-object relational pathway will be disrupted. Here are two examples: the narcissistic mother who requires that the baby attend to her, and the depressed mother whose own unresponsiveness compels the infant to take note of his own distress, interrupting the inner relaxation which underpins the security of this wholesome omnipotence. In such situations, the infant might feel a sense of futility or even breakdown, and might respond by molding himself to these challenging conditions, developing the compliant false self of which Winnicott wrote even facing so remarkably, with acute or chronic break-down looming in more troubled situations.

Winnicott thus rejects the usual analogy between "the infantile" and primitive psychopathology. Babies are dependent, but not in a state compa-rable to that of severe psychopathology, unless something has gone wrong. Generally, he doesn't refer to the primary situation as primitive, which car-ries a sense of something other than the "normal" or "civilized"; rather, it is in describing the products of the breakdown of the normal parent-infant relationship that he refers to "primitive emotional agonies." The infant's motivations are similar to those of the healthy adult, and indeed of culture overall. Babies are innately prepared to accommodate to and evoke "good-enough" care, which is to say they integrate and take comfort in what is there for them (as in Erikson's (1950/1959) account of "basic trust" as a matter of "getting what is given"). In this sense, babies are mostly not dis-organized, since there are usually caregivers who will organize them and be organized by them. These are basic phenomena that underlie the rather obvious fact that "whenever one finds an infant one finds maternal care, and without maternal care there can be no infant" (Winnicott, 1960/1965, p. 39).

This means that adult psychopathology is *not* a regression or fixation to normal infancy, nor, to put another way, a failure to be extricated from it. Rather, it is a fixation to the *abnormal* situation occurring when the usual good-enough caregiving has not been provided. (This is what Balint (1968/1979), in parallel to Erikson, calls "the basic fault."). For Winnicott, "the infantile" anxieties about destruction and the concomitant recourse to splitting and projective identification are outcomes of such environmental failure, deficit or other trauma. Klein's description of the infantile mind can now be read as a brilliant account of what happens when things go wrong, developed through the observation of older children and adults who had experienced developmental failures or traumas. (See Seligman, in prepara-tion, for a more extensive account.)

I take it that most of the infants that Winnicott followed in his pediatric practice weren't that perturbed, but rather, primed for growth and devel-opment. Some analytic observers see "primitive" anxieties when looking at babies who are generally doing well. But most in the extensive community of analytic infant clinicians with whom I am familiar would say that it is in those cases of trauma and deprivation where the "primitive" anxieties are observable. Most (though far from all) babies are leading comfortable-enough lives, especially when culture and political economy provide ade-quate support for their caregivers to take care of them. Although Winnicott doesn't refer often to his Middle Group colleague Bowlby's Attachment Theory, the commonalities are obvious. Current infant development re-search supports a similar view.

Conclusions and Extensions

In the seminal "theory of thinking" paper, Bion begins his own move away from the classical instinct-drive model and Mrs. Klein's emphasis on the Death Instinct in particular, which was further reflected in the bold and independent turn in the later work that emerged, largely after he left Lon-don. As he specifies the constructive possibilities of the infant's projective identifications and the mother's handling of them beyond hers, he goes forward with a more elaborate account of how psychic growth begins in the first relationship. Bion also indeed *suggested* that there is something in the baby that *supports* transformation, such that frustration can be transformed into another sort of mental process—"thinking," or "alpha-process."

But he still presents an infant organized *in the first place* around incom-plete or disorganizing states and pressures, like preconceptions, frustra-tion and beta elements, which must be regulated and transformed, as they emerging from the bedrock of the psyche and are, as such, inevitable. That is, in Bion's "Thinking" paper, the originary infantile appears as a matter of a more or less precipitous cycle of distress, or at least disorganization, leading to ongoing cycles of relief and renewed distress. Frustration is both taken-for-granted and psychically disruptive and the baby cannot handle it without projection, and this is the primary psychic dynamic in which he is interested. Although the mother may well be there to transform this, such that new functions develop, the baby is regularly uncomfortable and hence must repetitively resort to projective identification of problematic states, whether normal or otherwise. This is reflected in the essential Bionian inflection of contemporary Kleinian clinical technique, relying as it does on the analyst's management of the patient's projective identifications, in analogy with the mother's. The "Kleinian patient," like Bion's baby, is motivated by a kind of anxious incompleteness, absence, and existential risk.

Risking caricature, I'll say that while "Winnicottian patients" surely present with deep emotional pain, their analytic progress doesn't depend on a series of transformations through containment, "metabolism," or interpretation. Instead, they will move forward when they can regress toward recovering their traumatic and otherwise thwarted states of dire disorganization and need, and—from there—find a way to draw on the new and more helpful analytic environment. "Winnicott's babies" don't usually need such transformations. Instead, the analysis-infancy analogy points toward a reconstitution toward the more usual infantile situation, in which dependency is relatively comforting—albeit in these analyses, amidst acute psychic pain. (Sandler (1960) captured this when he referred to "the background of safety" (p. 352).) Winnicott's baby starts out in a generally integrated psychosomatic state as he is embedded in a protective and satisfactory environment. When this goes awry, a variety of quite difficult distortions ensue, usually enduring over the life cycle. More commonly, though, development proceeds adequately, leaving a more or less reliable core: this is the emergent core of the "place where we live" that finds itself in culture, potential space, and with more differentiated objects that can be "used."

All of this helps clarify the elusive difference between holding and containment. Bion's baby *has something problematic inside that must be contained*, while Winnicott's baby lives through a body that needs to be held to be *protected from environmental dangers* like being left alone, being projected onto, having too much demanded of him, falling, getting too cold, not having skin-to-skin contact, and hunger, all so that he can go on living comfortably enough. The Kleinian-Bionian patient presents something to the analyst that is more particular, such as an unsymbolized phantasy, that must be transformed, while the Winnicottian patient allows the analyst to facilitate the re-activation of previously derailed potentials for growth through sustaining a setting that allows collaboration with the analysand's creative capacity to experience a protective and reliable environment.

I believe that the following comment from Winnicott about Klein also applies to the Bionian image of the infant:

> there seems to me to be no specific reference to a stage at which the infant exists only because of the maternal care, together with which it forms a unit…. the work of Klein on the splitting defence mechanisms and on projections and introjections and so on, is an attempt to state the effects of failure of environmental provision in terms of the individual.
>
> (Winnicott, 1960/1965, p. 42)

Lesley Caldwell (personal communication) has recently called attention to Winnicott's radical move toward a spatially oriented psychoanalysis; I would add a sensory-motor orientation. We can see this in his image of the infant and the infantile: a mind constituted through a body which comes into being through activity, proximity, movement, and physical and emotional contact with other bodies; scents and fluids like milk, air, water, and inanimate objects like the mattress on which it lies; and direct experience of psychosomatic states like satiation and hunger, warmth and cold, gravity and support, sounds and sights, sucking, reaching, gazing, etc., and the whole range of affects and interactional and somatic rhythms, including the wave-like coordination of mother and infant's movements, breathing and cardiac pulses and sounds, and sleep patterns. The intrapsychic emerges in tandem with the psychesoma and object relations, both internal and external, and in relation to the space between. This yields the area of ordinary creativity that constitutes lived experience, in all its imagination, variation, and tribulation. I'm reminded of the seminal infant researcher Colwyn Trevarthen's (2009) declaration that motor activity and musicality are the first human motivations.

Finally: to repeat, Winnicott's account of infancy contests the traditional correlation of infancy, primitivity, and severe psychopathology into question. He builds his view of the infantile around presence, while Bion builds his around absence. Winnicott reverses the temporal and spatial order of the developmental and ontological process: destructiveness, disorientation, asociality originate in developmental failure, not in infantile instincts. Dependency is not intrinsically dangerous; rather, it is dangerous when it is met with unreliability, exploitation, domination, deprivation, and the like.

Notes

1 This chapter is drawn from a previous paper: Seligman, S. (2025). Holding and Containing: "The Metaphor of the Baby" in Winnicott, Bion, and Klein*, Psychoanalytic Dialogues, 35:1, 46–54, DOI: 10.1080/10481885.2024.2444197 *Psychoanalytic Dialogues: International Journal of Relational Perspectives*, 35, 1:46-54. Earlier versions were presented at the International Psychoanalytical Association Congress, London, 2019; James Grotstein Memorial Lecture, 2023: Institute of Psychoanalysis, London, 2023.

2 Winnicott's fundamental emphasis on the emergence of subjectivity in the process of discovering the separateness of others and the difference between inside and outside is conspicuous here (See, for example, Winnicott, 1963/1965).

3 I take "preconceptions" to be a Kantian-inflected way of re-describing (something like) drive-phantasy.

4 With regard to Klein "would not allow," some colleagues who do give substantial weight to environmental influences are nonetheless inclined to give Mrs. Klein "the benefit of the doubt" on this matter. But Klein (1957/1975) does indeed minimize those environmental effects. Here is her comment in her extraordinary, late essay, "Envy and Gratitude":

> ....I have often referred to the strength of the ego in relation to the anxieties it has to cope with as a constitutional factor....Another factor that influences development from the beginning is the variety of external experiences through which the infant goes....My accumulated observations, however, have convinced me that *the impact of these external experiences is in proportion to the constitutional strength of the innate destructive impulses and the ensuing paranoid anxieties.*
>
> (italics mine).... (pp. 229–230)

5 Winnicott is here claiming originality, much as in the first part of the 1967 letter to Bion, when he notes Clare's reminder that the "phrase memory and desire... is a quotation from T.S. Eliot...."

6 Note Winnicott's different use of "conception," which I am drawing from his (1962) paper on concern. (See also my review of that paper (Seligman, 2021).) As often, he stays closer to the ordinary sense of the term, differing from Bion's invocation of such esoteric and private language as "preconception," "conception," and the alpha and beta functions to which Winnicott refers as diversions.

7 This is nimbly presented in the "Parent-Infant Relationship" paper in which he takes up a footnote from the "two principles" paper. He notes that Freud (1911) bolstered his argument by asking the reader to follow what he (i.e., Freud) calls "a "fiction" of an infantile psychic "organization which...neglected the reality of the outside world..." without discussing the mother. Winnicott nimbly, if appreciatively, turns Freud against himself by proceeding instead, to write about how mothers and infants do indeed live interdependently. Freud, he says, "knows that he is taking for granted the very things that are under discussion in this paper" (Winnicott, 1960/1965, p. 39).

8 I follow Winnicott in using this spelling.

References

Balint, M. (1968/1979). *The basic fault: Therapeutic aspects of regression.* Evanston, Illinois: Northwestern University Press.

Bion, W. R. (1962). The psycho-analytic study of thinking. *International Journal of Psychoanalysis* 43:306–310.

Erikson, E. H. (1950/1959). *Childhood and society.* New York: Norton.

Freud, S. (1911). Formulations on the two principles of mental functioning. *The Standard Edition of the Complete Psychological Works of Sigmund Freud,* 12:213–226.

Klein, M. (1957/1975). Envy and gratitude. In Klein, M. (1975). *Envy and gratitude and other works, 1946–1963.* New York: The Free Press, pp. 176–235.

Sandler, J. (1960). The background of safety. *International Journal of Psychoanalysis* 41:352–356.

Seligman, S. (in preparation). *Beginning with Winnicott.* New York: Oxford University Press.

Seligman, S. (2018a). *Relationships in development: Infancy, intersubjectivity, and attachment*. London and New York: Routledge.

Seligman, S. (2018b). Illusion as a basic psychic principle: Winnicott, Freud, Oedipus, and Trump. *Journal of the American Psychoanalytic Association* 66:263–288.

Seligman, S. (2021). Reconstructing the depressive position: creativity and style in Winnicott's "Concern" paper. *Journal of the American Psychoanalytic Association* 69:491–512.

Trevarthen, C. (2009). The intersubjective psychobiology of human meaning: learning of culture depends on interest for co-operative practical work–and affection for the joyful art of good company. *Psychoanalytic Dialogues* 19:507–518.

Winnicott, D. W. (1953). Transitional objects and transitional phenomena—a study of the first not-me possession. *International Journal of Psychoanalysis* 34:89–97.

Winnicott, D. W. (1956/1975). Chapter XXIV. Primary maternal preoccupation. In *Through paediatrics to psycho-analysis*. New York: Brunner/Mazel, pp. 300–305.

Winnicott, D. W. (1960/65). The theory of the parent-infant relationship. In *The maturational processes and the facilitating environment*. Madison, CT: International Universities Press, pp. 37–55.

Winnicott, D. W. (1962/65). A personal view of the Kleinian contribution. In *The maturational processes and the facilitating environment*. Madison, CT: International Universities Press, pp. 171–178.

Winnicott, D. W. (1963/65). The development of the capacity for concern. In *The maturational processes and the facilitating environment*. Madison, CT: International Universities Press, pp. 73–82.

Winnicott, D. W. (1964). Letter to John O. Wisdom, 26 October 1964 (1987, Letter 89, p. 144–146) [CW 7:1:11]. In *The Collected Works of D.W. Winnicott*. Eds. Lesley Caldwell and Helen Taylor Robinson. Oxford and New York: Oxford University Press.

Winnicott, D. W. (1965). *The maturational processes and the facilitating environment*. New York: International Universities Press.

Winnicott, D. W. (1969). The use of an object. *International Journal of Psychoanalysis* 50:711–716.

Index

Note: Page numbers in bold refer to tables. Page numbers followed by "n" refer to notes.

Abraham, N. 69
Abram, J. 27, 31n5, 65, 92, 129, 139
actuality of the object 33–38, 40
adoption 113, 118, 121n1, 156
Adorno, T. 13
Aguayo, J. 36, 41, 61n3, 90, 158, 160
alpha function 49, 50, 65, 68, 72, 93, 177
Amati Mehler, J.: *Babel of the Unconscious, The* 15
Anderson, J. 163
Andreas-Salomé, L. 60n1
anxiety 47, 56, 72, 84–86, 107, 140, 172; castration 108; catastrophic 171; existential 9; infantile 177; and insecurity 10; intolerable 69; paranoid 180n4; primitive 177; separation 40
'Anxiety Associated with Insecurity' (Winnicott) 10, 131, 152
anxiety–defence dynamic, in analysts and carers 84, **84**
Apprey, M. 69
Argentieri, S.: *Babel of the Unconscious, The* 15
Aristotle 102; on *hypokeimenon* 110n1
asociality 179
atonement/at-one-ment 29, 46, 52, 60, 65, 75, 77, 78, 104, 106, 108
Attachment Theory 177
Attention and Interpretation (Bion) 2, 48, 73, 75, 80, 99–101, 111n7, 141
autistic O 110

Balint, M. 175
becoming O 22, 46, 48, 52, 60

being with and without desire, paradox of 35–37
Bell, D. 141
Benjamin, W. 20
Bergson, H. 156
beta elements 93, 178
Bion, W. R. 2; on being without memory and desire 35–37; as colonialist 155–157; on Gospels 24–25; on Imaginary Twin 9; intentions 81–83; on Language of Achievement 2–4, 54; on Language of Substitution 2–6; on love 3; responsibilities 81–83; stresses and strains 83–85; on waking dream thoughts 57, 96; and Winnicott, similarities and dissimilarities between 154–155; *see also individual entries*
Bollas, C. 121n7
Bott Spillius, E. 99
boundarilessness 169
Bowlby, J. 177
BPS *see* British Psychoanalytic Society (BPS)
Brentano, F. 19
British Psychoanalytic Society (BPS) 1, 5, 9–11, 17, 64–66, 88, 91, 95, 99–111, 124, 125, 127, 134, 141, 145, 152, 154, 157, 159, 163
Byung-Chul, H. 110

Canestri, J.: *Babel of the Unconscious, The* 15
Caper, R. 107
Carroll, L. 155

Cartesian solipsism 19
castration anxiety 108
"Catastrophic Change" (CC) 17,
   22–24, 123–125, 128, 130, 136, 141,
   145, 150n1
Cauldwell, L. 80
CC *see* "Catastrophic Change" (CC)
"Children" (Winnicott) 113
clinical psychoanalysis 93
Cogitations (Bion) 24, 29, 46
Collected Works of Donald Winnicott, The
   (Caldwell) 9
'Communicating and Not Communicating Leading to a Study of
   Certain Opposites (C&NC)'
   (Winnicott) 11, 134, 152–165
communication: attempts to directly
   157–160; indirect 152, 160; nonverbal
   156, 160; symbolic 160–161; theory
   of 68, 92
Complete Works of W.R. Bion, The (Bion)
   17, 99
consciousness 74, 105, 165; ecological
   78
container-contained model 11, 22, 27,
   30, 31n3, 52, 65, 85, 95, 107, 128, 156,
   159, 161
containment 49, 50, 61n5, 74, 76, 170,
   173–175, 178
Corbett, K. 39
countertransference 37, 52, 105, 160;
   objective 55; subjective 55
creative aggression 39–41
creative apperception 75
creative gesture 66, 67, 133, 153
creative perception 75
creativity 10, 11, 42, 49, 56, 59, 109, 129,
   132–134, 153, 173, 179
'Creativity and its Origins' (Winnicott)
   133
CW *see* Complete Works (CW)

Darwin, C. 22, 156
denial 7n1, 106
deprivation 7n1, 110, 172, 177
Derrida, J. 120
destruction 20, 30, 33, 35, 40–41, 58–60,
   104, 130, 133, 134, 145, 168, 177;
   constant 60; continuous 60;
   creative 41, 116; of object 113–117,
   120, 148, 149
destructiveness 58, 130, 148, 171,
   176, 179

developmental psychoanalysis 93
"Differentiation of the Psychotic from
   the Non-Psychotic Personalities"
   (Bion) 10, 51, 68, 94, 157
disorientation 179
dissociated self 73
Doyle, A. C.: 'Adventure of Silver
   Blaze, The' 97
dreams/dreaming 4, 12, 20–22, 27, 31,
   38, 41, 57, 67, 96, 102–105, 108–110,
   113–121, 123, 130, 144

early infant development 132; theories
   of 10
Eckhart, M. 129, 156, 164
ecological consciousness 78
Eigen, M. 103–104
Eliot, T. S. 6, 34, 67, 81, 130, 140, 180n5;
   Four Quartets 39, 164; *Tradition and
   the Individual Talent* 129; 'Wasteland,
   The' 80, 102, 133
empty thoughts 157
environmental object 82, 174
'envy and gratitude' 2, 5
'envy and greed' 2, 5
Erikson, E. 42
evolution 21–22, 48, 54, 102, 103,
   105, 107
existential anxiety 9
external object 37, 49, 61n5, 162

F (act of faith) 103, 104
"Fable for Our Time, A" (Bion) 29
Faimberg, H. 69
Ferenczi, S. 104
"fight/flight" assumption 109
Fischia il vento 109
formlessness 21, 22, 50, 56–57, 165
Foucault, M. 26
Four Quartets 39, 164
fragile self 72
Francesca.B. 93
freedom 10, 25, 136; to express 132;
   to talk 113; to think 132; of thought
   89, 117
Freud, A. 64, 65, 145
Freud, S. 20, 25, 26, 50, 59, 70, 72, 103,
   110n5, 123, 160, 168–170, 172, 175,
   180n7; *Beyond the Pleasure Principle*
   27; on free-floating attention 36;
   on helplessness *(Hilflosigkeit)* 27;
   on undifferentiated primary
   narcissism 174

genius 23, 38, 128
Glover, E. 64–65
Goldman, D. 156
"good-enough" care 177
Graves, R. 80, 81; *Nazarene Gospel Restored, The* 13, 23, 107, 128, 130, 131, 136
Green, A. 39, 68, 141
group behavior 68
group dynamics 9

hallucination 38, 55, 60
handling 75, 177
hate 37, 52, 69
hauntology 64
Hegel, G. W. F. 105; *Phenomenology of Spirit, The* 111n5
helplessness *(Hilflosigkeit)* 27, 69
holding 11, 33, 37–40, 52, 61n5, 67, 73, 75, 76, 149, 153, 157, 161, 172, 174, 178
Husserl, E. 19
hypokeimenon 110n1

'Imaginary Twin, The' (Winnicott) 9, 90
imaginative conjectures 15, 45
imprinting 96
incommunicado isolate/self 92
indirect communication 152, 160
infancy 96, 134–136, 138, 156, 159, 161, 168–180
infantile 168–180; dependency 69; desires 108; development 10
infants: creative gesture 67; and mother, relationship between 31, 55, 169
instinct theory 169, 172
intention/intentionality 18–20, 72, 76, 89–90, 102, 103, 105, 113, 116, 117, 149
internal analytic setting 92, 96
internal object 11, 49, 162, 169, 172, 174
internal world 11, 18, 56, 69, 96
intuition 19, 21, 22, 46, 50, 74, 76, 77, 90, 91, 101, 104, 105, 107, 155, 156
irrationality 169
Isaacs, S.: "Nature and Function of Phantasy, The" 64

Jung, C. 23, 104, 156; *Memories, Dreams and Reflections* 130–131

K (knowledge of self) 3, 7n1, 9, 22, 46, 77, 93, 103, 109, 110
Kant, I. 156, 157

Keats, J. 2, 54, 80, 81, 95, 143, 156
Kestenberg, J. S. 69
Khan, M.: "Silence as Communication" 161
Klein, M. 8, 10, 17–31, 49, 50, 59, 61n6, 64–70, 72, 79n3, 80, 82, 89, 96, 131–133, 136, 140, 152–153, 163, 168, 170, 171, 178; on catastrophic change 22–24; death of 93; "Envy and Gratitude" 180n4; on 'envy and gratitude' 5; on evolution 21–22; on 'memories and desires' 18–21; on paranoid-schizoid 126; on secular psychoanalysis 26–28; on shadowboxing 28–31
Kleinian group 11, 24, 27, 29, 30, 52, 94, 157, 158
Kleinianism 23
Kleinism 27, 132, 153, 154, 158, 162
"knowing about" phenomena 9

Lacan, J. 95, 103
Language of Achievement 2–4, 54
language of psychoanalysis 104–106
Language of Substitution 2–6
"Life of P, The" 114–115
'Location of Cultural Experience, The' (Winnicott) 123, 127, 133–136, 138, 143–145
Lollards 156
Los Angeles Psycho-Analytic Society 28
love 3, 4, 59, 69, 104, 121, 163
Luria, I. 129

'Making the Best of a Bad Job' (Bion) 14
Mancia, M. 158–159
maternal preoccupation 37–38
Mawson, C. 8, 11, 12, 15, 18; *Psychoanalysis and Anxiety – from Knowing to Being* 9
–MDC *see* memory, desire, and understanding (–MDC)
Meltzer, D. 11, 17, 29, 30, 125–127, 139–141, 145
Memoir of the Future, A (Bion) 28, 54, 93
'memories and desires' 5, 6, 7n1, 13, 18–21, 33–43, 46–48, 67, 73, 99, 100, 102, 113, 116, 141, 144, 145, 164; minimizing 74; playing without 117–120; rejection of 146, 147, 149; suspension of 51–52
memory, desire, and understanding (–MDC) 18–21, 46
mental growth 109

Merleau-Ponty, M. 20, 31n1
metabolization 39, 43, 74, 95
metapsychology 27, 31, 49, 83, 104, 157, 165
Milner, M. 11, 149, 160, 163
Möbius strip 120
Money-Kyrle, R. 154
moral education 130
mother–infant nonverbal communication 156
mother–infant relationship 31, 55, 169
muscle eroticism 75

NC *see* 'Negative Capability' (NC)
'Negative Capability' (NC) 1–3, 17, 18, 46–48, 51, 52, 61n3, 73–76, 80, 81, 89, 91, 95, 99, 100, 108, 111n8, 123–126, 131, 132, 141, 143, 145–146, 150n1, 156, 163
neurotic O 110
New York Psychoanalytic Society 129
Nietzsche, F. 27; on genius 23
Nissim, L. 100, 101, 103, 110n2
Noel-Smith, K. 156
non-communication 88–97
nonverbal communication 156, 160
'Notes made on a train' (Winnicott) 130–131
"Notes on Memory and Desire" (Bion) 17, 28, 33, 61n3, 73, 99, 100, 108, 141

O 3, 7n1, 9, 65, 75–77, 93, 103, 109, 157; autistic 110; becoming 22, 46, 48, 52, 60; neurotic 110; psychotic 110
object: actuality of 33–38, 40; destruction of 113–117, 120, 148, 149; environmental 82, 174; external 37, 49, 61n5, 162; internal 11, 49, 162, 169, 172, 174; subjective 55, 74, 75, 106, 130, 131, 139, 161, 162, 164, 165, 174, 176; use of 39–41, 56, 58–59
object relations theory 169, 172, 176
Oedipus complex 28
Ogden, T. H. 73, 85, 95, 129, 165
omnipotence 45, 55, 56, 58, 67, 69, 74, 75, 79n3, 97, 130, 139, 154, 168, 169, 175, 176
omnipotent control 33–35, 39, 54, 56, 105, 168
"On Arrogance" (Bion) 50, 159
'On memory and desire' (Bion) 80
ontological primacy 169
ontological self 9

oscillation 109, 116, 120; fertile 60
O'Shaughnessy, E. 85

parallel convergence 48–54, 61n4
paranoid-schizoid position 69, 101, 126, 131, 169, 176
"Parent-Infant Relationship" (Winnicott) 180n7
partial convergence 50
penis envy 53, 136–137, 140, 145
perception 55; creative 75; sensory 73, 74, 107, 108
"Personalities" (Bion) 68
personal self 121n7
"Personal View of the Kleinian Contribution," (Winnicott) 176
Place where we Live, The (Bion) 67
Plato 42
playing 56–58, 67, 90–91, 113–121
"Playing, Creativity, and the Search for the Self" (Winnocott) 41–42
'Playing and Culture' (Winnicott) 138–139
Playing and Reality (Winnocott) 13, 14, 67
pluperfect errands 64–70
Podro, J. 80, 81; *Nazarene Gospel Restored, The* 13, 23, 107, 128, 130, 131, 136
post-Bionian field theory 117
precariousness 57
primitive agonies 72
primitive emotional agonies 176
Primitive Emotional Development (Winnicott) 37, 155–156, 165n4
projective identification 11, 23, 27, 30, 31n3, 39, 50, 51, 65, 74, 77, 159, 161, 169, 170, 172, 175, 177, 178
Proust, M. 20
psyche-soma 49, 52, 53, 72, 77
psychoanalytical theory 115–117
Psychoanalytic Forum (1967) 17, 21, 48, 99
psychoanalytic theory 17, 69, 88, 100, 105, 157, 169
"psychoanalytic theory of thinking, The" (Bion) 177
psychological turbulence 7n1
psychosexuality 27
psychosis 11, 49, 65, 169, 175
psychosomatic disorders 113
psychotic O 110

rationality, abstract 20
Reeves, C. 164

relaxation 56
religion 107–108, 130
"Reverence and Awe" (Bion) 28–29
rêverie 19, 22, 24, 25, 36, 38, 39, 41–43, 49, 50, 65, 67, 76, 81, 96, 109, 160, 164, 165, 171; hermeneutic 20, 31n1; maternal 156
Rickman, J. 27, 31n4, 64, 65
Riviere, J. 65
Rodman, F. R. 80, 137, 165n3
role-responsiveness 39
Rosenfeld, H. 96, 154
Roussillon, R. 39, 88

Said, E. 13, 14
Saint Augustine 129
Savery, D. 9
Schützenberger, A. A. 69
Sechehaye, A. 25
Second Thoughts (Bion) 100, 106
secular psychoanalysis 26–28
seduction theory 70
Segal, H. 65–66, 96, 154
self 14, 15, 108; dissociated 73; fragile 72; incommunicado 92; ontological 9; personal 121n7; true 102, 103, 113, 116, 118
self-communication 97
self-consciousness 25
self-containment 119
sensory perception 73, 74, 107, 108
sensory symbiosis 75
sensuous engagement 76–77
separateness 58, 82, 83, 104, 168, 180n2
separation anxiety 40
shadowboxing 28–31
shared sensoriality 75
Sharpe, E. F.: "Psycho-Physical Problems Revealed in Language: an examination of metaphor" 156
Shelley, P. B.: "Defense of Poetry, A" 39
"snack bar therapy" formula 19
social self mix 121n7
Southern California Psycho-Analytic Society 29
Spelman, M. 163
Spillius, B.: *Cogitations* 17; *Melanie Klein Today* 17
spontaneity 43, 67, 109, 124, 125, 136, 173
spontaneous gesture 75
Stiegler, B. 42
St John of the Cross 6, 7n1, 51, 106, 107, 156, 164

Strachey, J. 65, 133, 134, 138, 140
subjective object 55, 74, 75, 106, 130, 131, 139, 161, 162, 164, 165, 174, 176
symbolic communication 160–161
symbolic realization 25

Taipale, J. 152, 153
Taylor Robinson, H. 80; *Collected Works of Donald Winnicott, The* 9
telepathy 104, 105
"Theory of Functions, A" (Bion) 67
thing-in-itself 156, 157
things-in-themselves 157
"thought without a thinker" 30
Torres, N. 156
transference 34, 38–40, 42, 46, 52, 58, 105, 108, 160, 164; countertransference *see* countertransference; delusional 60
transference-countertransference 40, 43, 52
transformation 4, 9, 27, 39, 52–54, 72, 77, 78, 93, 96, 103, 109, 120, 164, 168, 170, 173, 177, 178
Transformation: Change from Learning to Growth (Bion) 7n1, 9, 21, 22, 99
'Transitional Object' (Winnicott) 95
transitional phenomena 57, 75, 103, 134, 140
Trevarthen, C. 179
true self 102, 103, 113, 116, 118
Tustin, F. 3

unconscious 18, 22, 26, 31, 38, 41, 49, 52, 53, 57, 58, 69, 83–86, 89, 93, 96, 113, 130, 136, 144, 164; emotions 120; fantasy 18, 39, 40, 60, 104, 148, 149
'Use of an Object and Relating Through Identifications, The' (Winnicott) 123, 129, 130, 139, 145, 148, 149, 164

Vermote, R. 92–93, 164

waking dream thoughts 57, 96
Wesley, J. 156
Whitehead, A. N. 156
Wilson, M. 94
Winnicott, D. W.: on actuality of the object 33–38; on being with and without desire 35–37; and Bion, similarities and dissimilarities between 154–155; collaboration 163–165; collegial love 163–165;

on creative aggression 39–41; death of 137; as gatherer 155–157; influence of 163–165; intentions 81–83; on maternal preoccupation 37–38; on 'memories and desires' 6, 33–43; on omnipotence 75, 79n3; on Primitive Emotional Development 37; responsibilities 81–83; rivalry 163–165; stresses and strains 83–85; "Theory of the Parent-Infant Relationship" 175; uniqueness of research 54–59; *see also individual entries*

Wisdom, J. O. 11, 25, 36, 96, 159–160, 170

Wittgenstein, L. 5

Yehoshua, A.: *Mr. Mani* 45

For Product Safety Concerns and Information please contact our EU
representative GPSR@taylorandfrancis.com
Taylor & Francis Verlag GmbH, Kaufingerstraße 24, 80331 München, Germany

www.ingramcontent.com/pod-product-compliance
Lightning Source LLC
Chambersburg PA
CBHW070334270326
41926CB00017B/3864

* 9 7 8 1 0 3 2 8 1 9 2 1 1 *